GRACE RANDOLPH'S
SUPURBIA™

VOLUME TWO
THE VILLAIN NEXT DOOR

⟿ GRACE RANDOLPH'S ⟿
SUPURBIA ™

ROSS RICHIE Chief Executive Officer • **MATT GAGNON** Editor-in-Chief • **FILIP SABLIK** VP-Publishing & Marketing • **LANCE KREITER** VP-Licensing & Merchandising • **PHIL BARBARO** Director of Finance • **BRYCE CARLSON** Managing Editor
DAFNA PLEBAN Editor • **SHANNON WATTERS** Editor • **ERIC HARBURN** Editor • **CHRIS ROSA** Assistant Editor • **ALEX GALER** Assistant Editor • **STEPHANIE GONZAGA** Graphic Designer • **KASSANDRA HELLER** Production Designer
MIKE LOPEZ Production Designer • **JASMINE AMIRI** Operations Coordinator • **DEVIN FUNCHES** E-Commerce & Inventory Coordinator • **VINCE FREDERICK** Event Coordinator • **BRIANNA HART** Executive Assistant

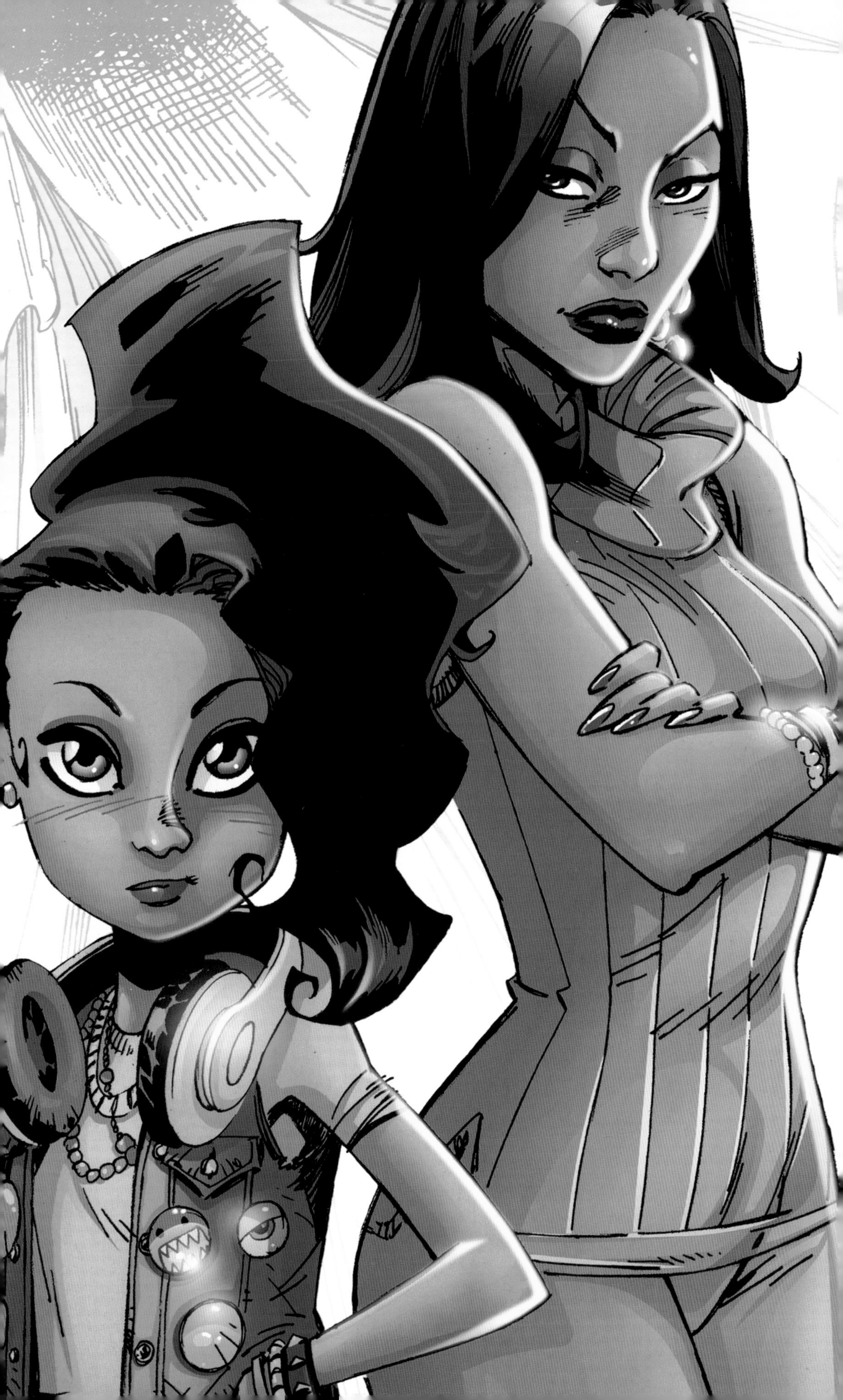

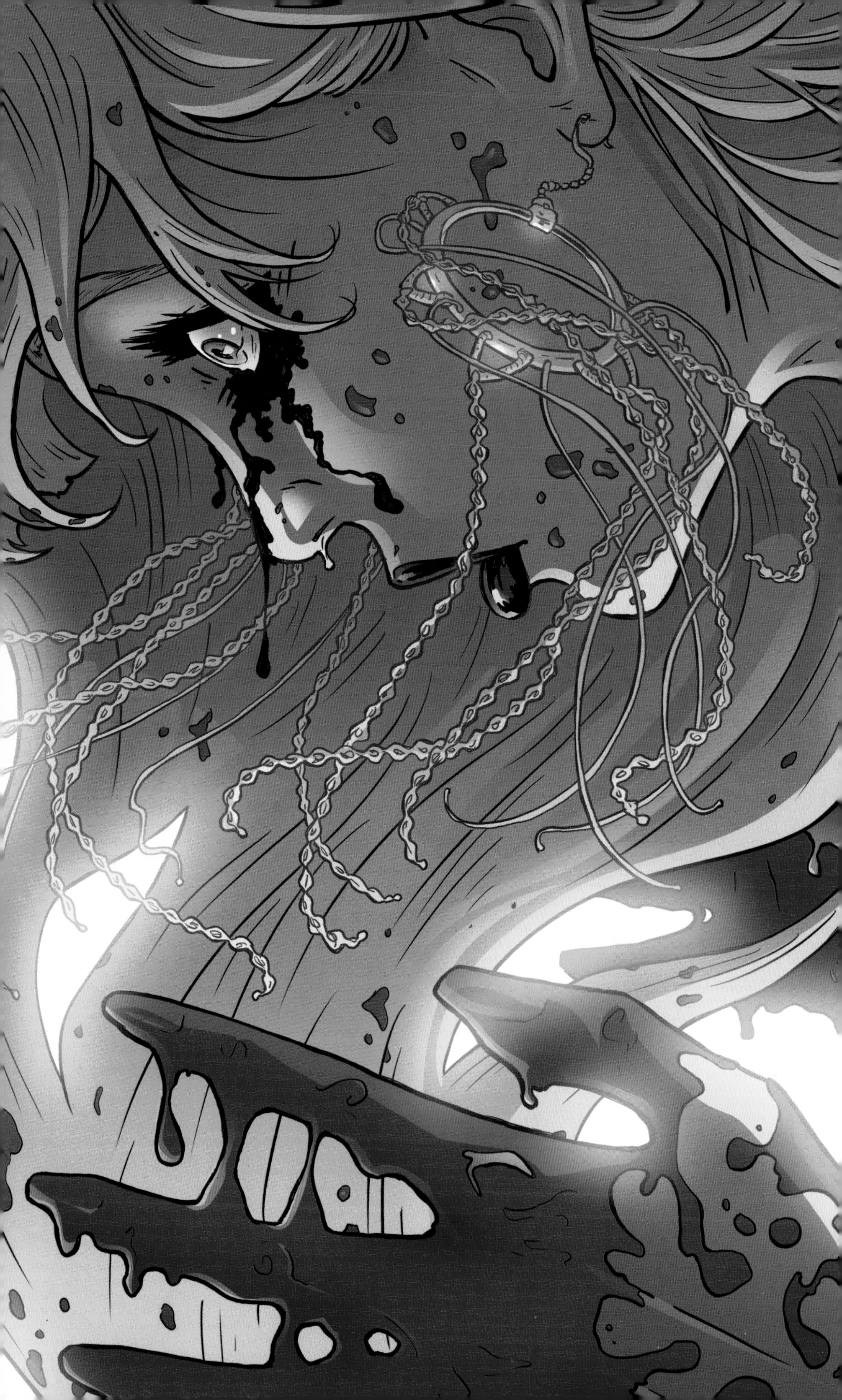

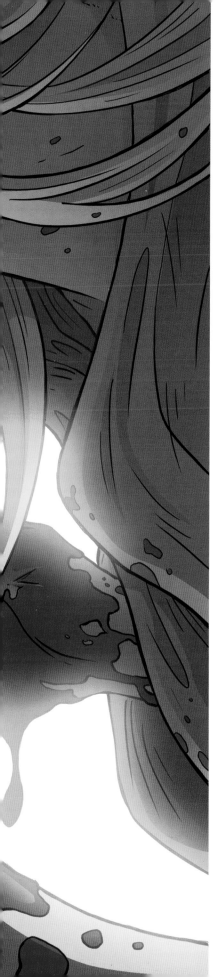

CREATED AND WRITTEN BY

GRACE RANDOLPH

ART BY

RUSSELL DAUTERMAN

COLORS BY

GABRIEL CASSATA

LETTERS BY

STEVE WANDS

COVER BY

STEPHANE ROUX

EDITOR

ERIC HARBURN

DESIGNER

MIKE LOPEZ

Chapter 1

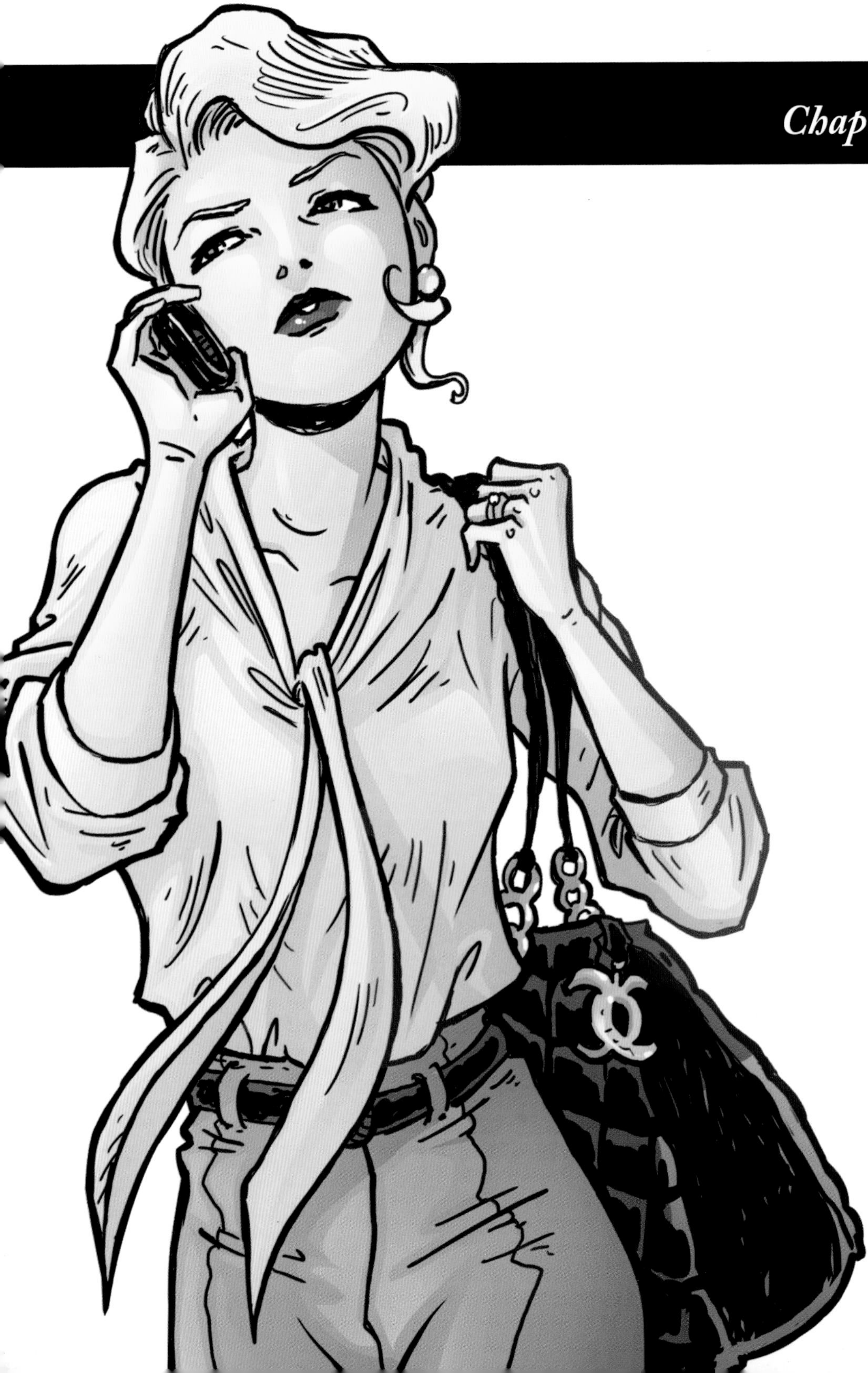

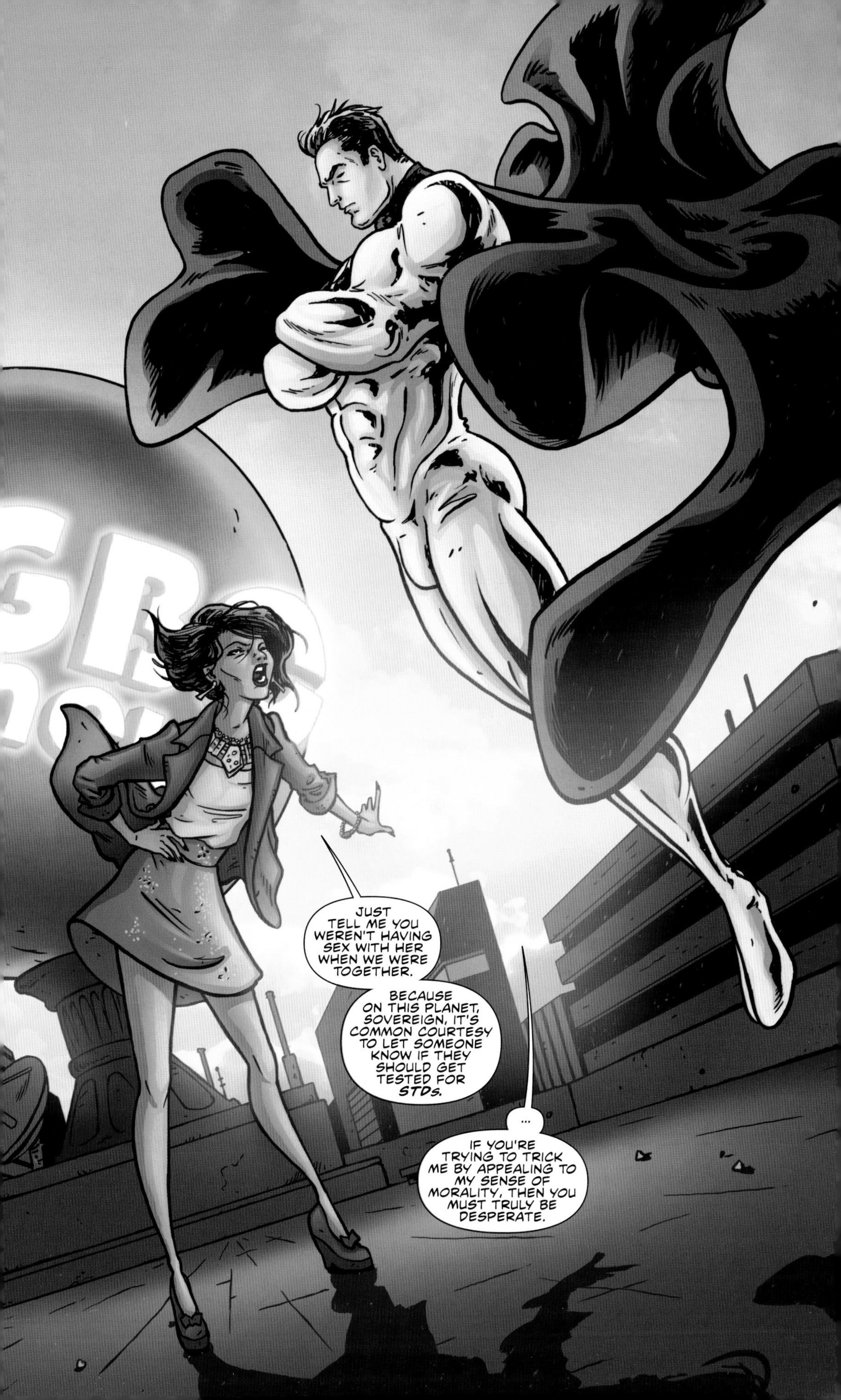
JUST TELL ME YOU WEREN'T HAVING SEX WITH HER WHEN WE WERE TOGETHER.
BECAUSE ON THIS PLANET, SOVEREIGN, IT'S COMMON COURTESY TO LET SOMEONE KNOW IF THEY SHOULD GET TESTED FOR STDs.
...
IF YOU'RE TRYING TO TRICK ME BY APPEALING TO MY SENSE OF MORALITY, THEN YOU MUST TRULY BE DESPERATE.

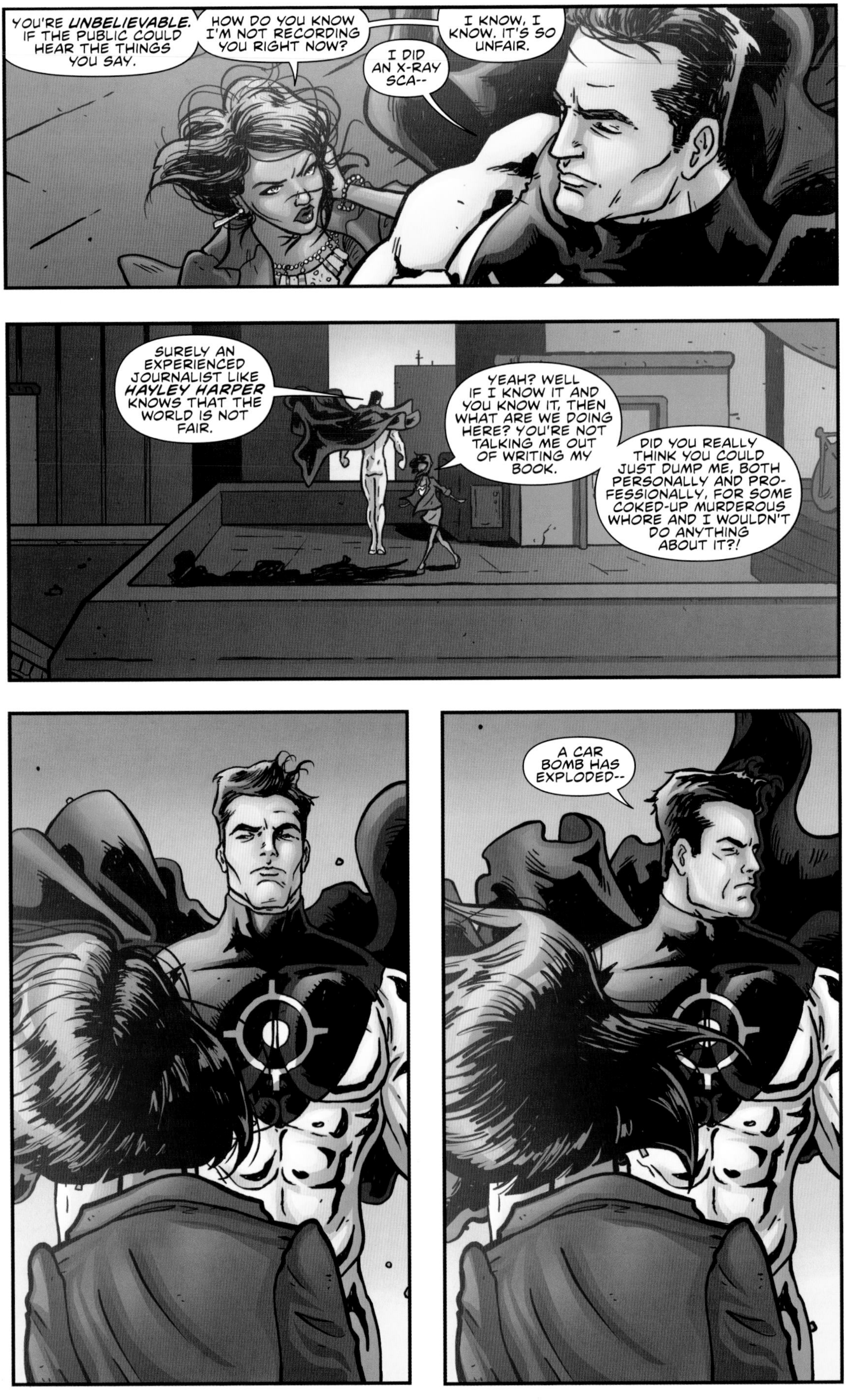

YOU'RE UNBELIEVABLE. IF THE PUBLIC COULD HEAR THE THINGS YOU SAY.
HOW DO YOU KNOW I'M NOT RECORDING YOU RIGHT NOW?
I DID AN X-RAY SCA--
I KNOW, I KNOW. IT'S SO UNFAIR.
SURELY AN EXPERIENCED JOURNALIST LIKE HAYLEY HARPER KNOWS THAT THE WORLD IS NOT FAIR.
YEAH? WELL IF I KNOW IT AND YOU KNOW IT, THEN WHAT ARE WE DOING HERE? YOU'RE NOT TALKING ME OUT OF WRITING MY BOOK.
DID YOU REALLY THINK YOU COULD JUST DUMP ME, BOTH PERSONALLY AND PROFESSIONALLY, FOR SOME COKED-UP MURDEROUS WHORE AND I WOULDN'T DO ANYTHING ABOUT IT?!
A CAR BOMB HAS EXPLODED--

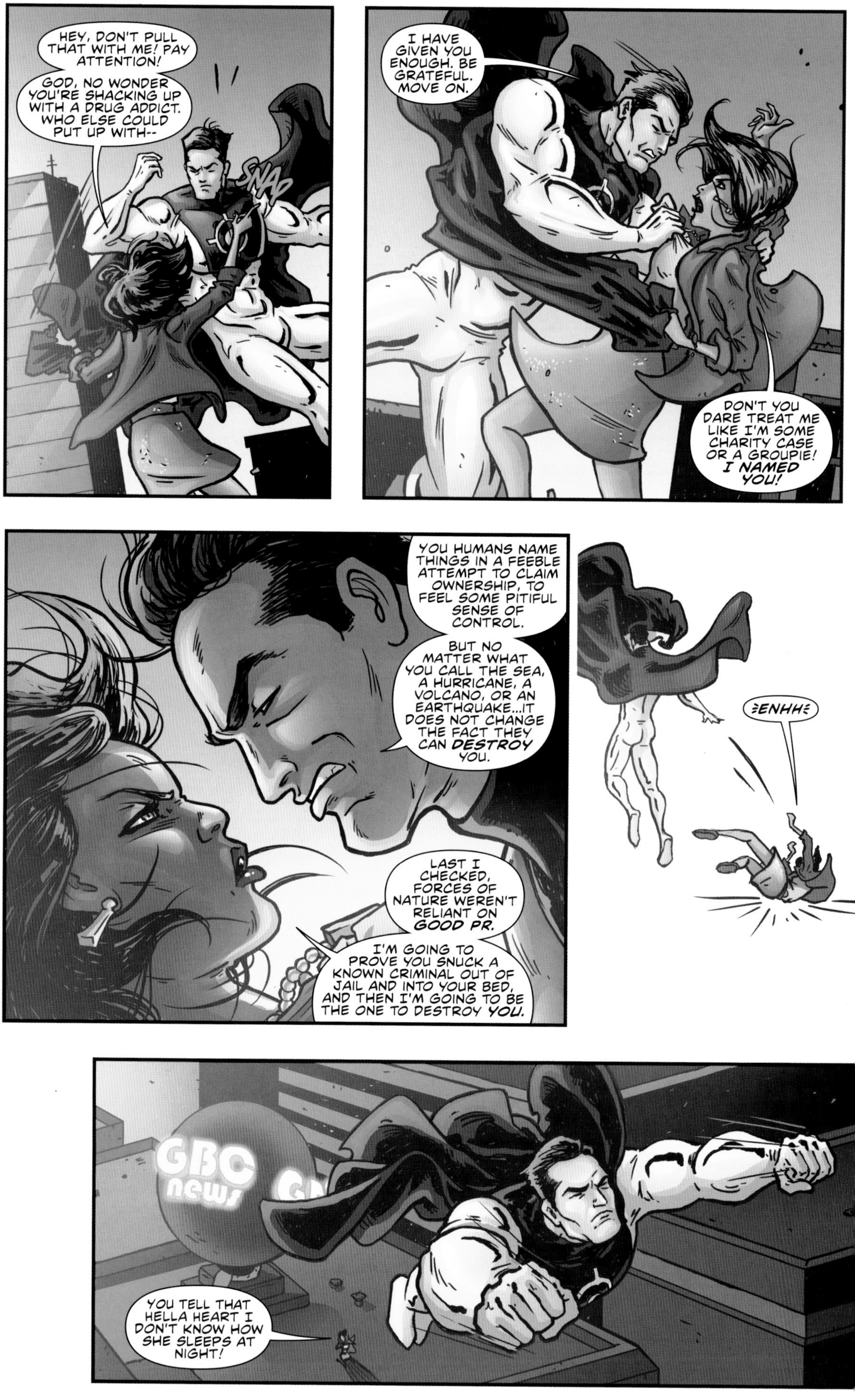
HEY, DON'T PULL THAT WITH ME! PAY ATTENTION!
GOD, NO WONDER YOU'RE SHACKING UP WITH A DRUG ADDICT. WHO ELSE COULD PUT UP WITH--
SNAP
I HAVE GIVEN YOU ENOUGH. BE GRATEFUL. MOVE ON.
DON'T YOU DARE TREAT ME LIKE I'M SOME CHARITY CASE OR A GROUPIE! I NAMED YOU!
YOU HUMANS NAME THINGS IN A FEEBLE ATTEMPT TO CLAIM OWNERSHIP, TO FEEL SOME PITIFUL SENSE OF CONTROL.
BUT NO MATTER WHAT YOU CALL THE SEA, A HURRICANE, A VOLCANO, OR AN EARTHQUAKE...IT DOES NOT CHANGE THE FACT THEY CAN DESTROY YOU.
LAST I CHECKED, FORCES OF NATURE WEREN'T RELIANT ON GOOD PR.
I'M GOING TO PROVE YOU SNUCK A KNOWN CRIMINAL OUT OF JAIL AND INTO YOUR BED, AND THEN I'M GOING TO BE THE ONE TO DESTROY YOU.
ENHH
GBC news
YOU TELL THAT HELLA HEART I DON'T KNOW HOW SHE SLEEPS AT NIGHT!

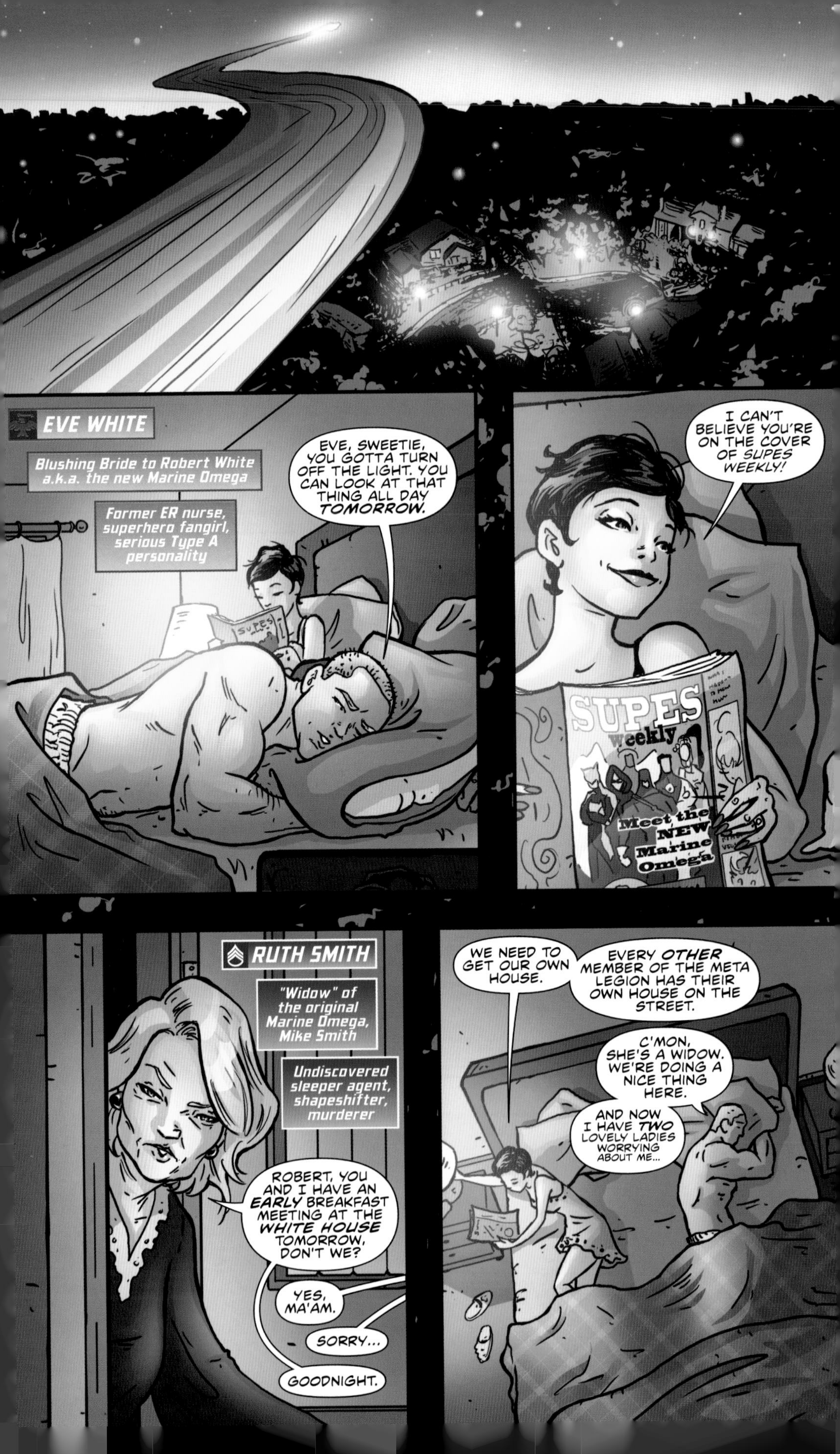
EVE WHITE
Blushing Bride to Robert White a.k.a. the new Marine Omega
Former ER nurse, superhero fangirl, serious Type A personality
EVE, SWEETIE, YOU GOTTA TURN OFF THE LIGHT. YOU CAN LOOK AT THAT THING ALL DAY TOMORROW.
I CAN'T BELIEVE YOU'RE ON THE COVER OF SUPES WEEKLY!
SUPES weekly
Meet the NEW Marine Omega
RUTH SMITH
"Widow" of the original Marine Omega, Mike Smith
Undiscovered sleeper agent, shapeshifter, murderer
ROBERT, YOU AND I HAVE AN EARLY BREAKFAST MEETING AT THE WHITE HOUSE TOMORROW, DON'T WE?
YES, MA'AM.
SORRY...
GOODNIGHT.
WE NEED TO GET OUR OWN HOUSE.
EVERY OTHER MEMBER OF THE META LEGION HAS THEIR OWN HOUSE ON THE STREET.
C'MON, SHE'S A WIDOW. WE'RE DOING A NICE THING HERE.
AND NOW I HAVE TWO LOVELY LADIES WORRYING ABOUT ME...

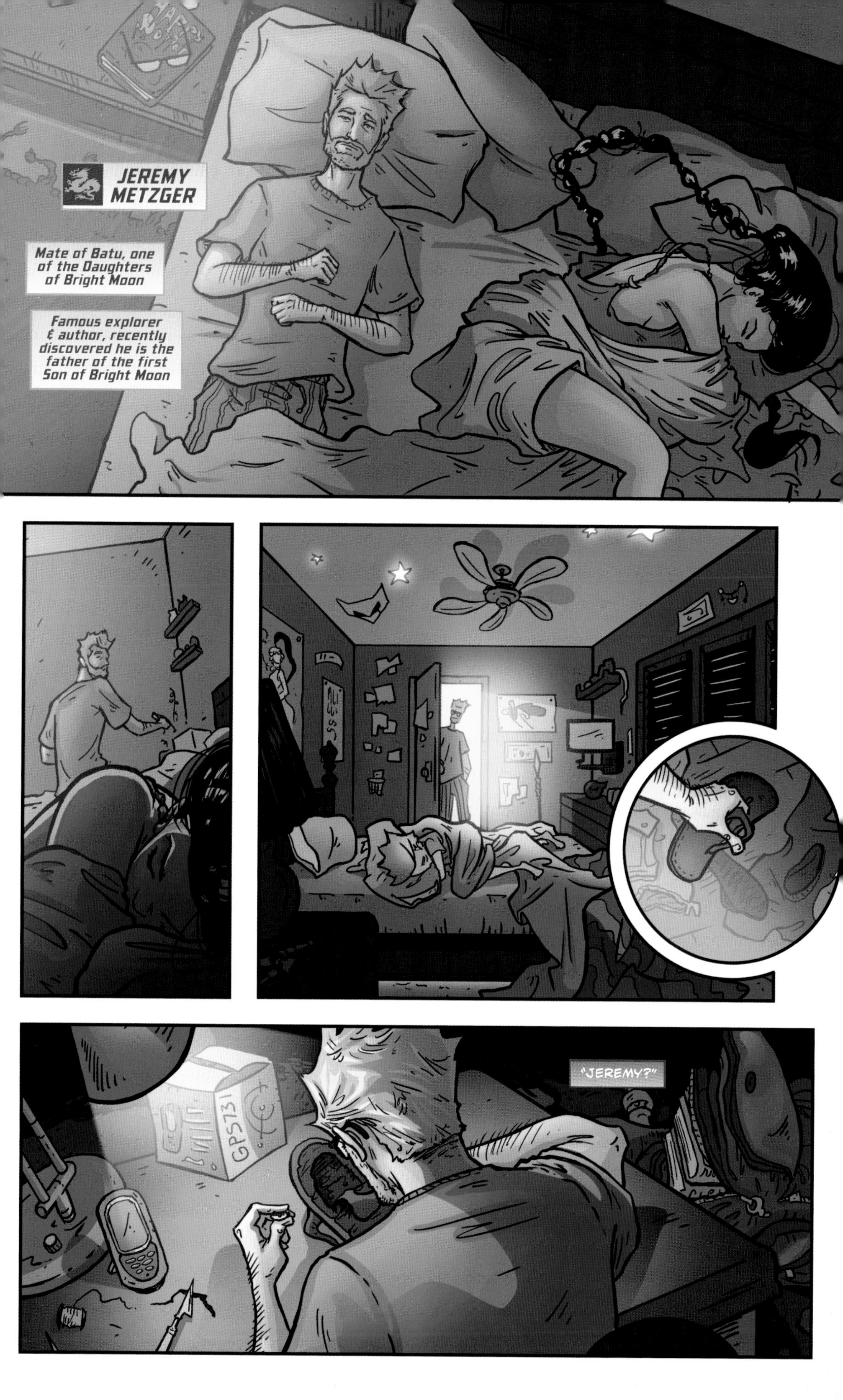
JEREMY METZGER
Mate of Batu, one of the Daughters of Bright Moon
Famous explorer & author, recently discovered he is the father of the first Son of Bright Moon
GPS731
"JEREMY?"

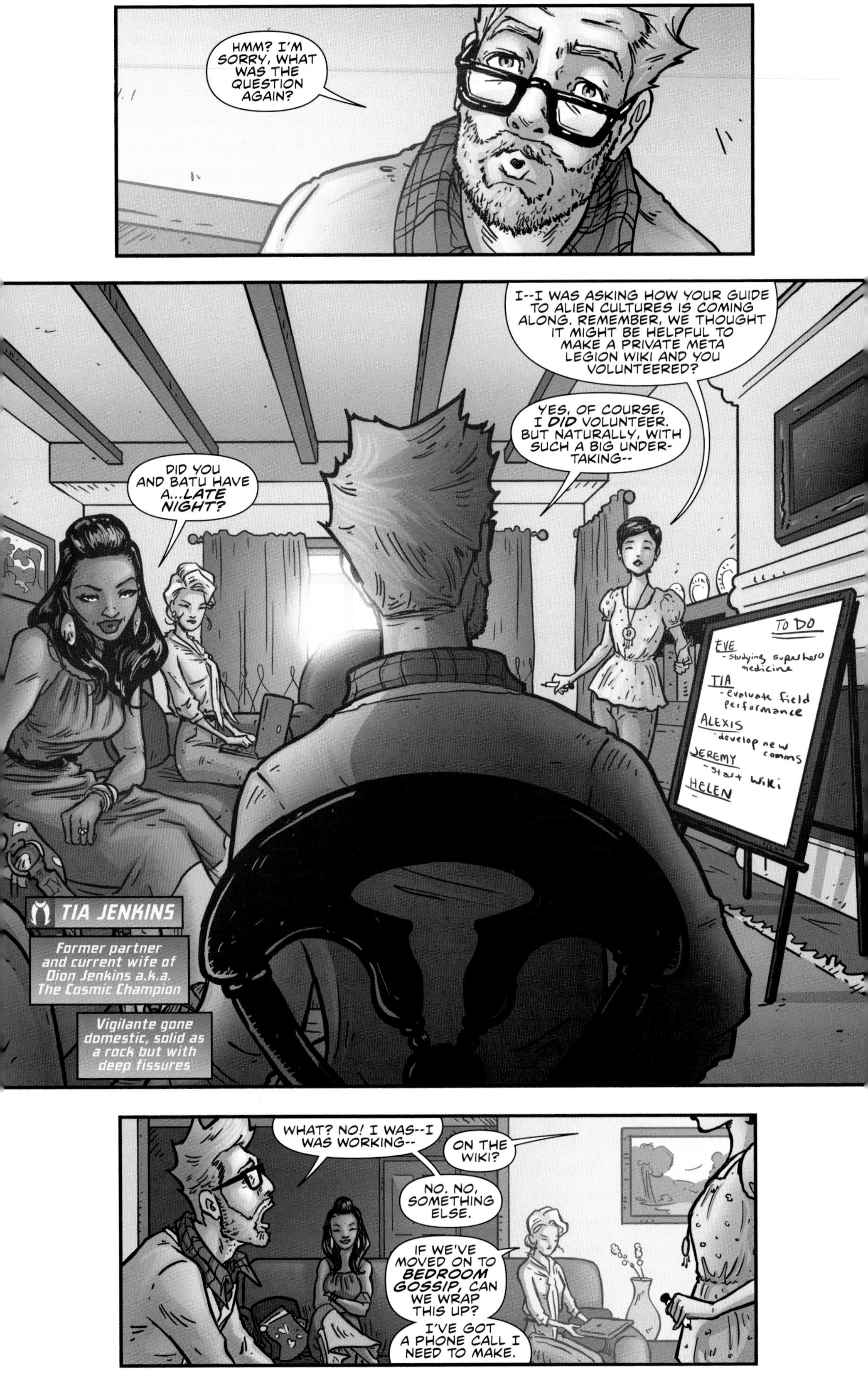
HMM? I'M SORRY, WHAT WAS THE QUESTION AGAIN?
I--I WAS ASKING HOW YOUR GUIDE TO ALIEN CULTURES IS COMING ALONG. REMEMBER, WE THOUGHT IT MIGHT BE HELPFUL TO MAKE A PRIVATE META LEGION WIKI AND YOU VOLUNTEERED?
YES, OF COURSE, I DID VOLUNTEER. BUT NATURALLY, WITH SUCH A BIG UNDER-TAKING--
DID YOU AND BATU HAVE A...LATE NIGHT?
TO DO
EVE
-studying superhero medicine
TIA
-evaluate field performance
ALEXIS
-develop new comms
JEREMY
-start wiki
HELEN
TIA JENKINS
Former partner and current wife of Dion Jenkins a.k.a. The Cosmic Champion
Vigilante gone domestic, solid as a rock but with deep fissures
WHAT? NO! I WAS--I WAS WORKING--
ON THE WIKI?
NO. NO, SOMETHING ELSE.
IF WE'VE MOVED ON TO BEDROOM GOSSIP, CAN WE WRAP THIS UP?
I'VE GOT A PHONE CALL I NEED TO MAKE.

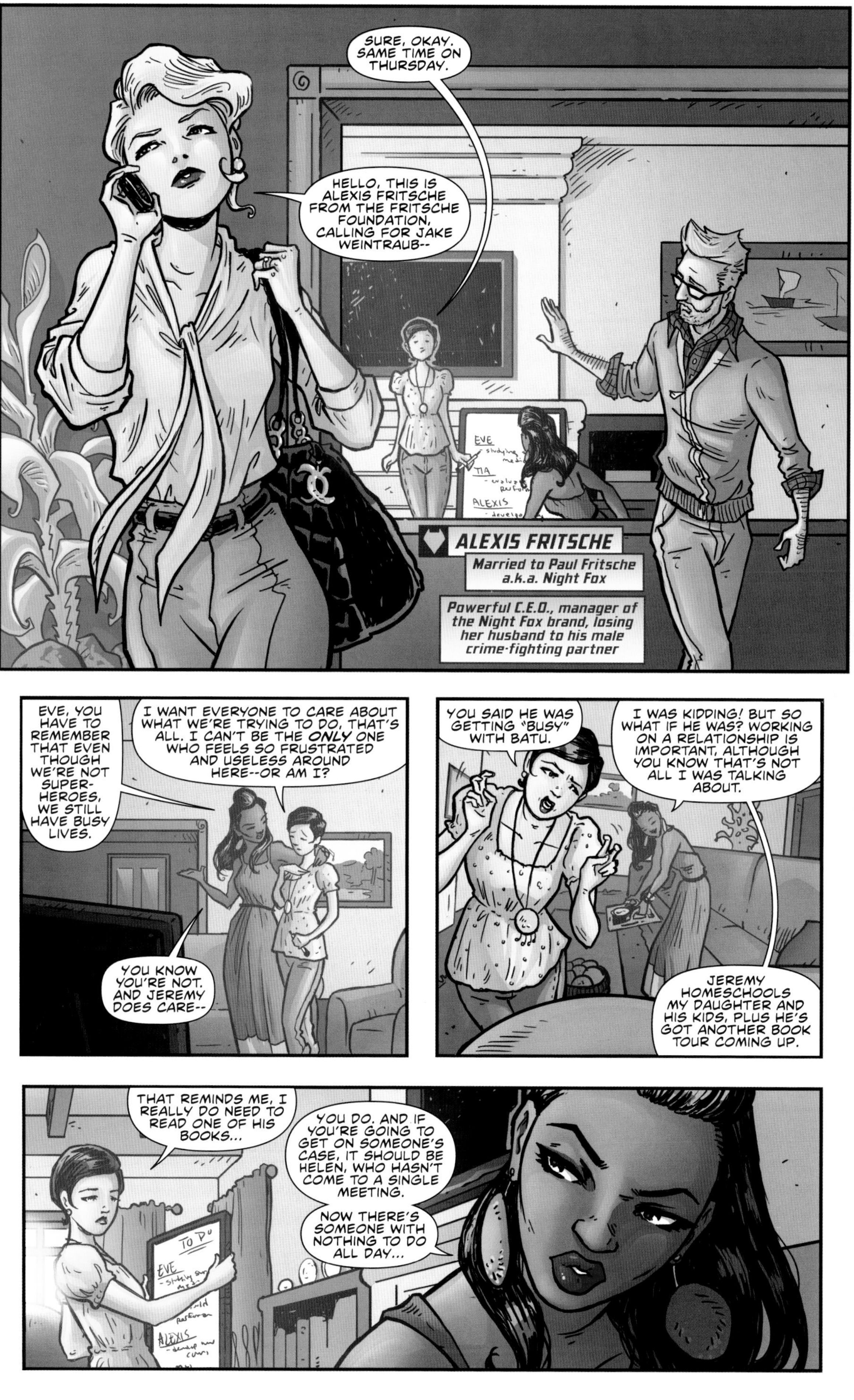
HELLO, THIS IS ALEXIS FRITSCHE FROM THE FRITSCHE FOUNDATION, CALLING FOR JAKE WEINTRAUB--
SURE, OKAY. SAME TIME ON THURSDAY.
ALEXIS FRITSCHE
Married to Paul Fritsche a.k.a. Night Fox
Powerful C.E.O., manager of the Night Fox brand, losing her husband to his male crime-fighting partner
I WANT EVERYONE TO CARE ABOUT WHAT WE'RE TRYING TO DO, THAT'S ALL. I CAN'T BE THE ONLY ONE WHO FEELS SO FRUSTRATED AND USELESS AROUND HERE--OR AM I?
EVE, YOU HAVE TO REMEMBER THAT EVEN THOUGH WE'RE NOT SUPER-HEROES, WE STILL HAVE BUSY LIVES.
YOU KNOW YOU'RE NOT. AND JEREMY DOES CARE--
YOU SAID HE WAS GETTING "BUSY" WITH BATU.
I WAS KIDDING! BUT SO WHAT IF HE WAS? WORKING ON A RELATIONSHIP IS IMPORTANT, ALTHOUGH YOU KNOW THAT'S NOT ALL I WAS TALKING ABOUT.
JEREMY HOMESCHOOLS MY DAUGHTER AND HIS KIDS, PLUS HE'S GOT ANOTHER BOOK TOUR COMING UP.
THAT REMINDS ME, I REALLY DO NEED TO READ ONE OF HIS BOOKS...
YOU DO. AND IF YOU'RE GOING TO GET ON SOMEONE'S CASE, IT SHOULD BE HELEN, WHO HASN'T COME TO A SINGLE MEETING.
NOW THERE'S SOMEONE WITH NOTHING TO DO ALL DAY...

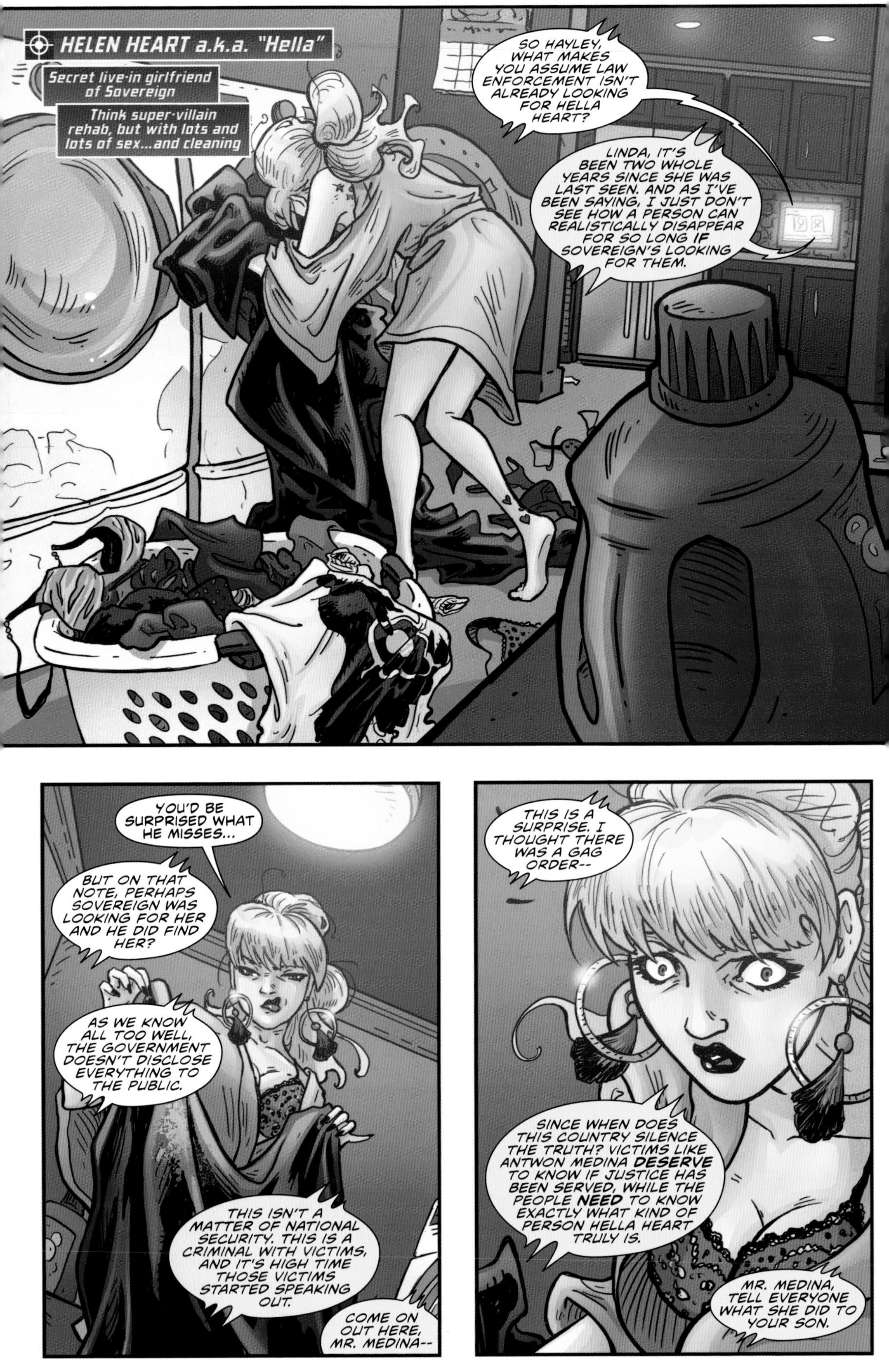
HELEN HEART a.k.a. "Hella"
Secret live-in girlfriend of Sovereign
Think super-villain rehab, but with lots and lots of sex...and cleaning
SO HAYLEY, WHAT MAKES YOU ASSUME LAW ENFORCEMENT ISN'T ALREADY LOOKING FOR HELLA HEART?
LINDA, IT'S BEEN TWO WHOLE YEARS SINCE SHE WAS LAST SEEN. AND AS I'VE BEEN SAYING, I JUST DON'T SEE HOW A PERSON CAN REALISTICALLY DISAPPEAR FOR SO LONG IF SOVEREIGN'S LOOKING FOR THEM.
YOU'D BE SURPRISED WHAT HE MISSES...
BUT ON THAT NOTE, PERHAPS SOVEREIGN WAS LOOKING FOR HER AND HE DID FIND HER?
AS WE KNOW ALL TOO WELL, THE GOVERNMENT DOESN'T DISCLOSE EVERYTHING TO THE PUBLIC.
THIS ISN'T A MATTER OF NATIONAL SECURITY. THIS IS A CRIMINAL WITH VICTIMS, AND IT'S HIGH TIME THOSE VICTIMS STARTED SPEAKING OUT.
COME ON OUT HERE, MR. MEDINA--
THIS IS A SURPRISE. I THOUGHT THERE WAS A GAG ORDER--
SINCE WHEN DOES THIS COUNTRY SILENCE THE TRUTH? VICTIMS LIKE ANTWON MEDINA DESERVE TO KNOW IF JUSTICE HAS BEEN SERVED, WHILE THE PEOPLE NEED TO KNOW EXACTLY WHAT KIND OF PERSON HELLA HEART TRULY IS.
MR. MEDINA, TELL EVERYONE WHAT SHE DID TO YOUR SON.

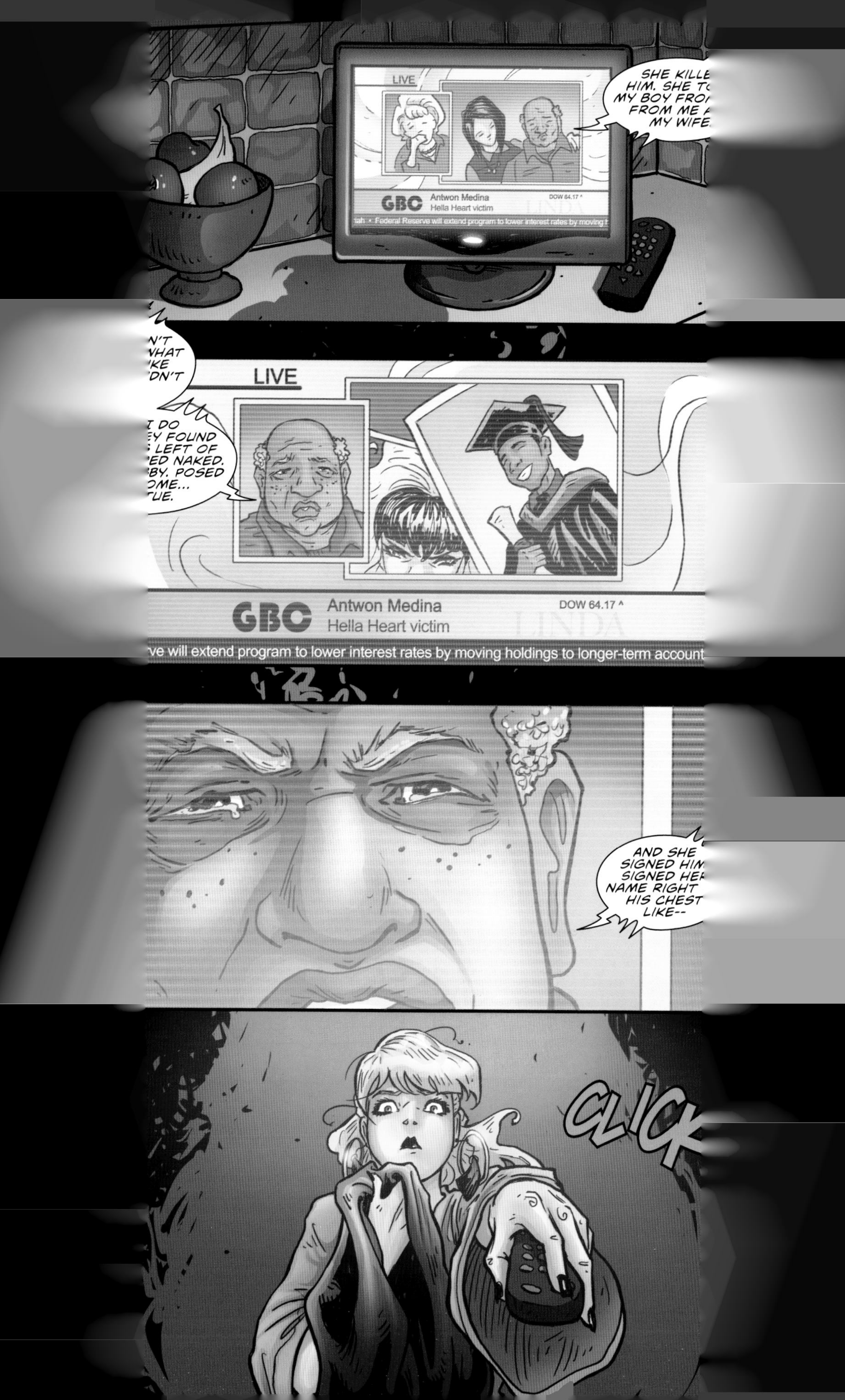
LIVE
GBC
Antwon Medina
Hella Heart victim
DOW 64.17
Federal Reserve will extend program to lower interest rates by moving
SHE KILLE HIM. SHE TO MY BOY FROM FROM ME A MY WIFE.
LIVE
GBC
Antwon Medina
Hella Heart victim
DOW 64.17 ^
ve will extend program to lower interest rates by moving holdings to longer-term account
AND SHE SIGNED HIM SIGNED HER NAME RIGHT HIS CHEST LIKE--
CLICK

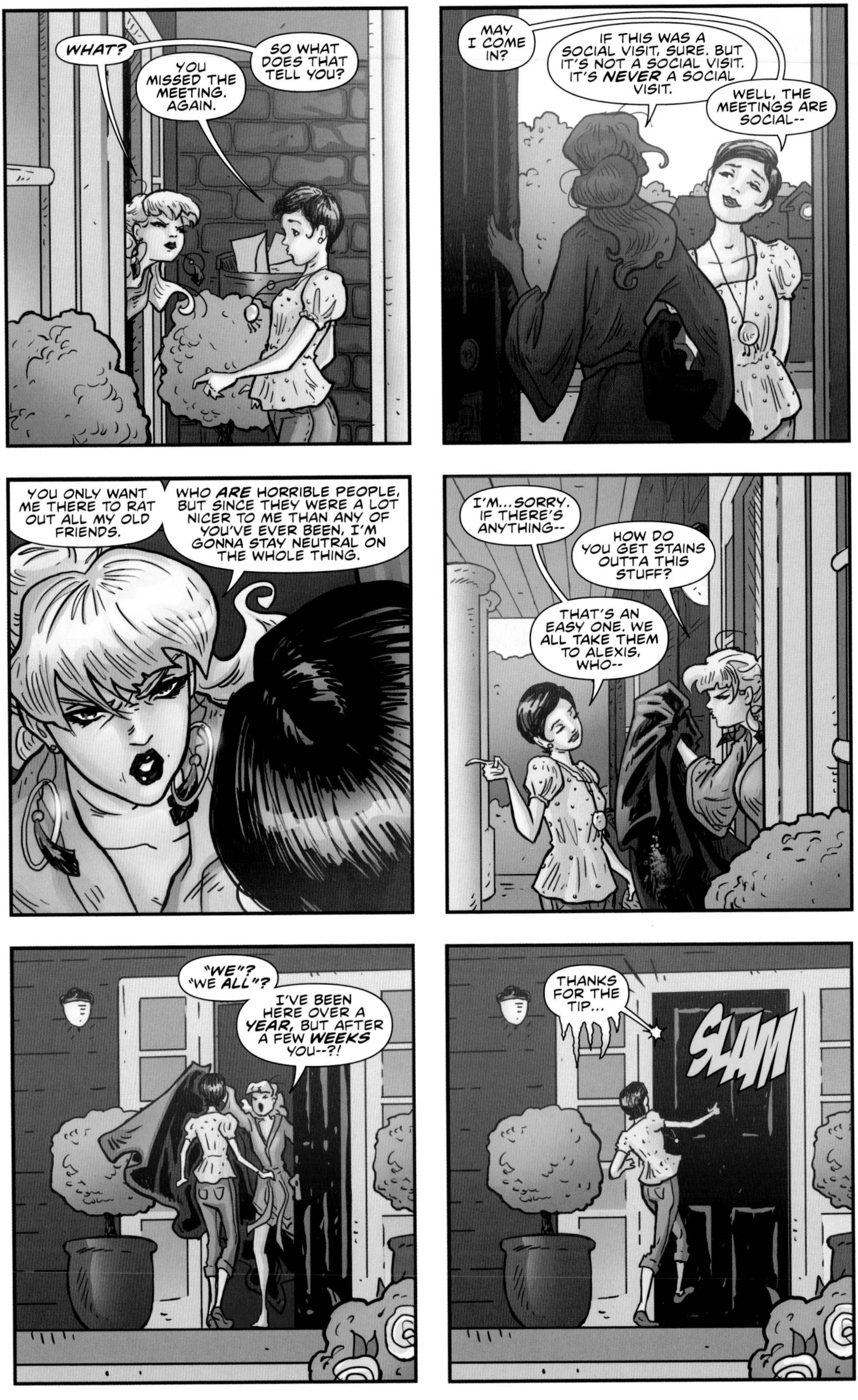

WHAT?
YOU MISSED THE MEETING. AGAIN.
SO WHAT DOES THAT TELL YOU?
MAY I COME IN?
IF THIS WAS A SOCIAL VISIT, SURE. BUT IT'S NOT A SOCIAL VISIT. IT'S *NEVER* A SOCIAL VISIT.
WELL, THE MEETINGS ARE SOCIAL--
YOU ONLY WANT ME THERE TO RAT OUT ALL MY OLD FRIENDS.
WHO *ARE* HORRIBLE PEOPLE, BUT SINCE THEY WERE A LOT NICER TO ME THAN ANY OF YOU'VE EVER BEEN, I'M GONNA STAY NEUTRAL ON THE WHOLE THING.
I'M...SORRY. IF THERE'S ANYTHING--
HOW DO YOU GET STAINS OUTTA THIS STUFF?
THAT'S AN EASY ONE. WE ALL TAKE THEM TO ALEXIS, WHO--
"WE"? "WE *ALL*"?
I'VE BEEN HERE OVER A *YEAR*, BUT AFTER A FEW *WEEKS* YOU--?!
THANKS FOR THE TIP...
SLAM

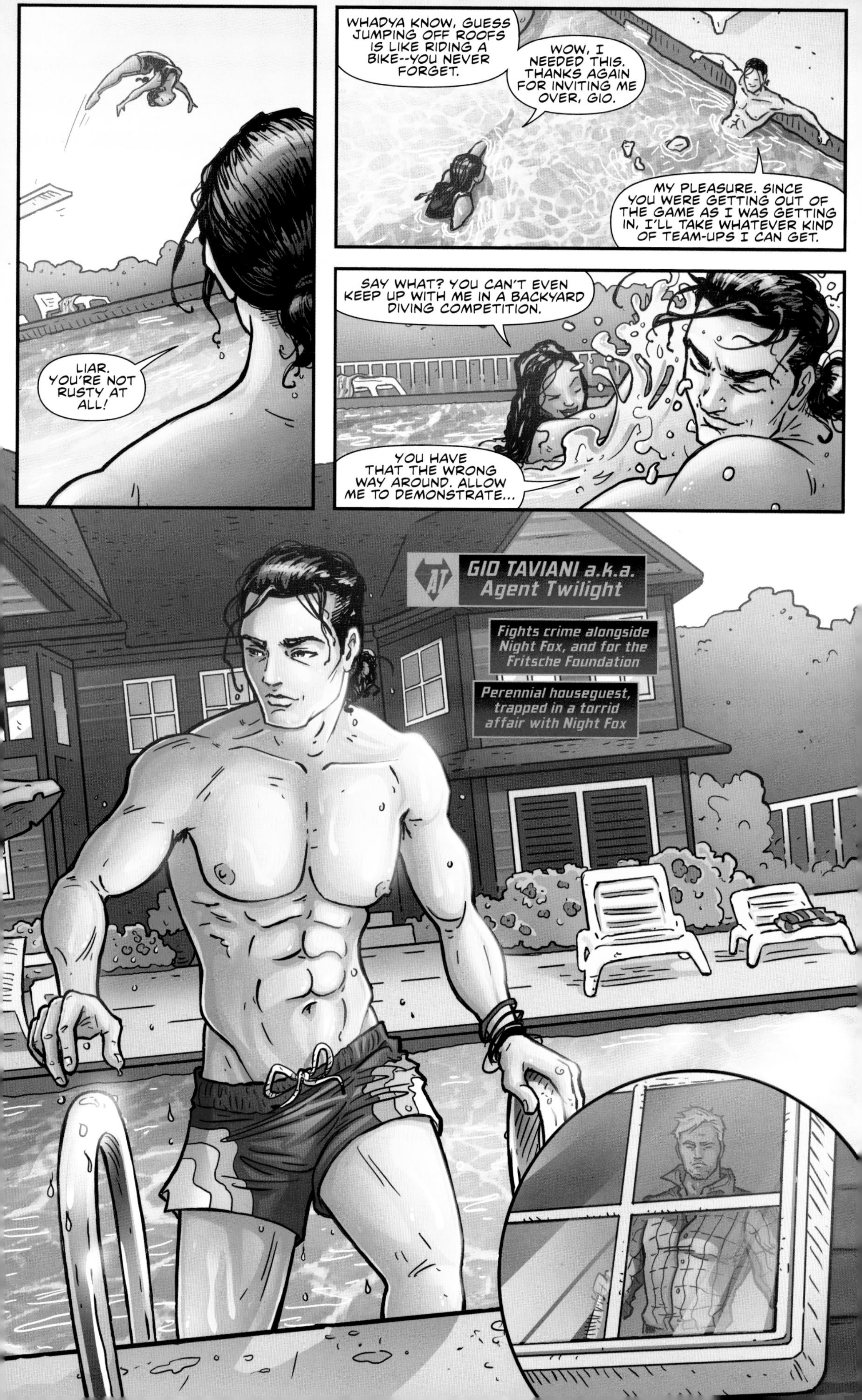
LIAR. YOU'RE NOT RUSTY AT ALL!
WHADYA KNOW, GUESS JUMPING OFF ROOFS IS LIKE RIDING A BIKE--YOU NEVER FORGET.
WOW, I NEEDED THIS. THANKS AGAIN FOR INVITING ME OVER, GIO.
MY PLEASURE. SINCE YOU WERE GETTING OUT OF THE GAME AS I WAS GETTING IN, I'LL TAKE WHATEVER KIND OF TEAM-UPS I CAN GET.
SAY WHAT? YOU CAN'T EVEN KEEP UP WITH ME IN A BACKYARD DIVING COMPETITION.
YOU HAVE THAT THE WRONG WAY AROUND. ALLOW ME TO DEMONSTRATE...
AT
GIO TAVIANI a.k.a. Agent Twilight
Fights crime alongside Night Fox, and for the Fritsche Foundation
Perennial houseguest, trapped in a torrid affair with Night Fox

ARE YOU GOING TO DIVE TODAY, OR WHAT?

I'M LETTING YOU SAVOR YOUR SHORT-LIVED VICTORY.

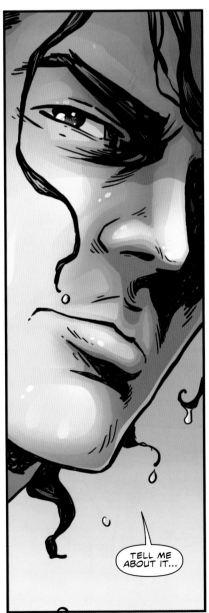

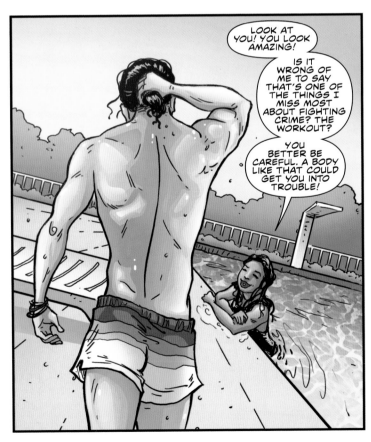

LOOK AT YOU! YOU LOOK AMAZING!

IS IT WRONG OF ME TO SAY THAT'S ONE OF THE THINGS I MISS MOST ABOUT FIGHTING CRIME? THE WORKOUT?

YOU BETTER BE CAREFUL. A BODY LIKE THAT COULD GET YOU INTO TROUBLE!

TELL ME ABOUT IT...

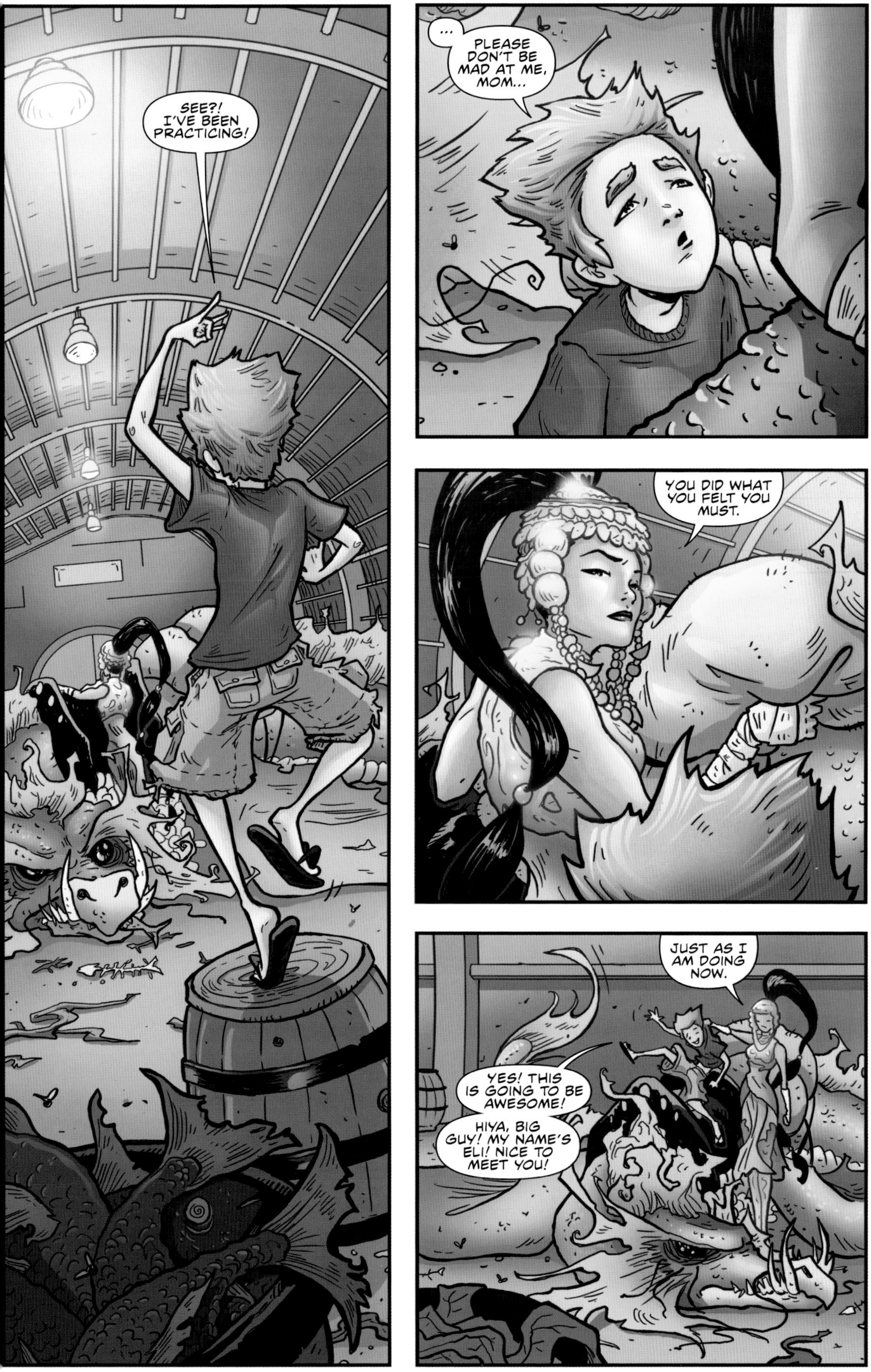
SEE?! I'VE BEEN PRACTICING!
... PLEASE DON'T BE MAD AT ME, MOM...
YOU DID WHAT YOU FELT YOU MUST.
JUST AS I AM DOING NOW.
YES! THIS IS GOING TO BE AWESOME!
HIYA, BIG GUY! MY NAME'S ELI! NICE TO MEET YOU!

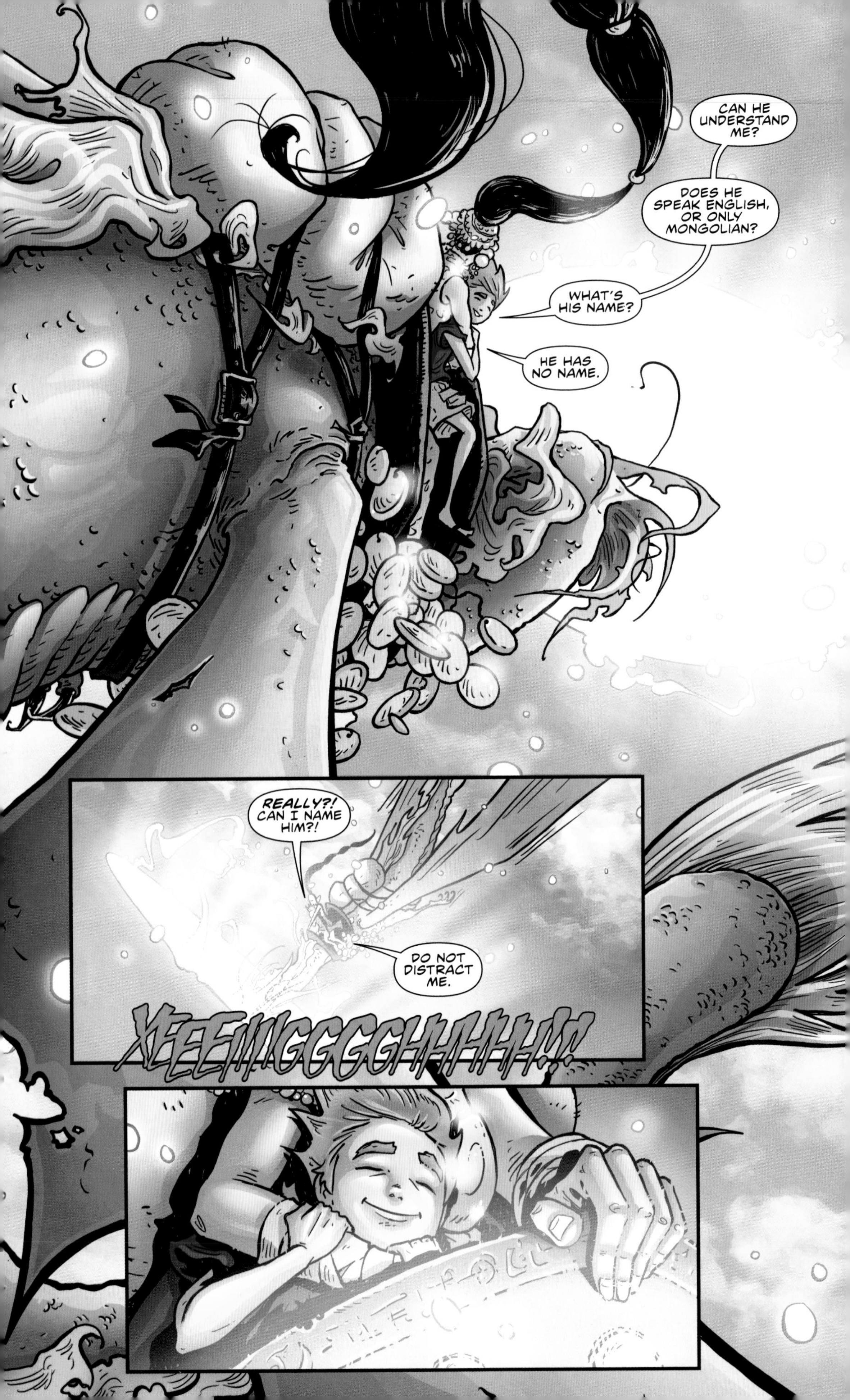
CAN HE UNDERSTAND ME?
DOES HE SPEAK ENGLISH, OR ONLY MONGOLIAN?
WHAT'S HIS NAME?
HE HAS NO NAME.
REALLY?! CAN I NAME HIM?!
DO NOT DISTRACT ME.
XEEEIIIGGGGHHHHH!!!

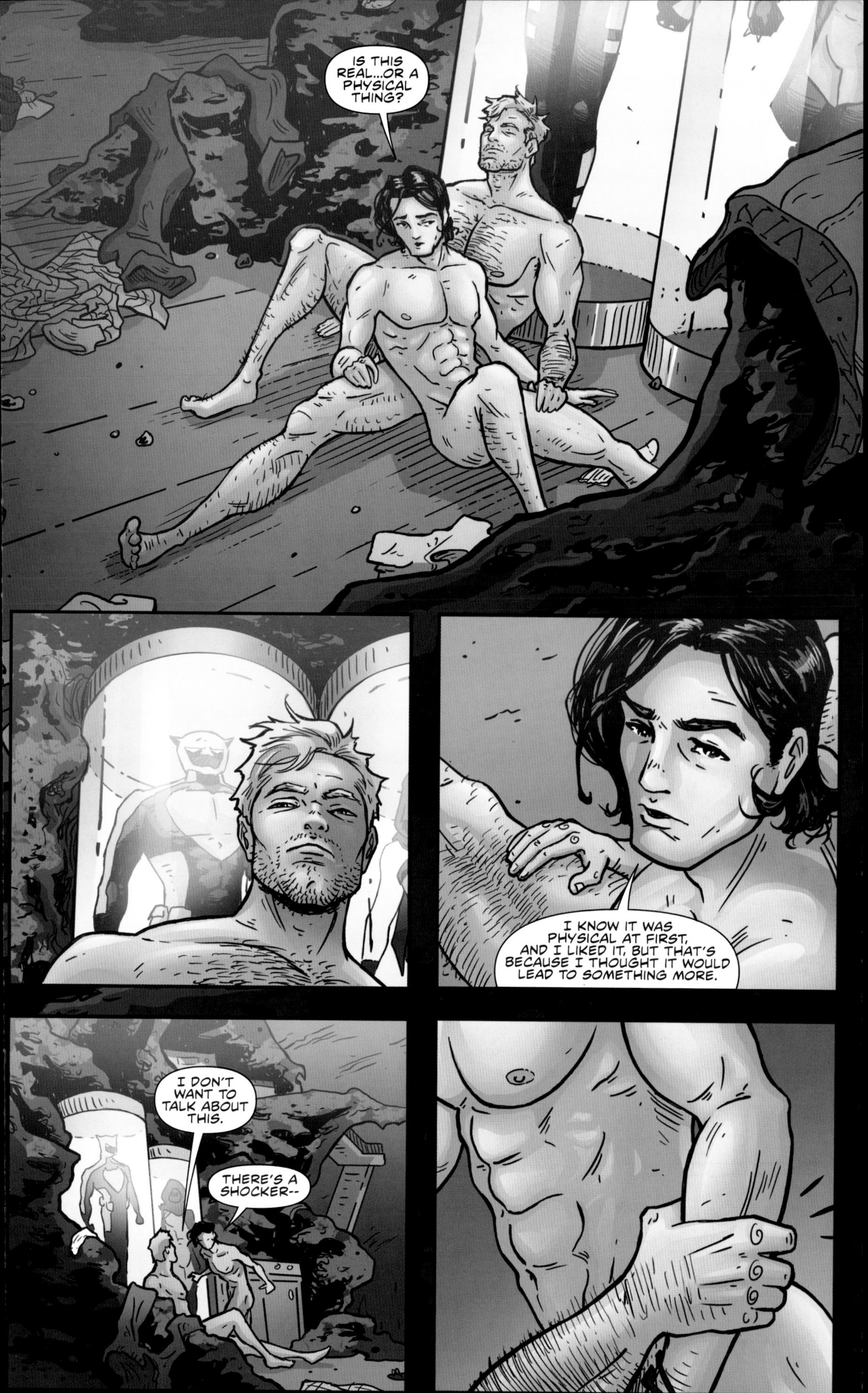
IS THIS REAL...OR A PHYSICAL THING?
I KNOW IT WAS PHYSICAL AT FIRST, AND I LIKED IT, BUT THAT'S BECAUSE I THOUGHT IT WOULD LEAD TO SOMETHING MORE.
I DON'T WANT TO TALK ABOUT THIS.
THERE'S A SHOCKER--

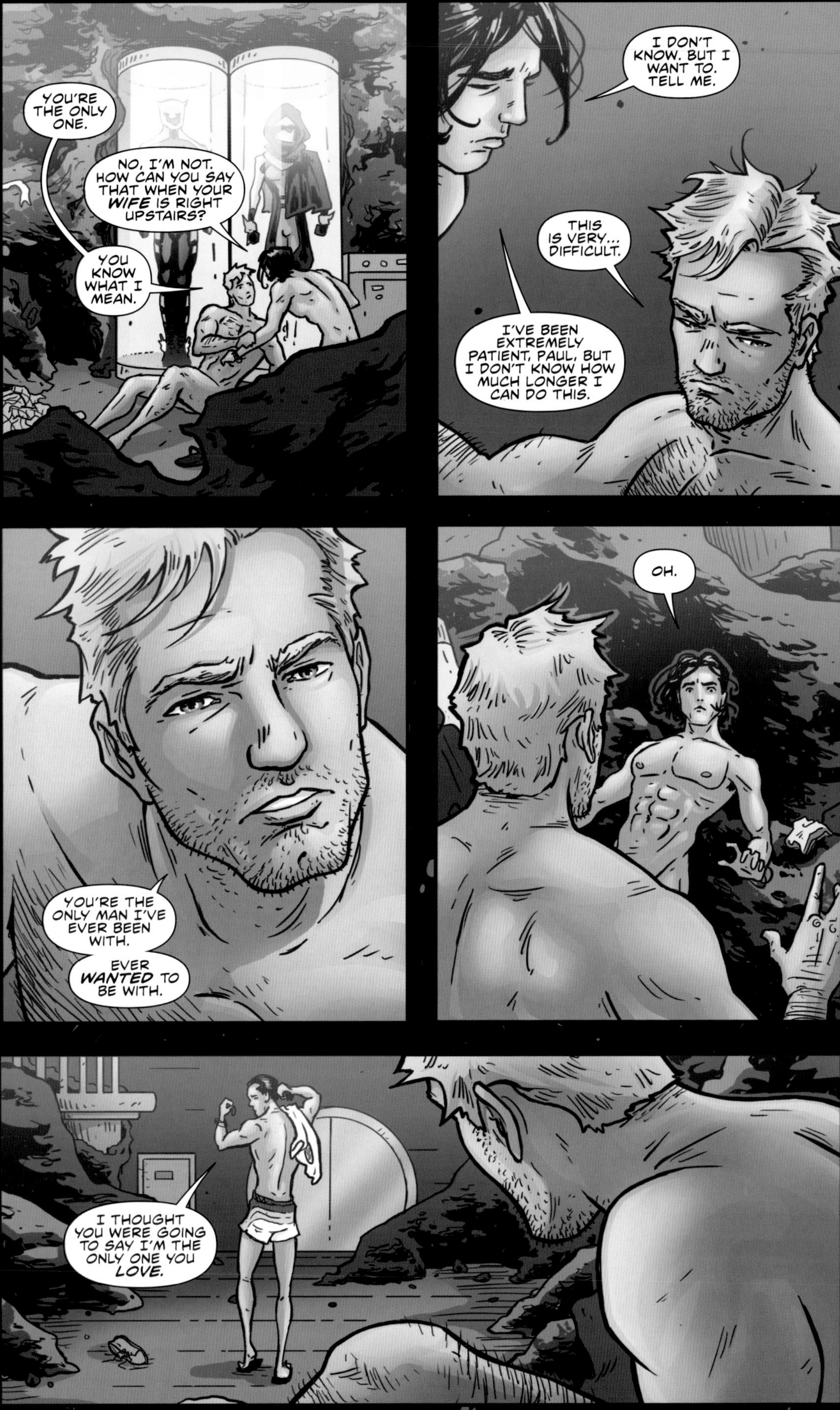
YOU'RE THE ONLY ONE.
NO, I'M NOT. HOW CAN YOU SAY THAT WHEN YOUR **WIFE** IS RIGHT UPSTAIRS?
YOU KNOW WHAT I MEAN.
I DON'T KNOW. BUT I WANT TO. TELL ME.
THIS IS VERY... DIFFICULT.
I'VE BEEN EXTREMELY PATIENT, PAUL, BUT I DON'T KNOW HOW MUCH LONGER I CAN DO THIS.
YOU'RE THE ONLY MAN I'VE EVER BEEN WITH.
EVER **WANTED** TO BE WITH.
OH.
I THOUGHT YOU WERE GOING TO SAY I'M THE ONLY ONE YOU **LOVE**.

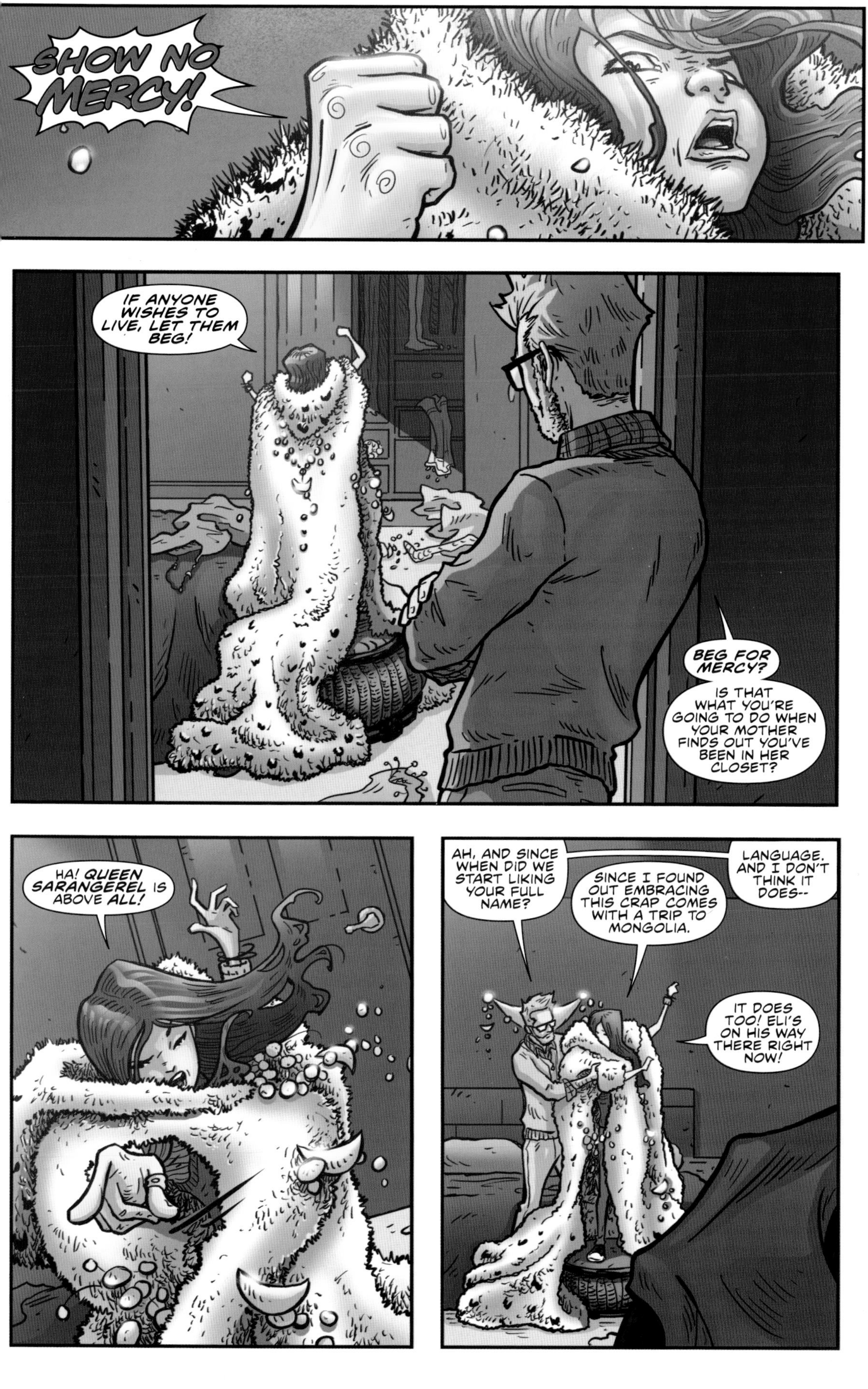
SHOW NO MERCY!
IF ANYONE WISHES TO LIVE, LET THEM BEG!
BEG FOR MERCY?
IS THAT WHAT YOU'RE GOING TO DO WHEN YOUR MOTHER FINDS OUT YOU'VE BEEN IN HER CLOSET?
HA! QUEEN SARANGEREL IS ABOVE ALL!
AH, AND SINCE WHEN DID WE START LIKING YOUR FULL NAME?
SINCE I FOUND OUT EMBRACING THIS CRAP COMES WITH A TRIP TO MONGOLIA.
LANGUAGE. AND I DON'T THINK IT DOES--
IT DOES TOO! ELI'S ON HIS WAY THERE RIGHT NOW!

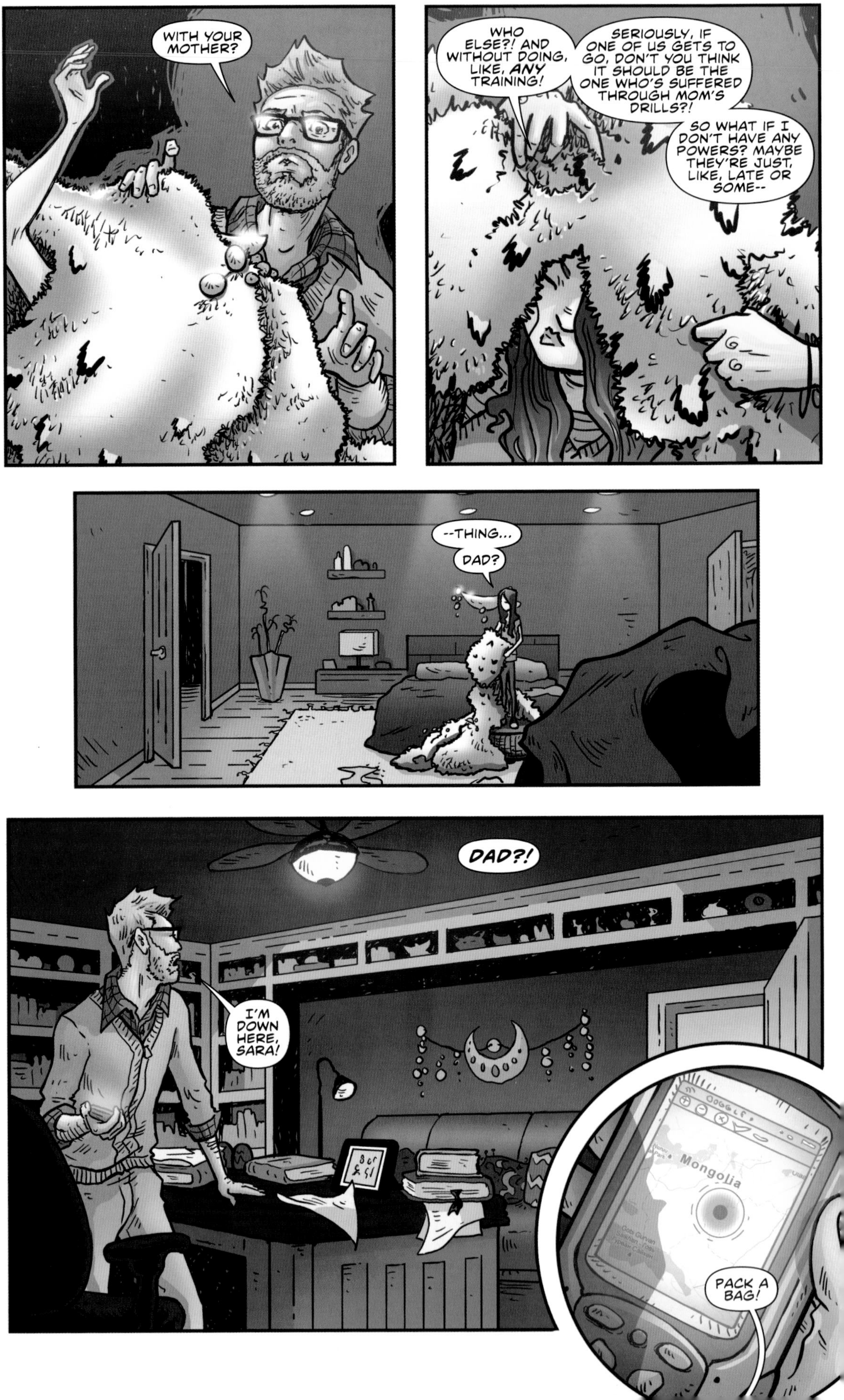
WITH YOUR MOTHER?
WHO ELSE?! AND WITHOUT DOING, LIKE, *ANY* TRAINING!
SERIOUSLY, IF ONE OF US GETS TO GO, DON'T YOU THINK IT SHOULD BE THE ONE WHO'S SUFFERED THROUGH MOM'S DRILLS?!
SO WHAT IF I DON'T HAVE ANY POWERS? MAYBE THEY'RE JUST, LIKE, LATE OR SOME--
--THING...
DAD?
DAD?!
I'M DOWN HERE, SARA!
Mongolia
PACK A BAG!

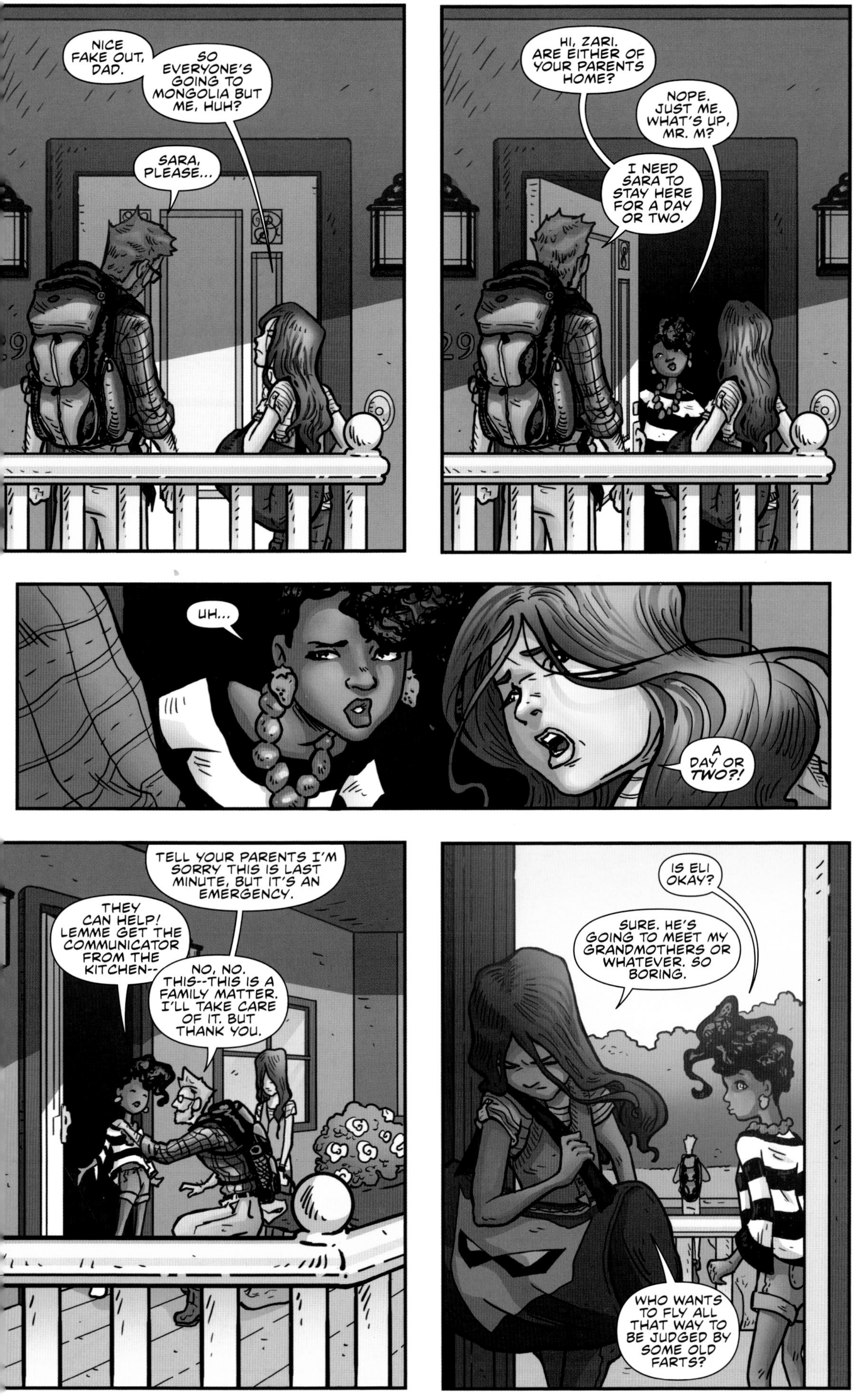
NICE FAKE OUT, DAD.
SO EVERYONE'S GOING TO MONGOLIA BUT ME, HUH?
SARA, PLEASE...
HI, ZARI. ARE EITHER OF YOUR PARENTS HOME?
NOPE. JUST ME. WHAT'S UP, MR. M?
I NEED SARA TO STAY HERE FOR A DAY OR TWO.
UH...
A DAY OR *TWO?!*
TELL YOUR PARENTS I'M SORRY THIS IS LAST MINUTE, BUT IT'S AN EMERGENCY.
THEY CAN HELP! LEMME GET THE COMMUNICATOR FROM THE KITCHEN--
NO, NO. THIS--THIS IS A FAMILY MATTER. I'LL TAKE CARE OF IT. BUT THANK YOU.
IS ELI OKAY?
SURE. HE'S GOING TO MEET MY GRANDMOTHERS OR WHATEVER. SO BORING.
WHO WANTS TO FLY ALL THAT WAY TO BE JUDGED BY SOME OLD FARTS?

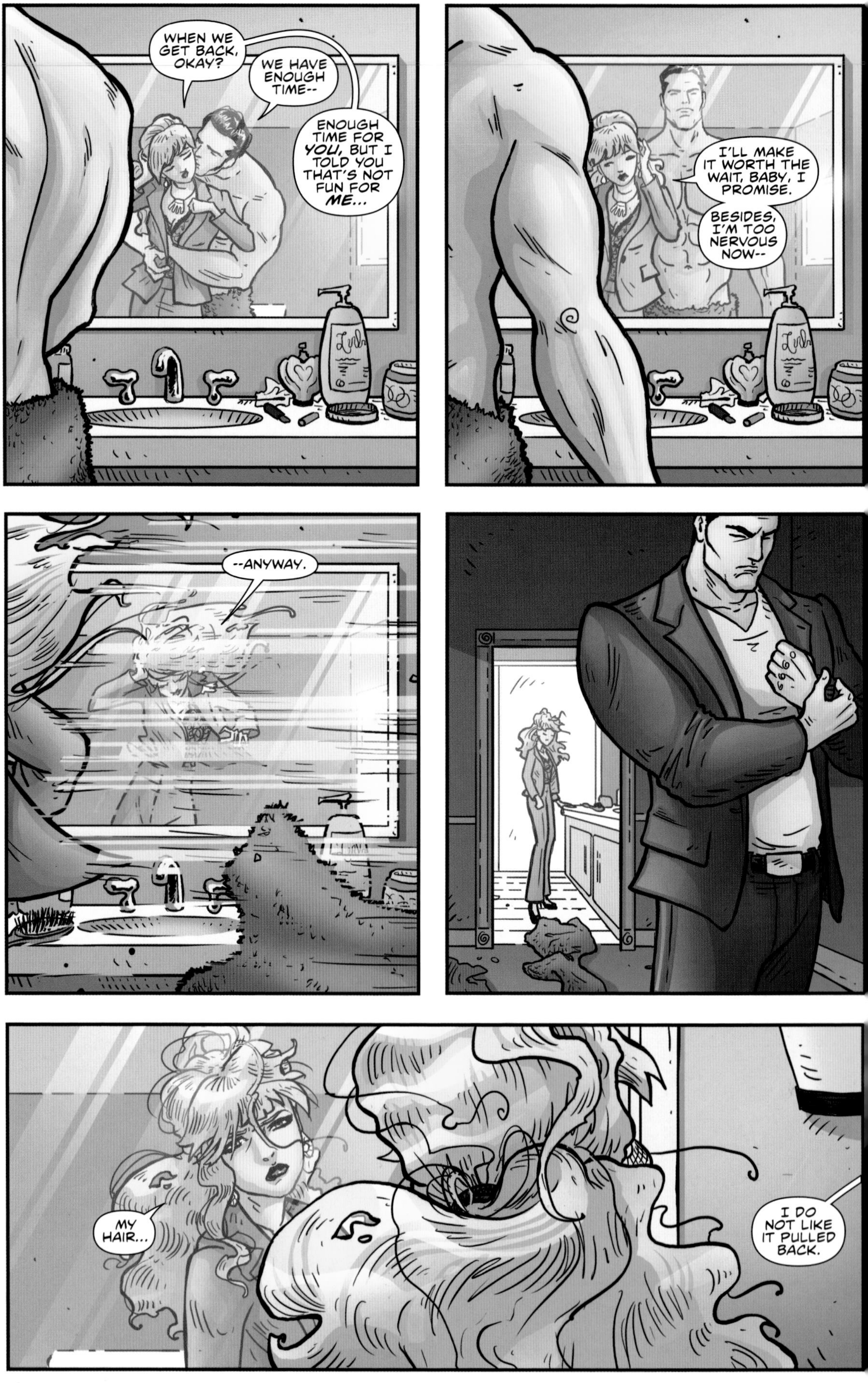
WHEN WE GET BACK, OKAY?
WE HAVE ENOUGH TIME--
ENOUGH TIME FOR *YOU*, BUT I TOLD YOU THAT'S NOT FUN FOR *ME*...
I'LL MAKE IT WORTH THE WAIT, BABY, I PROMISE.
BESIDES, I'M TOO NERVOUS NOW--
--ANYWAY.
MY HAIR...
I DO NOT LIKE IT PULLED BACK.

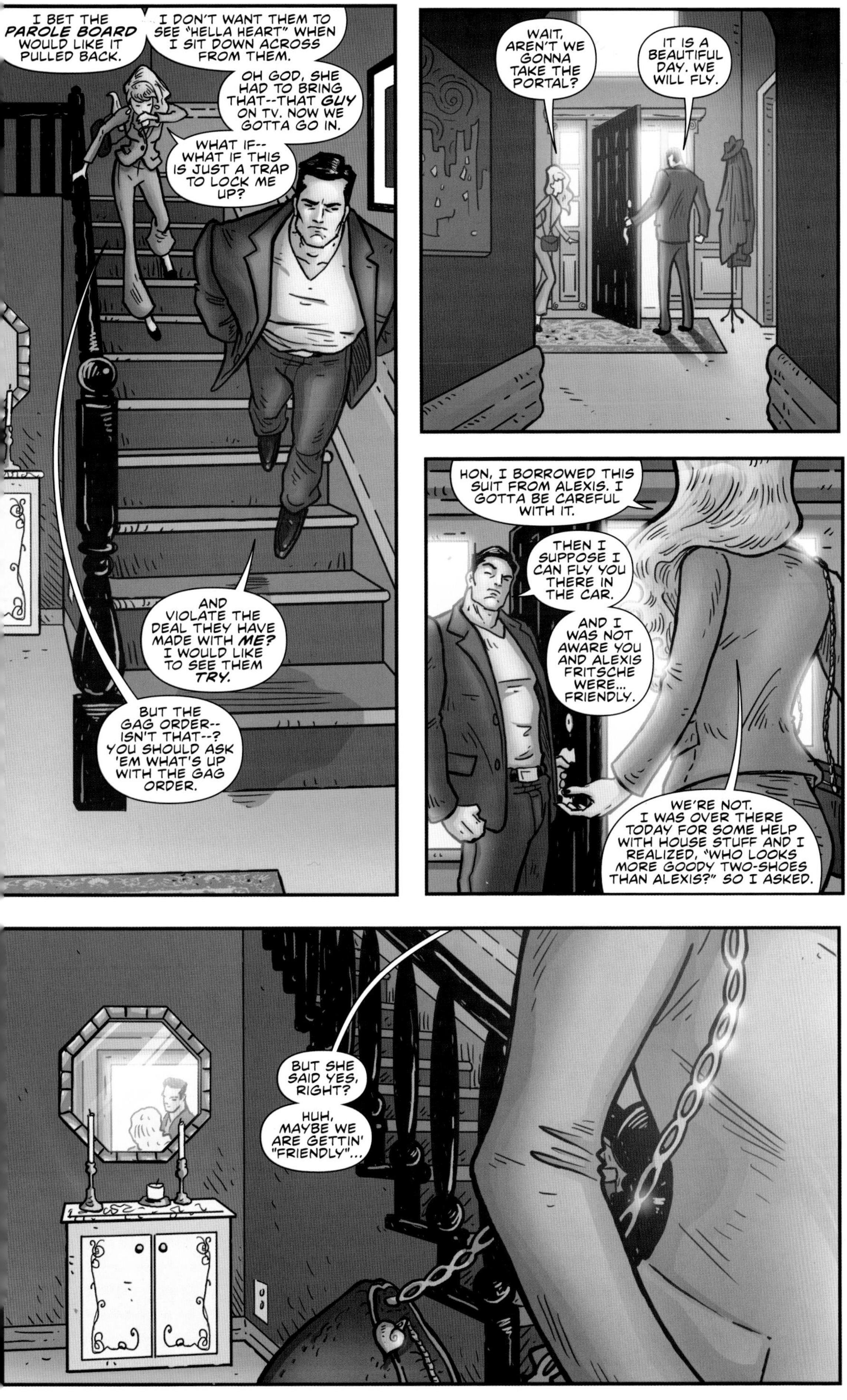
I BET THE PAROLE BOARD WOULD LIKE IT PULLED BACK.
I DON'T WANT THEM TO SEE "HELLA HEART" WHEN I SIT DOWN ACROSS FROM THEM.
OH GOD, SHE HAD TO BRING THAT--THAT GUY ON TV. NOW WE GOTTA GO IN.
WHAT IF-- WHAT IF THIS IS JUST A TRAP TO LOCK ME UP?
AND VIOLATE THE DEAL THEY HAVE MADE WITH ME? I WOULD LIKE TO SEE THEM TRY.
BUT THE GAG ORDER-- ISN'T THAT--? YOU SHOULD ASK 'EM WHAT'S UP WITH THE GAG ORDER.
WAIT, AREN'T WE GONNA TAKE THE PORTAL?
IT IS A BEAUTIFUL DAY. WE WILL FLY.
HON, I BORROWED THIS SUIT FROM ALEXIS. I GOTTA BE CAREFUL WITH IT.
THEN I SUPPOSE I CAN FLY YOU THERE IN THE CAR.
AND I WAS NOT AWARE YOU AND ALEXIS FRITSCHE WERE... FRIENDLY.
WE'RE NOT. I WAS OVER THERE TODAY FOR SOME HELP WITH HOUSE STUFF AND I REALIZED, "WHO LOOKS MORE GOODY TWO-SHOES THAN ALEXIS?" SO I ASKED.
BUT SHE SAID YES, RIGHT?
HUH, MAYBE WE ARE GETTIN' "FRIENDLY"...

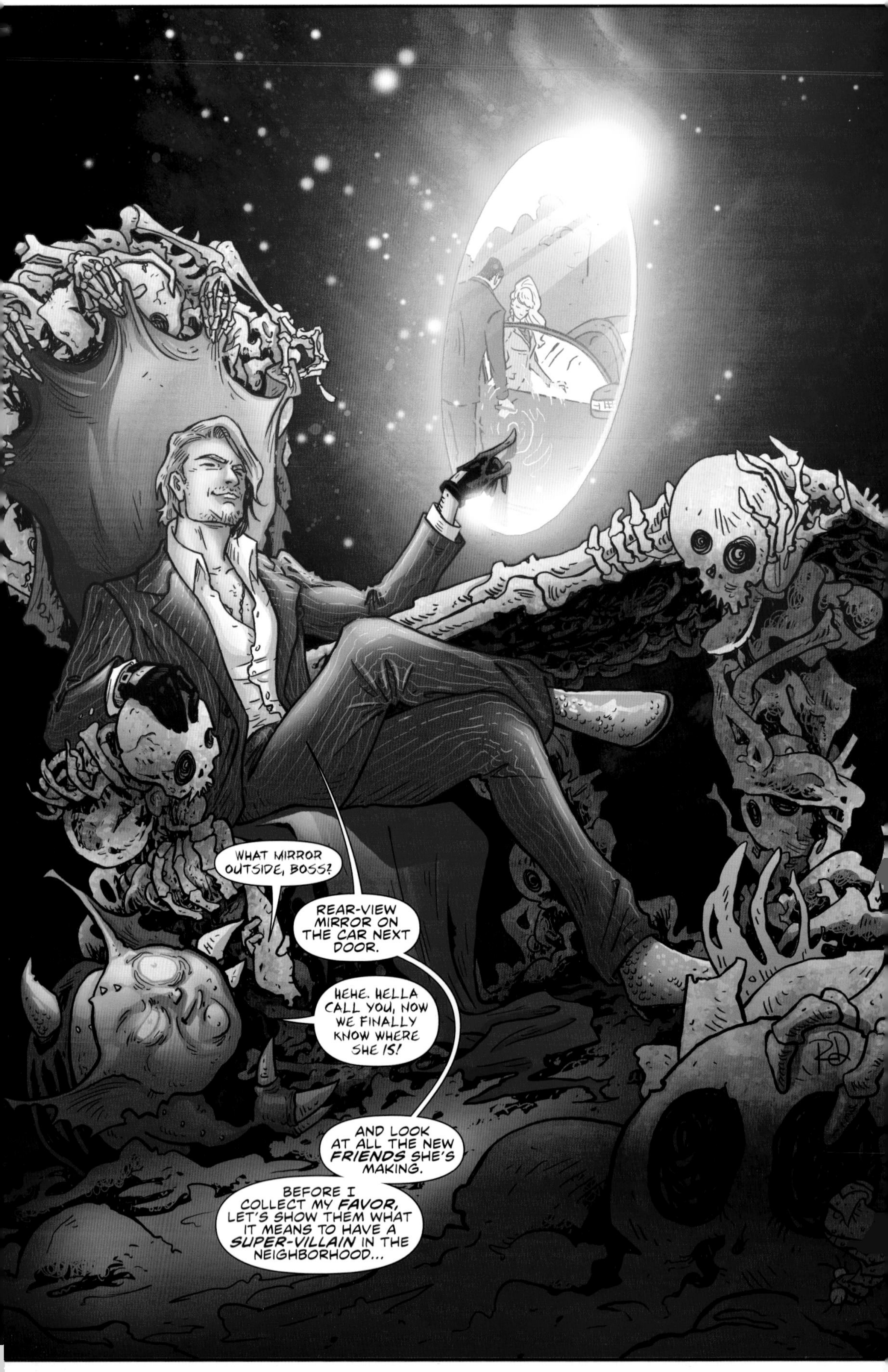
WHAT MIRROR OUTSIDE, BOSS?
REAR-VIEW MIRROR ON THE CAR NEXT DOOR.
HEHE. HELLA CALL YOU, NOW WE FINALLY KNOW WHERE SHE IS!
AND LOOK AT ALL THE NEW FRIENDS SHE'S MAKING.
BEFORE I COLLECT MY FAVOR, LET'S SHOW THEM WHAT IT MEANS TO HAVE A SUPER-VILLAIN IN THE NEIGHBORHOOD...

Chapter 2

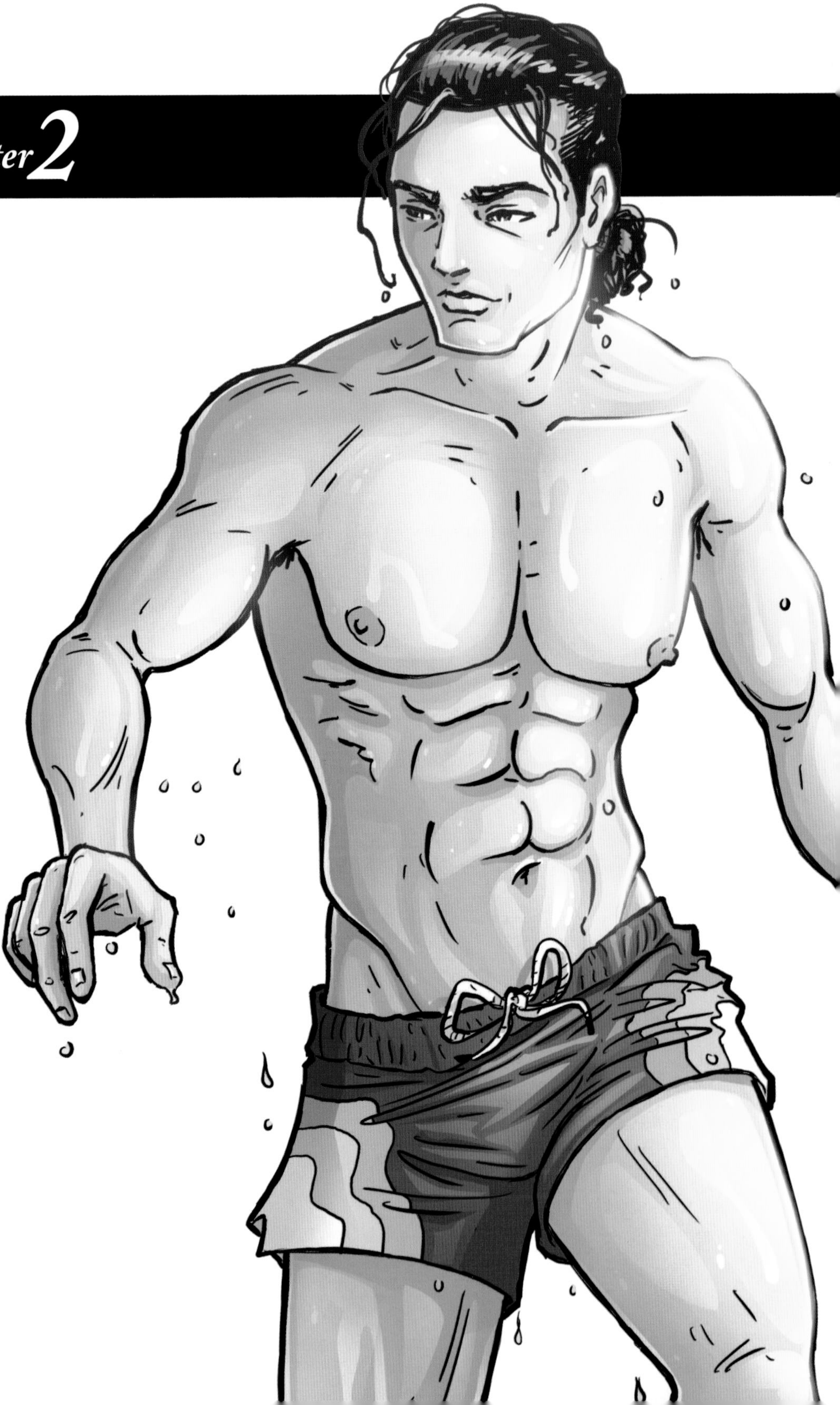

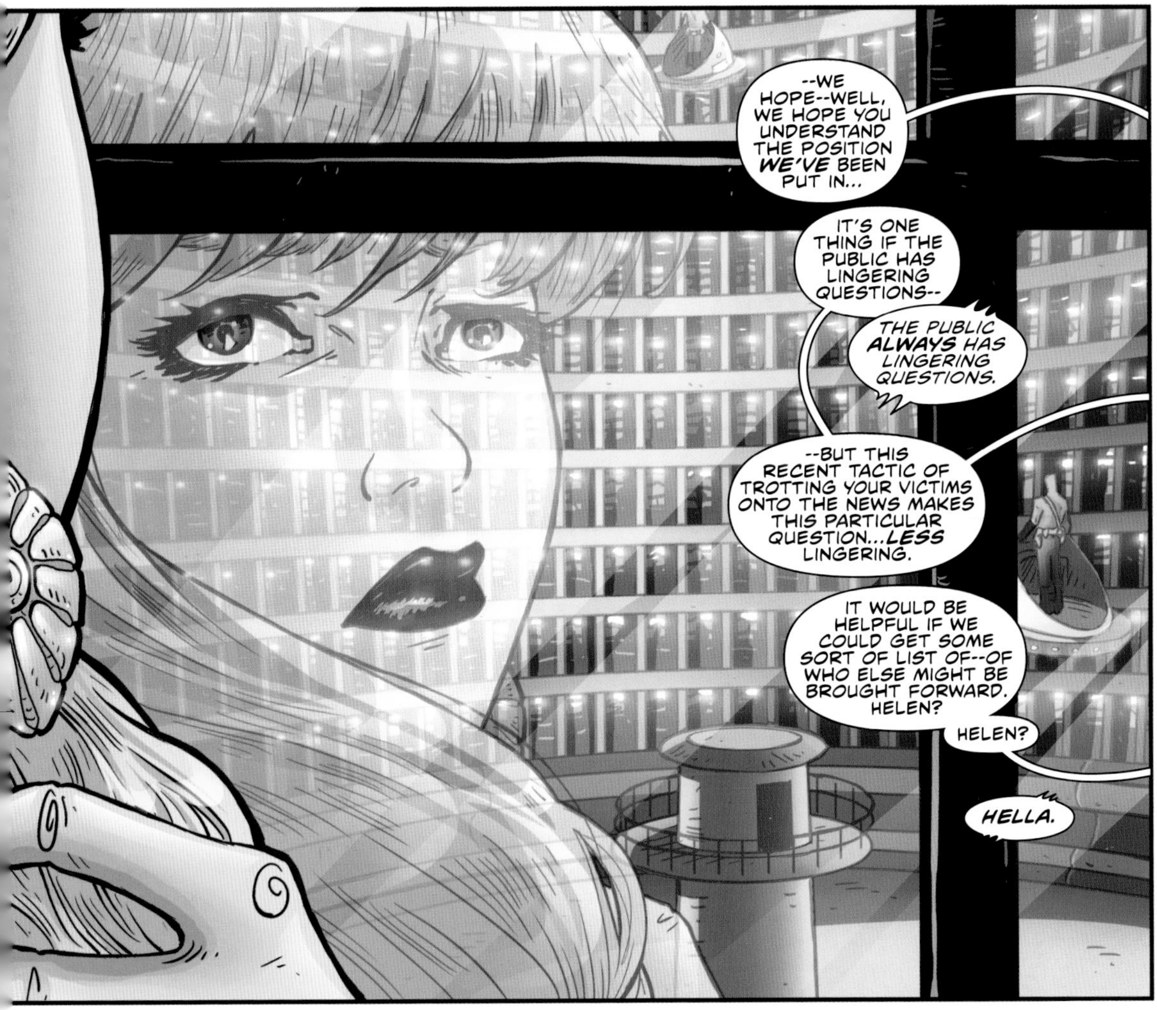
--WE HOPE--WELL, WE HOPE YOU UNDERSTAND THE POSITION WE'VE BEEN PUT IN...
IT'S ONE THING IF THE PUBLIC HAS LINGERING QUESTIONS--
THE PUBLIC ALWAYS HAS LINGERING QUESTIONS.
--BUT THIS RECENT TACTIC OF TROTTING YOUR VICTIMS ONTO THE NEWS MAKES THIS PARTICULAR QUESTION...LESS LINGERING.
IT WOULD BE HELPFUL IF WE COULD GET SOME SORT OF LIST OF--OF WHO ELSE MIGHT BE BROUGHT FORWARD. HELEN?
HELEN?
HELLA.

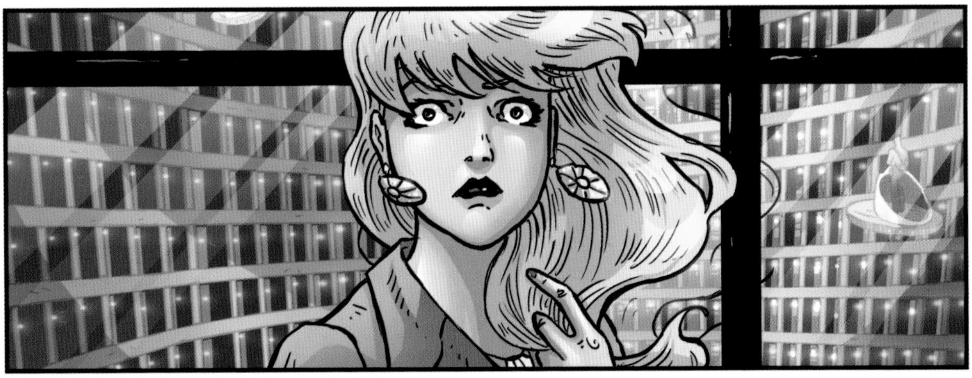

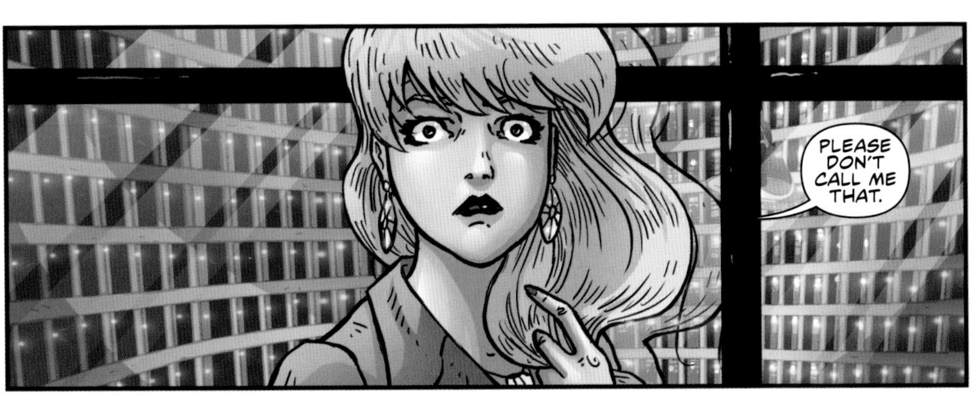
PLEASE DON'T CALL ME THAT.

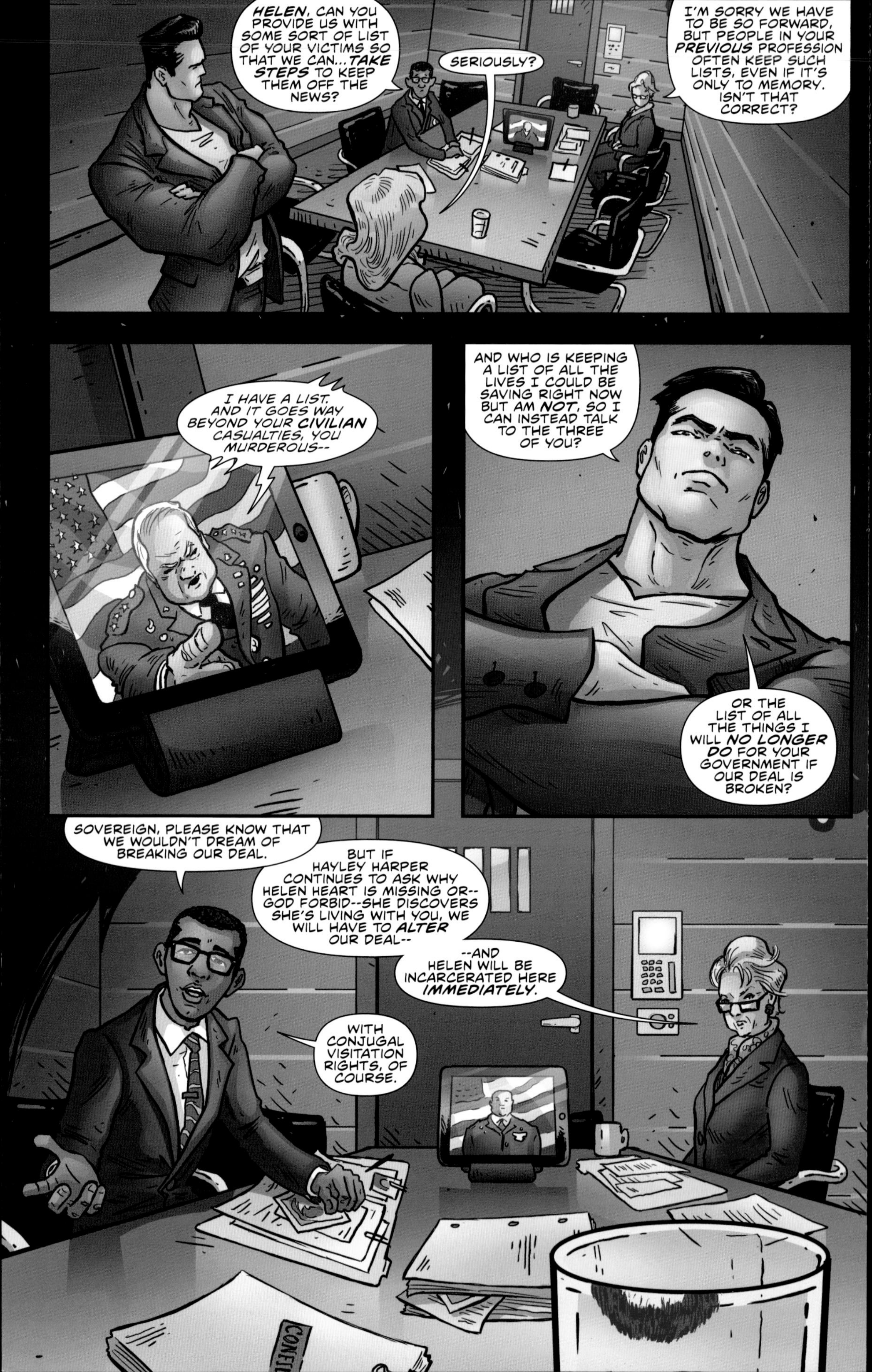
HELEN, CAN YOU PROVIDE US WITH SOME SORT OF LIST OF YOUR VICTIMS SO THAT WE CAN...TAKE STEPS TO KEEP THEM OFF THE NEWS?
SERIOUSLY?
I'M SORRY WE HAVE TO BE SO FORWARD, BUT PEOPLE IN YOUR PREVIOUS PROFESSION OFTEN KEEP SUCH LISTS, EVEN IF IT'S ONLY TO MEMORY. ISN'T THAT CORRECT?
I HAVE A LIST. AND IT GOES WAY BEYOND YOUR CIVILIAN CASUALTIES, YOU MURDEROUS--
AND WHO IS KEEPING A LIST OF ALL THE LIVES I COULD BE SAVING RIGHT NOW BUT AM NOT, SO I CAN INSTEAD TALK TO THE THREE OF YOU?
OR THE LIST OF ALL THE THINGS I WILL NO LONGER DO FOR YOUR GOVERNMENT IF OUR DEAL IS BROKEN?
SOVEREIGN, PLEASE KNOW THAT WE WOULDN'T DREAM OF BREAKING OUR DEAL.
BUT IF HAYLEY HARPER CONTINUES TO ASK WHY HELEN HEART IS MISSING OR--GOD FORBID--SHE DISCOVERS SHE'S LIVING WITH YOU, WE WILL HAVE TO ALTER OUR DEAL--
--AND HELEN WILL BE INCARCERATED HERE IMMEDIATELY.
WITH CONJUGAL VISITATION RIGHTS, OF COURSE.

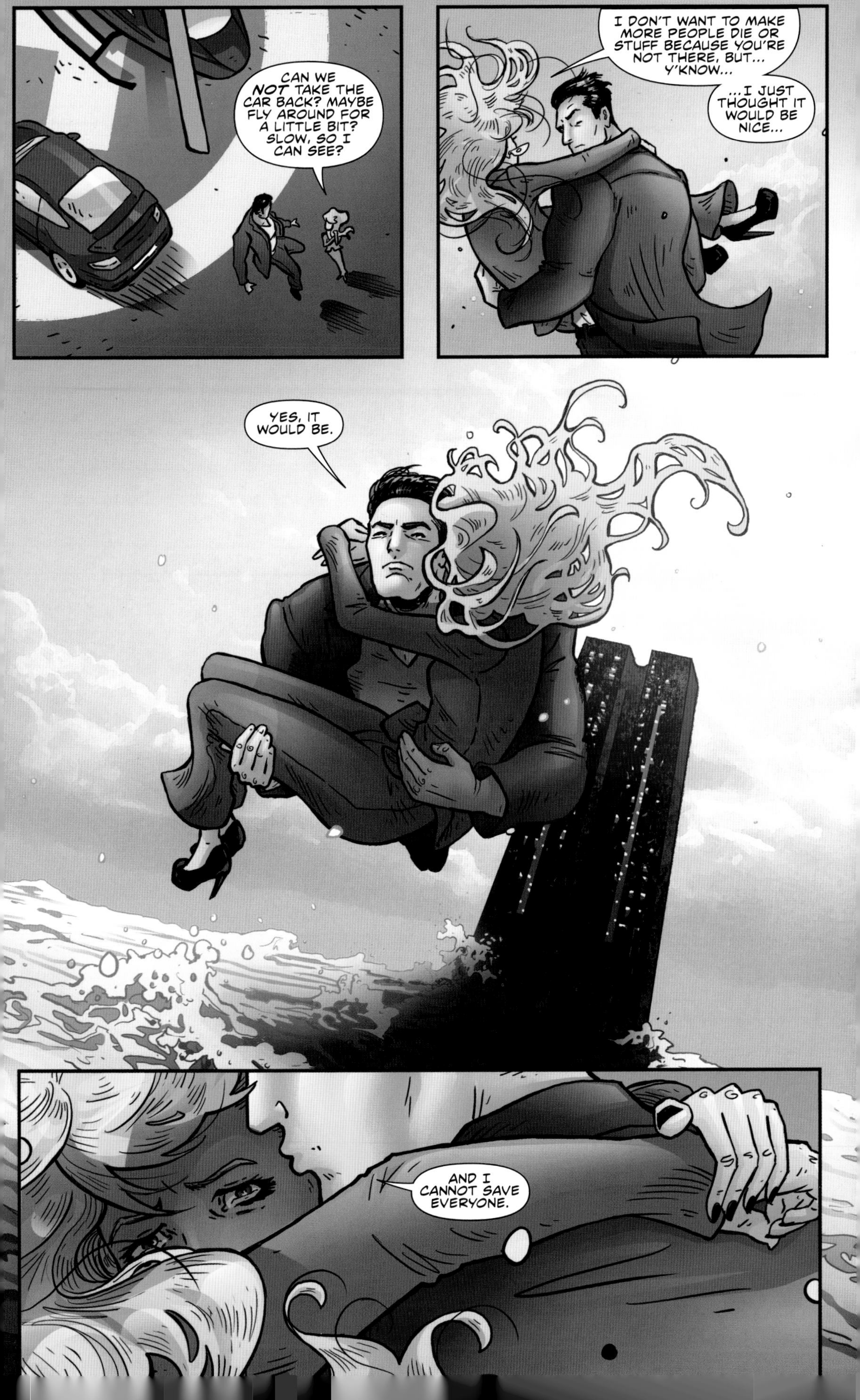
CAN WE NOT TAKE THE CAR BACK? MAYBE FLY AROUND FOR A LITTLE BIT? SLOW, SO I CAN SEE?
I DON'T WANT TO MAKE MORE PEOPLE DIE OR STUFF BECAUSE YOU'RE NOT THERE, BUT... Y'KNOW...
...I JUST THOUGHT IT WOULD BE NICE...
YES, IT WOULD BE.
AND I CANNOT SAVE EVERYONE.

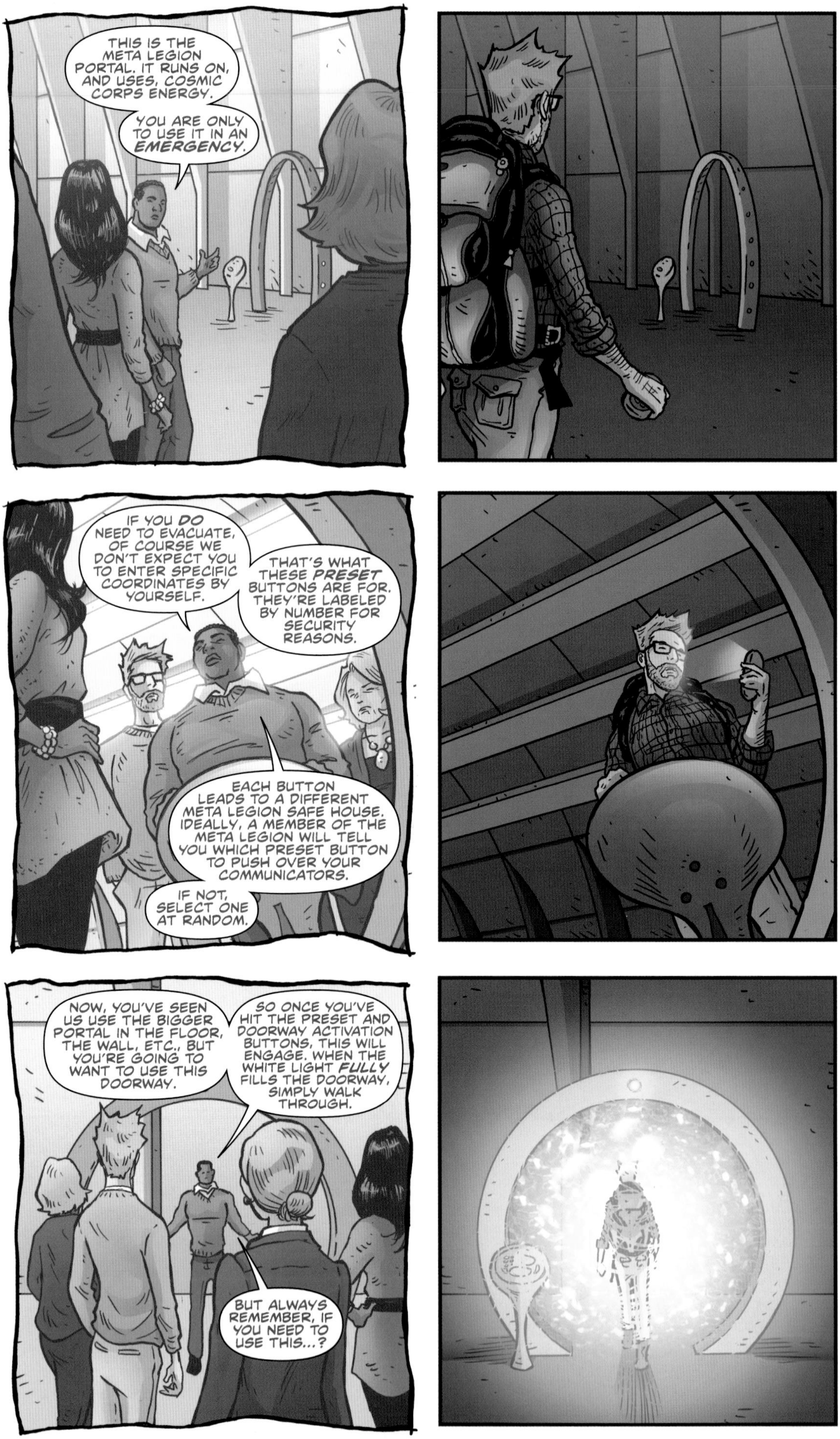

THIS IS THE META LEGION PORTAL. IT RUNS ON, AND USES, COSMIC CORPS ENERGY.
YOU ARE ONLY TO USE IT IN AN *EMERGENCY*.
IF YOU *DO* NEED TO EVACUATE, OF COURSE WE DON'T EXPECT YOU TO ENTER SPECIFIC COORDINATES BY YOURSELF.
THAT'S WHAT THESE *PRESET* BUTTONS ARE FOR. THEY'RE LABELED BY NUMBER FOR SECURITY REASONS.
EACH BUTTON LEADS TO A DIFFERENT META LEGION SAFE HOUSE. IDEALLY, A MEMBER OF THE META LEGION WILL TELL YOU WHICH PRESET BUTTON TO PUSH OVER YOUR COMMUNICATORS.
IF NOT, SELECT ONE AT RANDOM.
NOW, YOU'VE SEEN US USE THE BIGGER PORTAL IN THE FLOOR, THE WALL, ETC., BUT YOU'RE GOING TO WANT TO USE THIS DOORWAY.
SO ONCE YOU'VE HIT THE PRESET AND DOORWAY ACTIVATION BUTTONS, THIS WILL ENGAGE. WHEN THE WHITE LIGHT *FULLY* FILLS THE DOORWAY, SIMPLY WALK THROUGH.
BUT ALWAYS REMEMBER, IF YOU NEED TO USE THIS...?

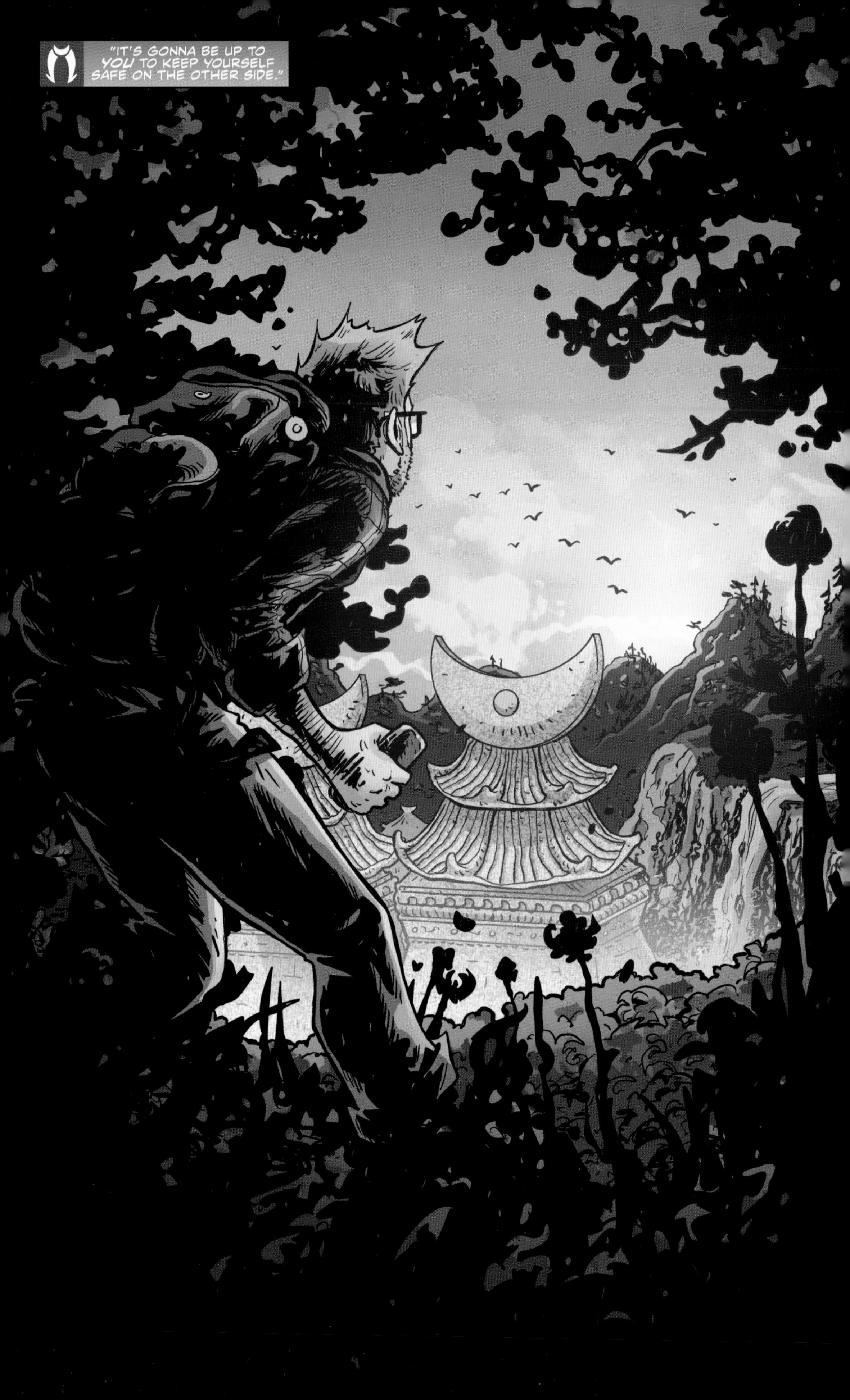
"IT'S GONNA BE UP TO YOU TO KEEP YOURSELF SAFE ON THE OTHER SIDE."

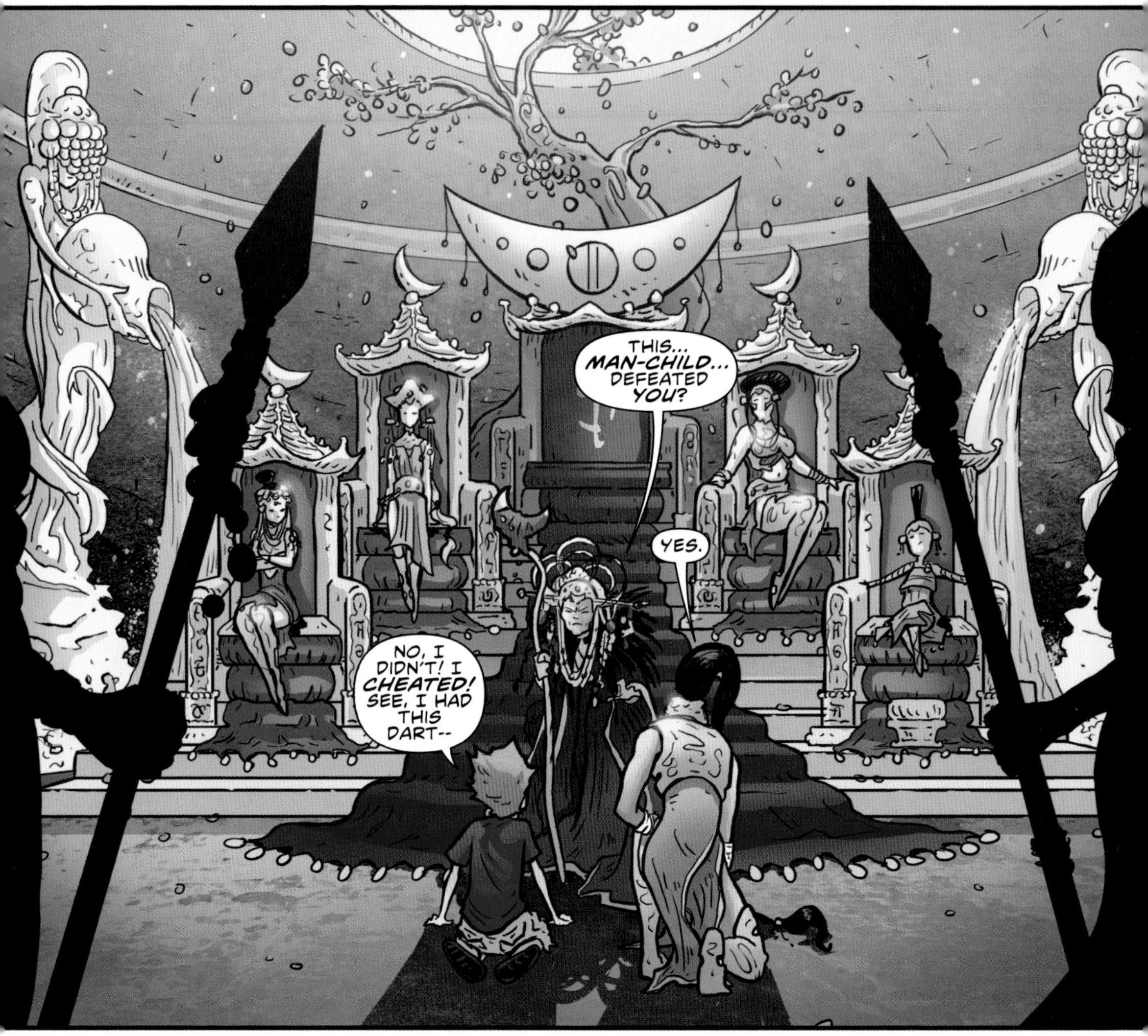
THIS... MAN-CHILD... DEFEATED YOU?
YES.
NO, I DIDN'T! I CHEATED! SEE, I HAD THIS DART--

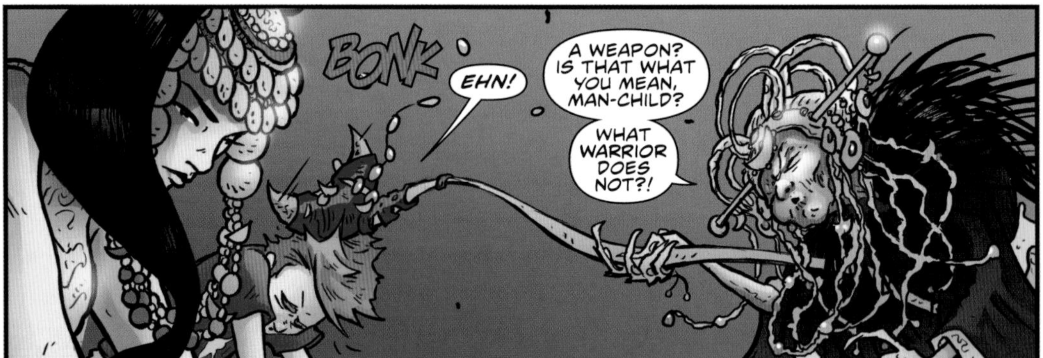
BONK
EHN!
A WEAPON? IS THAT WHAT YOU MEAN, MAN-CHILD?
WHAT WARRIOR DOES NOT?!

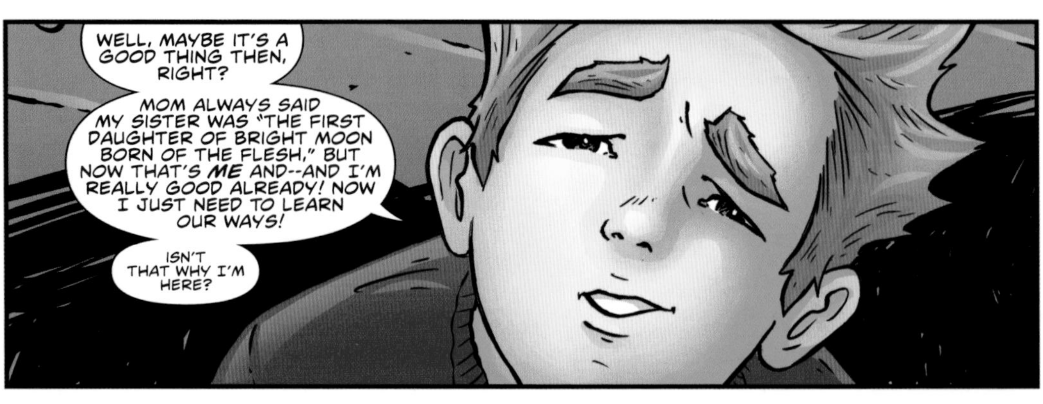
WELL, MAYBE IT'S A GOOD THING THEN, RIGHT?
MOM ALWAYS SAID MY SISTER WAS "THE FIRST DAUGHTER OF BRIGHT MOON BORN OF THE FLESH," BUT NOW THAT'S ME AND--AND I'M REALLY GOOD ALREADY! NOW I JUST NEED TO LEARN OUR WAYS!
ISN'T THAT WHY I'M HERE?

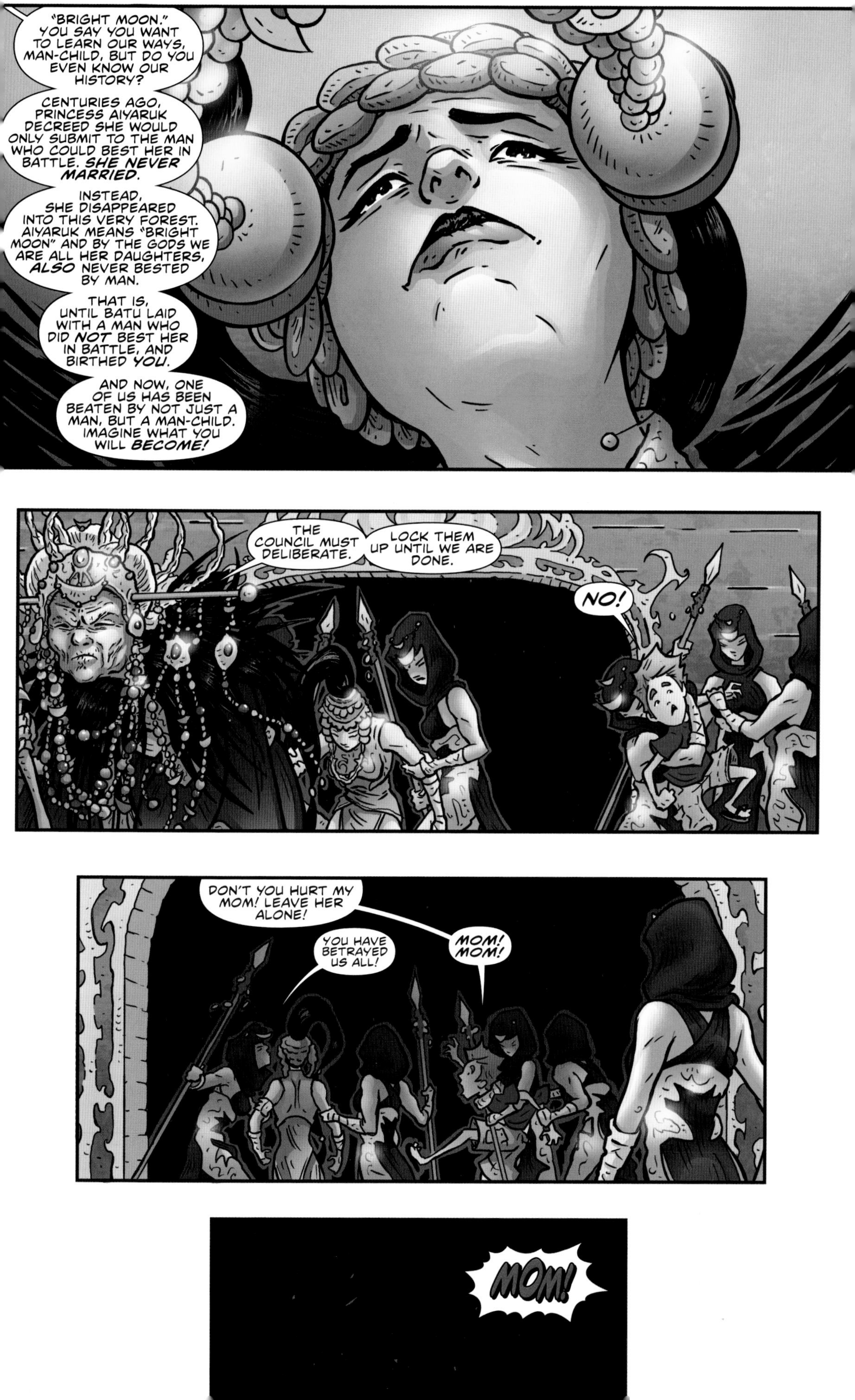

"BRIGHT MOON." YOU SAY YOU WANT TO LEARN OUR WAYS, MAN-CHILD, BUT DO YOU EVEN KNOW OUR HISTORY?
CENTURIES AGO, PRINCESS AIYARUK DECREED SHE WOULD ONLY SUBMIT TO THE MAN WHO COULD BEST HER IN BATTLE. ***SHE NEVER MARRIED.***
INSTEAD, SHE DISAPPEARED INTO THIS VERY FOREST. AIYARUK MEANS "BRIGHT MOON" AND BY THE GODS WE ARE ALL HER DAUGHTERS, ***ALSO*** NEVER BESTED BY MAN.
THAT IS, UNTIL BATU LAID WITH A MAN WHO DID ***NOT*** BEST HER IN BATTLE, AND BIRTHED ***YOU.***
AND NOW, ONE OF US HAS BEEN BEATEN BY NOT JUST A MAN, BUT A MAN-CHILD. IMAGINE WHAT YOU WILL ***BECOME!***
THE COUNCIL MUST DELIBERATE.
LOCK THEM UP UNTIL WE ARE DONE.
NO!
DON'T YOU HURT MY MOM! LEAVE HER ALONE!
YOU HAVE BETRAYED US ALL!
MOM! MOM!
MOM!

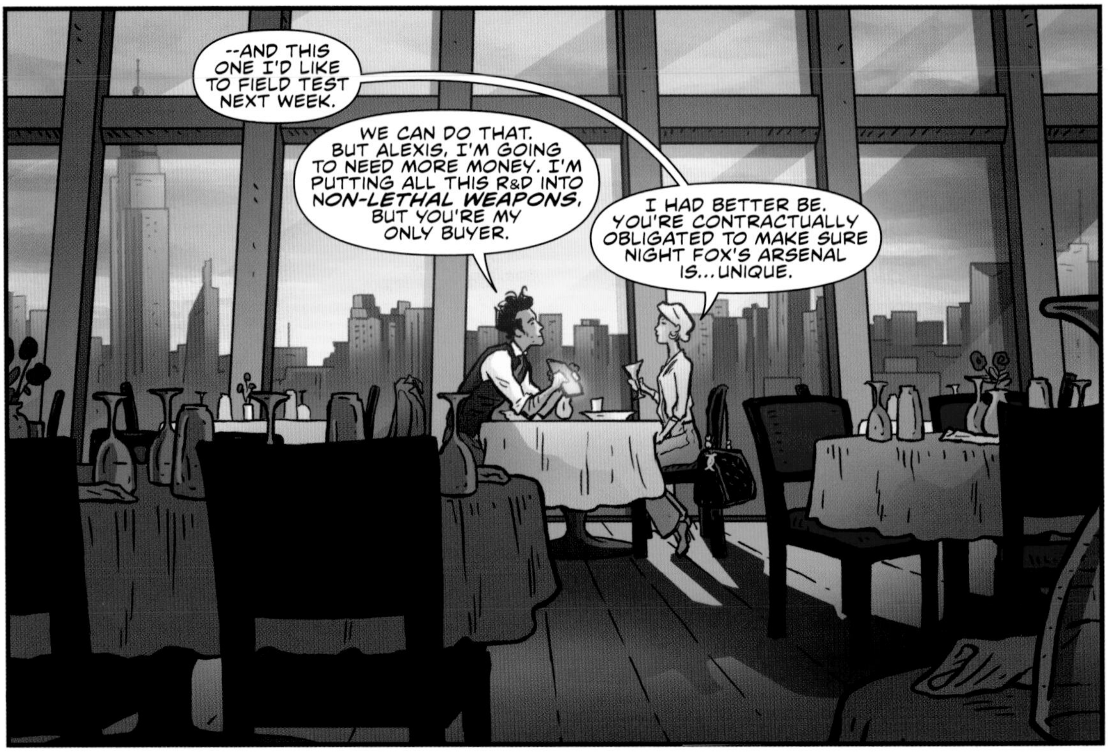
--AND THIS ONE I'D LIKE TO FIELD TEST NEXT WEEK.
WE CAN DO THAT. BUT ALEXIS, I'M GOING TO NEED MORE MONEY. I'M PUTTING ALL THIS R&D INTO *NON-LETHAL WEAPONS*, BUT YOU'RE MY ONLY BUYER.
I HAD BETTER BE. YOU'RE CONTRACTUALLY OBLIGATED TO MAKE SURE NIGHT FOX'S ARSENAL IS...UNIQUE.

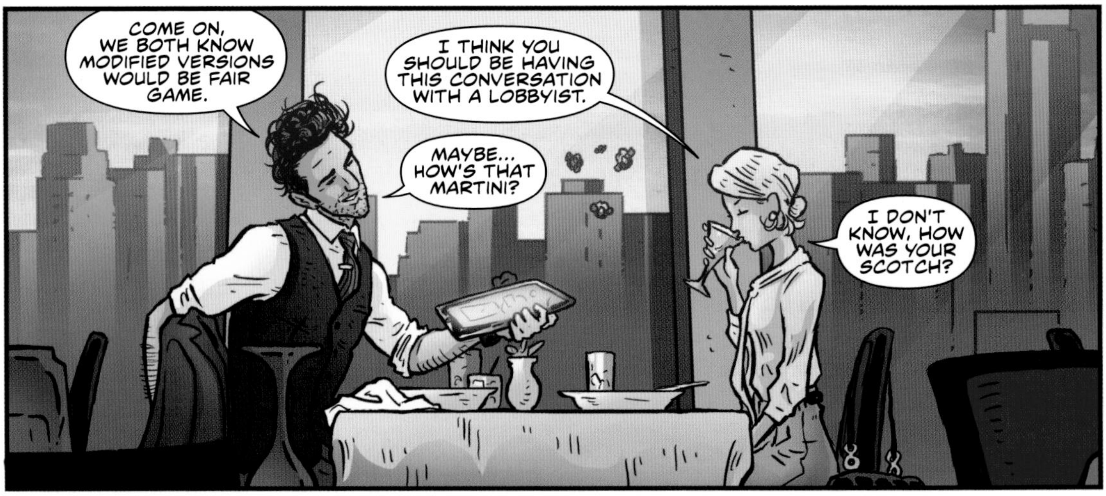
COME ON, WE BOTH KNOW MODIFIED VERSIONS WOULD BE FAIR GAME.
I THINK YOU SHOULD BE HAVING THIS CONVERSATION WITH A LOBBYIST.
MAYBE... HOW'S THAT MARTINI?
I DON'T KNOW, HOW WAS YOUR SCOTCH?

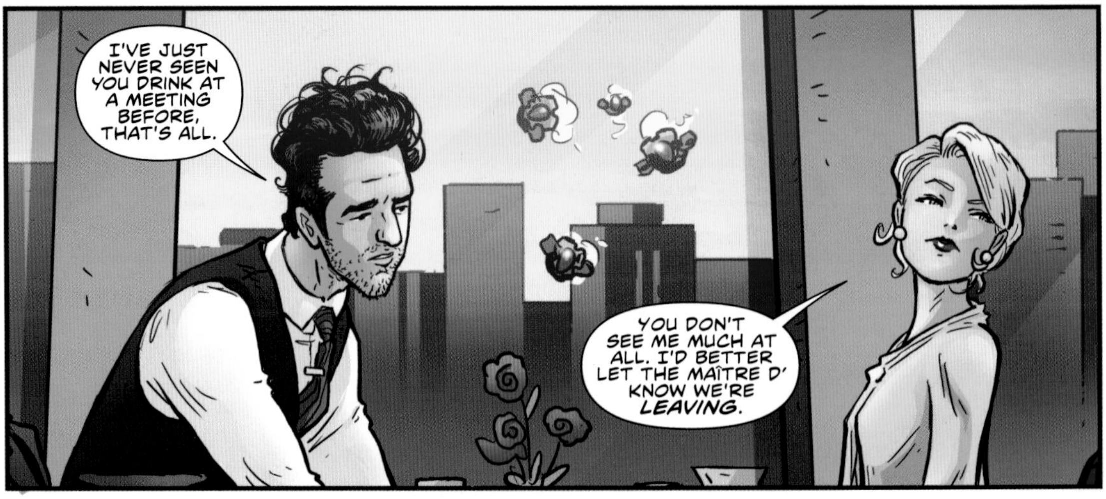
I'VE JUST NEVER SEEN YOU DRINK AT A MEETING BEFORE, THAT'S ALL.
YOU DON'T SEE ME MUCH AT ALL. I'D BETTER LET THE MAÎTRE D' KNOW WE'RE *LEAVING*.

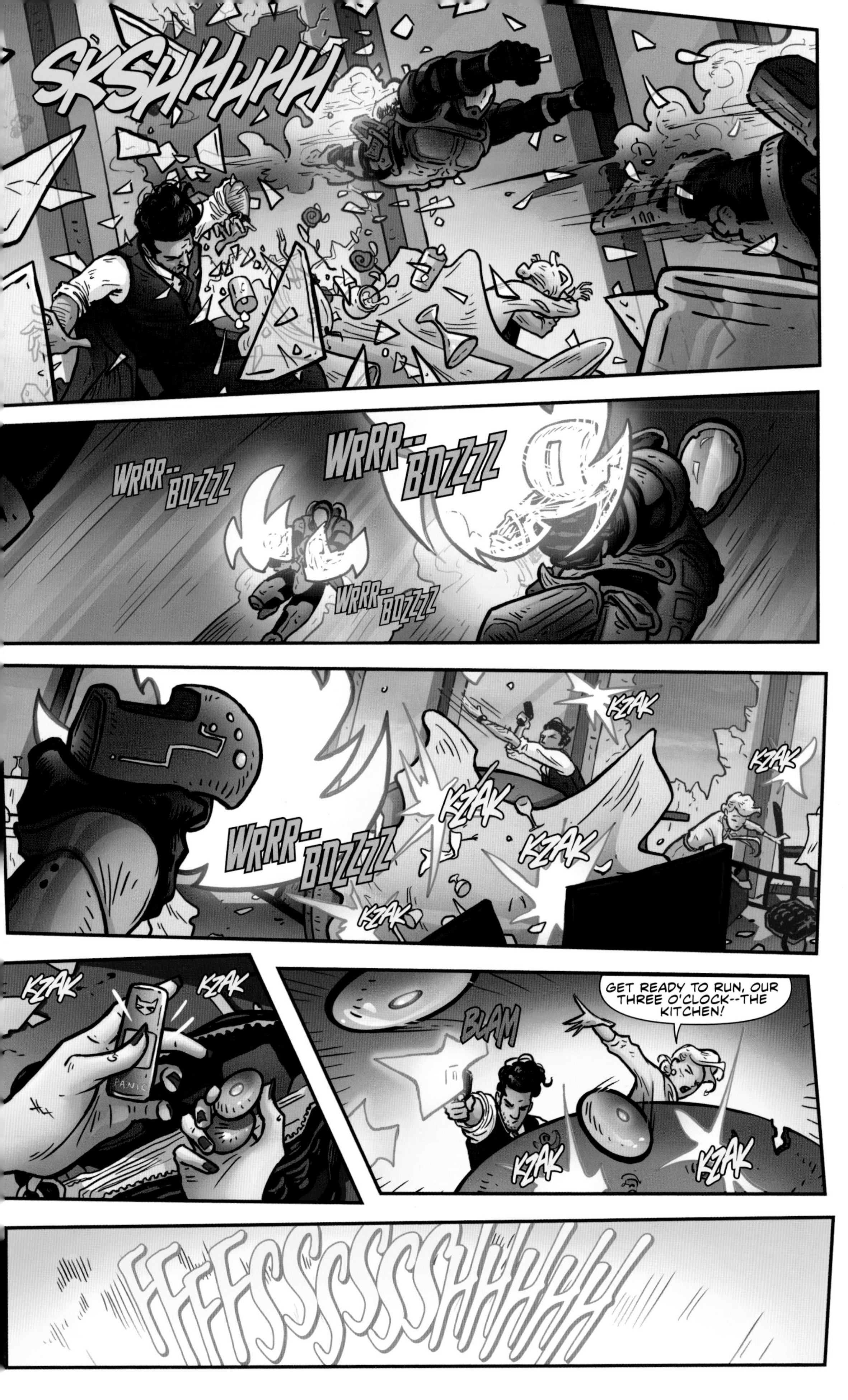
SKSHHHHH
WRRR-- BOZZZ
WRRR-- BOZZZ
WRRR-- BOZZZ
KZAK
WRRR-- BOZZZZ
KZAK
KZAK
KZAK
KZAK
KZAK
KZAK
PANIC
BLAM
GET READY TO RUN, OUR THREE O'CLOCK--THE KITCHEN!
KZAK
KZAK
FFFFSSSSSCHHHHH

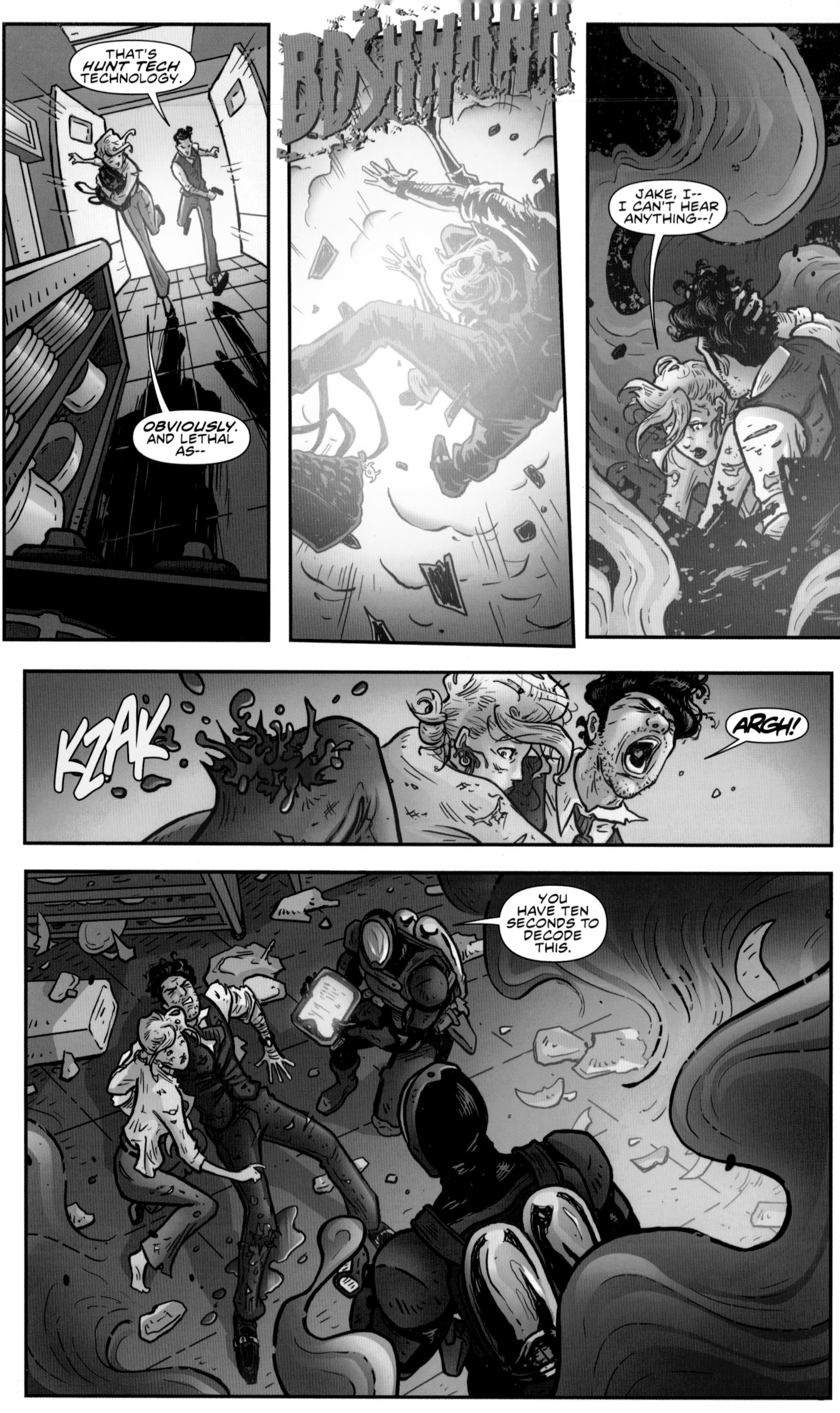
THAT'S HUNT TECH TECHNOLOGY.
OBVIOUSLY. AND LETHAL AS--
BOSHHHHH
JAKE, I-- I CAN'T HEAR ANYTHING--!
KZAK
ARGH!
YOU HAVE TEN SECONDS TO DECODE THIS.

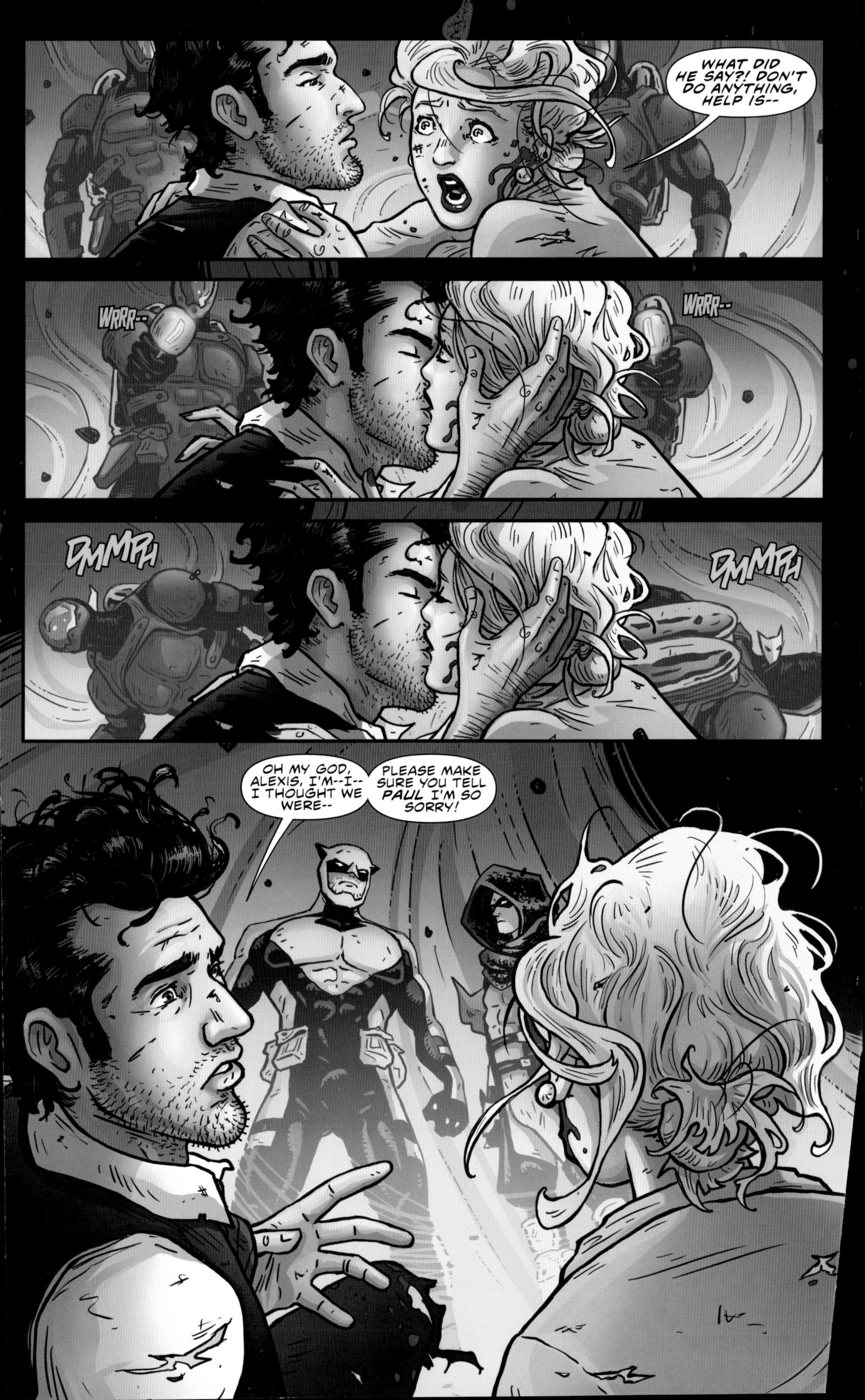
WHAT DID HE SAY?! DON'T DO ANYTHING, HELP IS--
WRRR--
WRRR--
DMMPH
DMMPH
OH MY GOD, ALEXIS, I'M--I-- I THOUGHT WE WERE--
PLEASE MAKE SURE YOU TELL PAUL I'M SO SORRY!

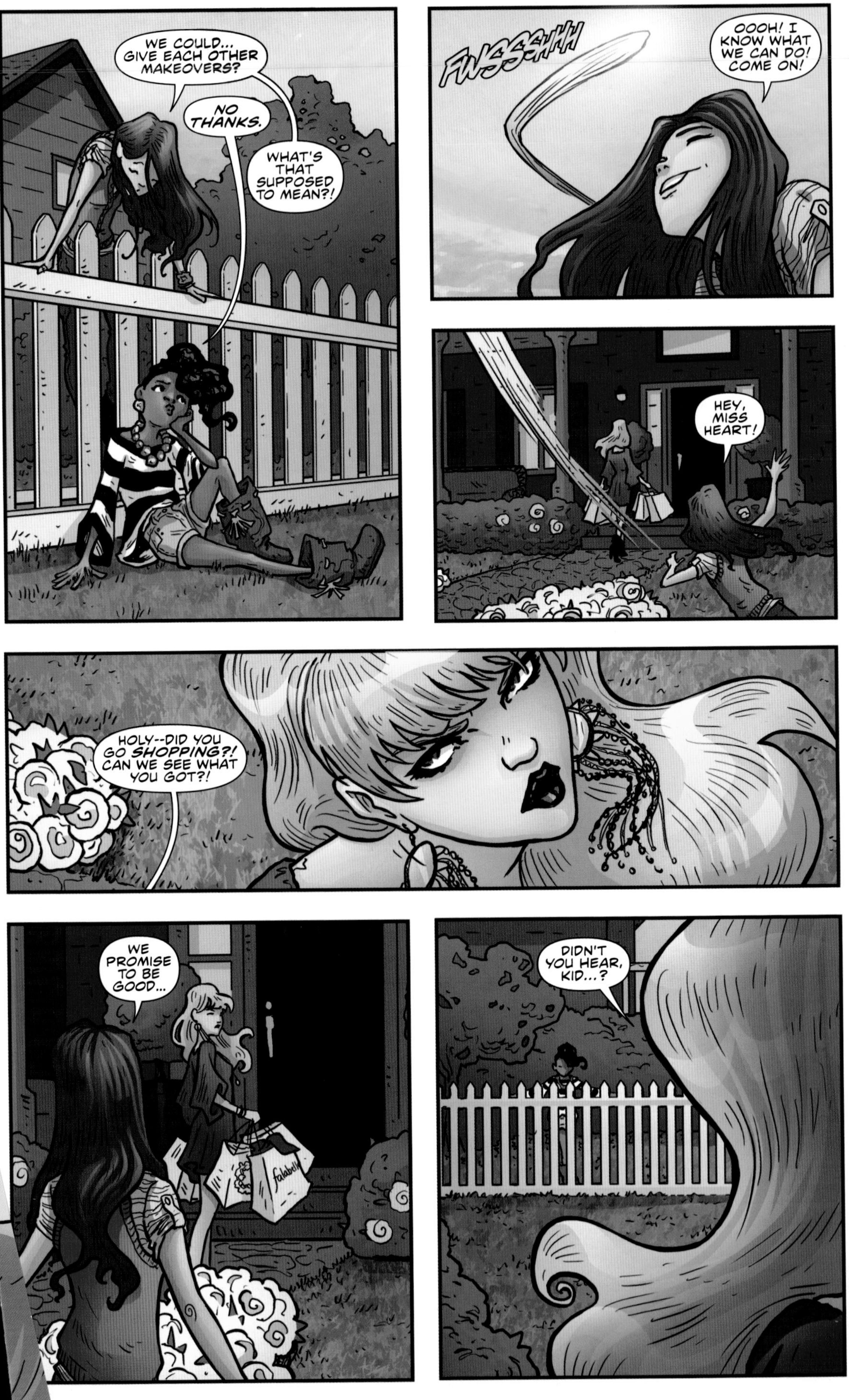
WE COULD... GIVE EACH OTHER MAKEOVERS?
NO THANKS.
WHAT'S THAT SUPPOSED TO MEAN?!
FWSSSHHH
OOOH! I KNOW WHAT WE CAN DO! COME ON!
HEY, MISS HEART!
HOLY--DID YOU GO SHOPPING?! CAN WE SEE WHAT YOU GOT?!
WE PROMISE TO BE GOOD...
DIDN'T YOU HEAR, KID...?

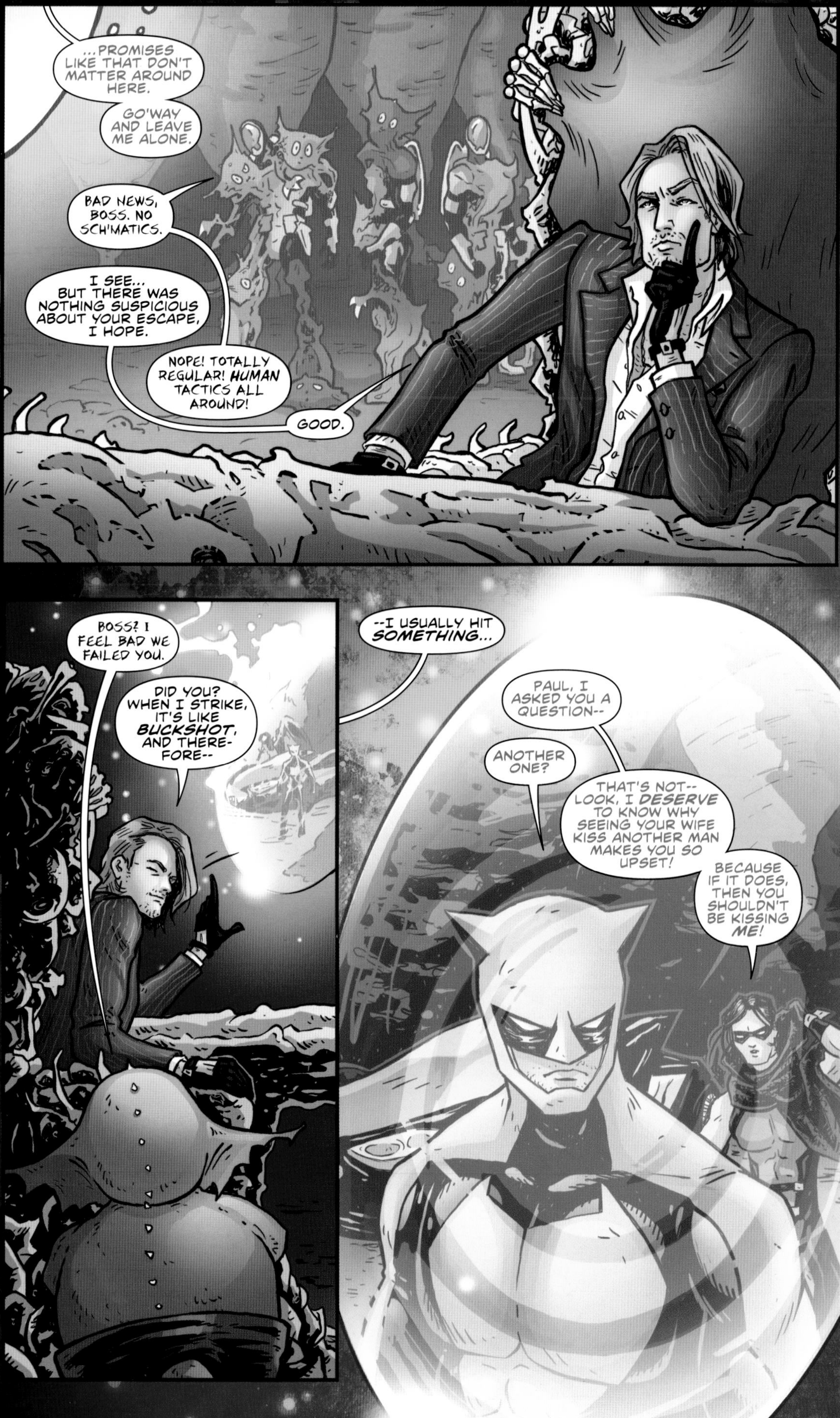
...PROMISES LIKE THAT DON'T MATTER AROUND HERE.
GO'WAY AND LEAVE ME ALONE.
BAD NEWS, BOSS. NO SCH'MATICS.
I SEE... BUT THERE WAS NOTHING SUSPICIOUS ABOUT YOUR ESCAPE, I HOPE.
NOPE! TOTALLY REGULAR! HUMAN TACTICS ALL AROUND!
GOOD.
BOSS? I FEEL BAD WE FAILED YOU.
DID YOU? WHEN I STRIKE, IT'S LIKE BUCKSHOT, AND THERE-FORE--
--I USUALLY HIT SOMETHING...
PAUL, I ASKED YOU A QUESTION--
ANOTHER ONE?
THAT'S NOT-- LOOK, I DESERVE TO KNOW WHY SEEING YOUR WIFE KISS ANOTHER MAN MAKES YOU SO UPSET!
BECAUSE IF IT DOES, THEN YOU SHOULDN'T BE KISSING ME!

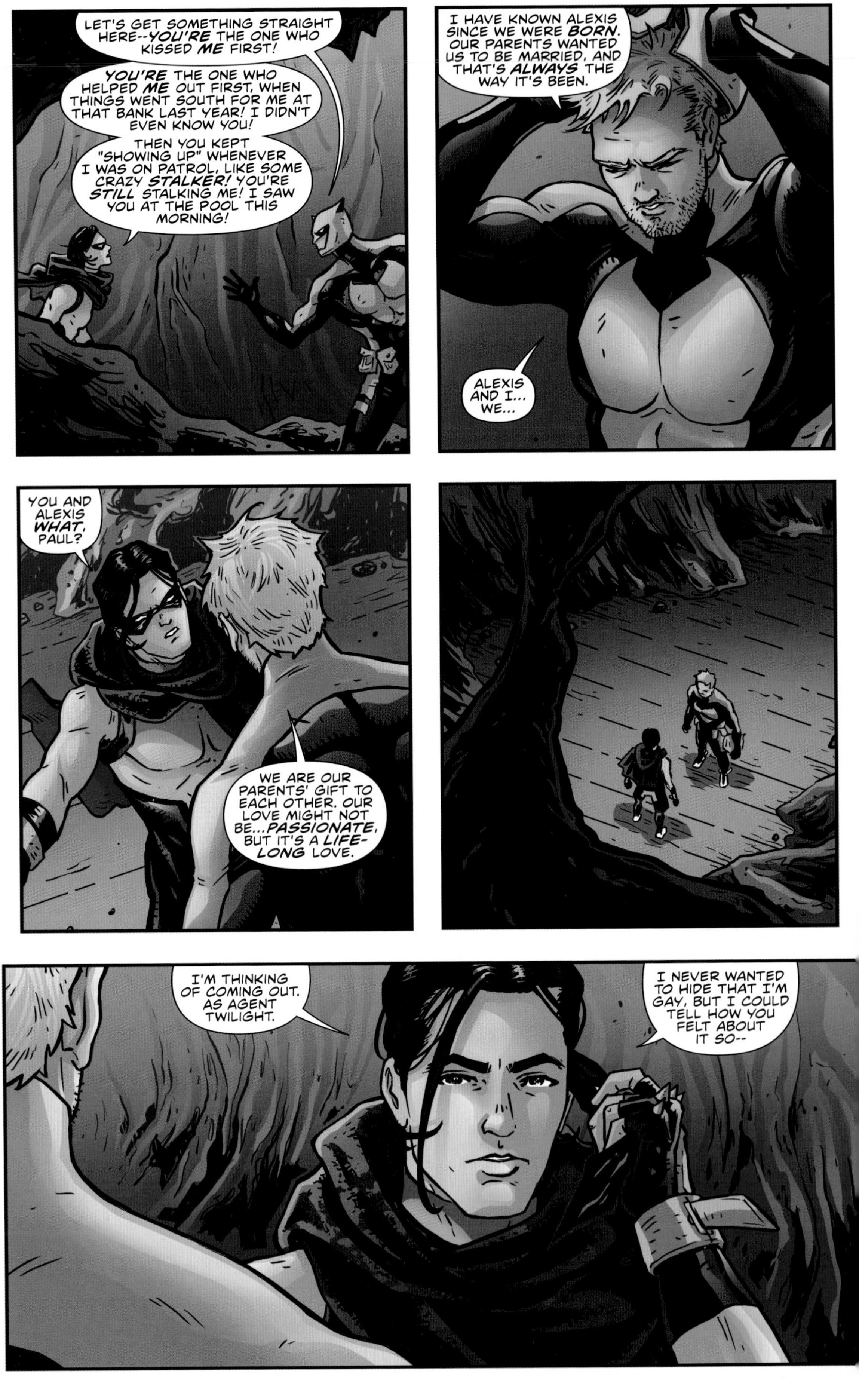
LET'S GET SOMETHING STRAIGHT HERE--YOU'RE THE ONE WHO KISSED ME FIRST!
YOU'RE THE ONE WHO HELPED ME OUT FIRST, WHEN THINGS WENT SOUTH FOR ME AT THAT BANK LAST YEAR! I DIDN'T EVEN KNOW YOU!
THEN YOU KEPT "SHOWING UP" WHENEVER I WAS ON PATROL, LIKE SOME CRAZY STALKER! YOU'RE STILL STALKING ME! I SAW YOU AT THE POOL THIS MORNING!
I HAVE KNOWN ALEXIS SINCE WE WERE BORN. OUR PARENTS WANTED US TO BE MARRIED, AND THAT'S ALWAYS THE WAY IT'S BEEN.
ALEXIS AND I... WE...
YOU AND ALEXIS WHAT, PAUL?
WE ARE OUR PARENTS' GIFT TO EACH OTHER. OUR LOVE MIGHT NOT BE...PASSIONATE, BUT IT'S A LIFE-LONG LOVE.
I'M THINKING OF COMING OUT. AS AGENT TWILIGHT.
I NEVER WANTED TO HIDE THAT I'M GAY, BUT I COULD TELL HOW YOU FELT ABOUT IT SO--

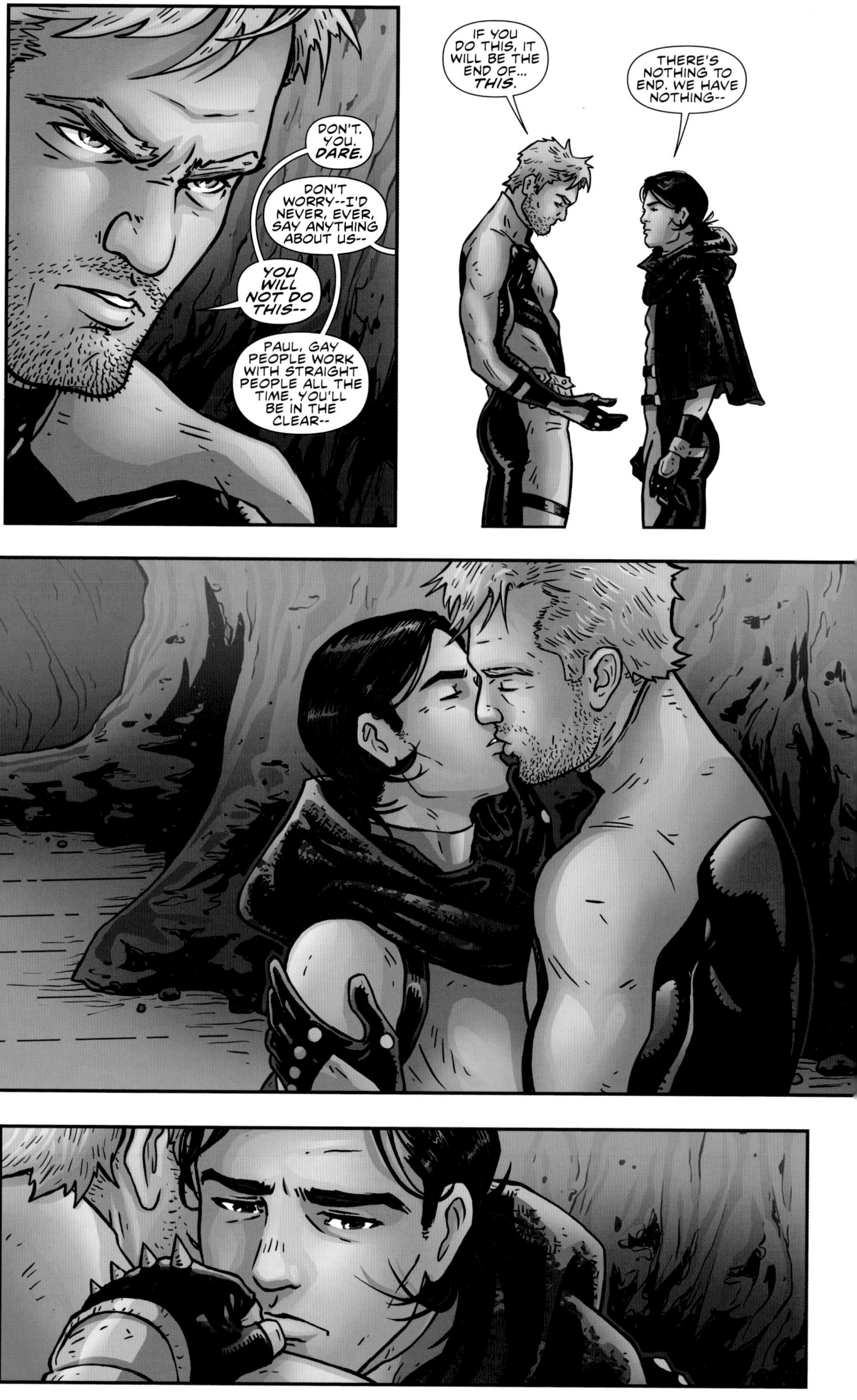
DON'T. YOU. DARE.
DON'T WORRY--I'D NEVER, EVER, SAY ANYTHING ABOUT US--
YOU WILL NOT DO THIS--
PAUL, GAY PEOPLE WORK WITH STRAIGHT PEOPLE ALL THE TIME. YOU'LL BE IN THE CLEAR--
IF YOU DO THIS, IT WILL BE THE END OF... THIS.
THERE'S NOTHING TO END. WE HAVE NOTHING--

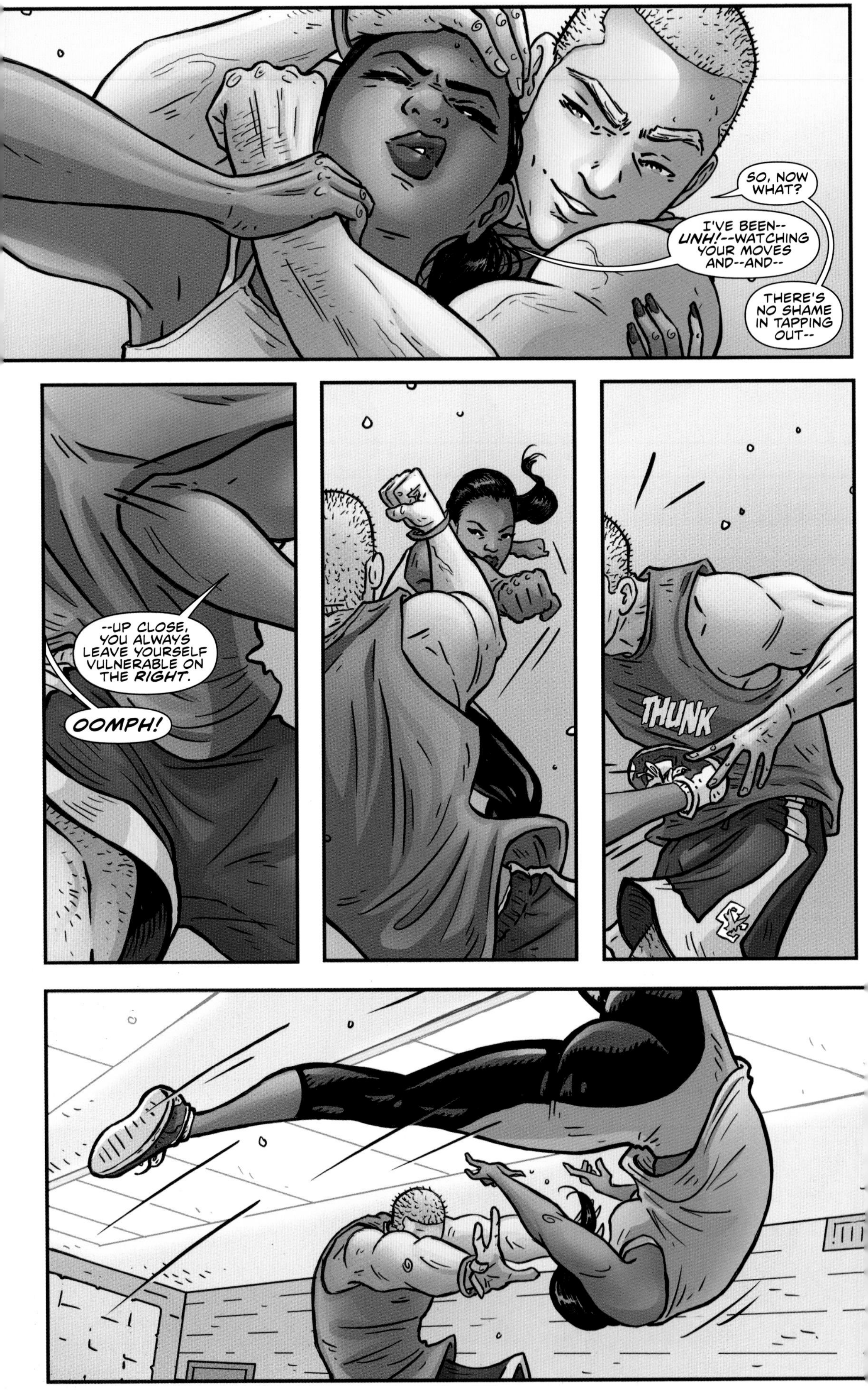

SO, NOW WHAT?
I'VE BEEN-- UNH!--WATCHING YOUR MOVES AND--AND--
THERE'S NO SHAME IN TAPPING OUT--
--UP CLOSE, YOU ALWAYS LEAVE YOURSELF VULNERABLE ON THE RIGHT.
OOMPH!
THUNK

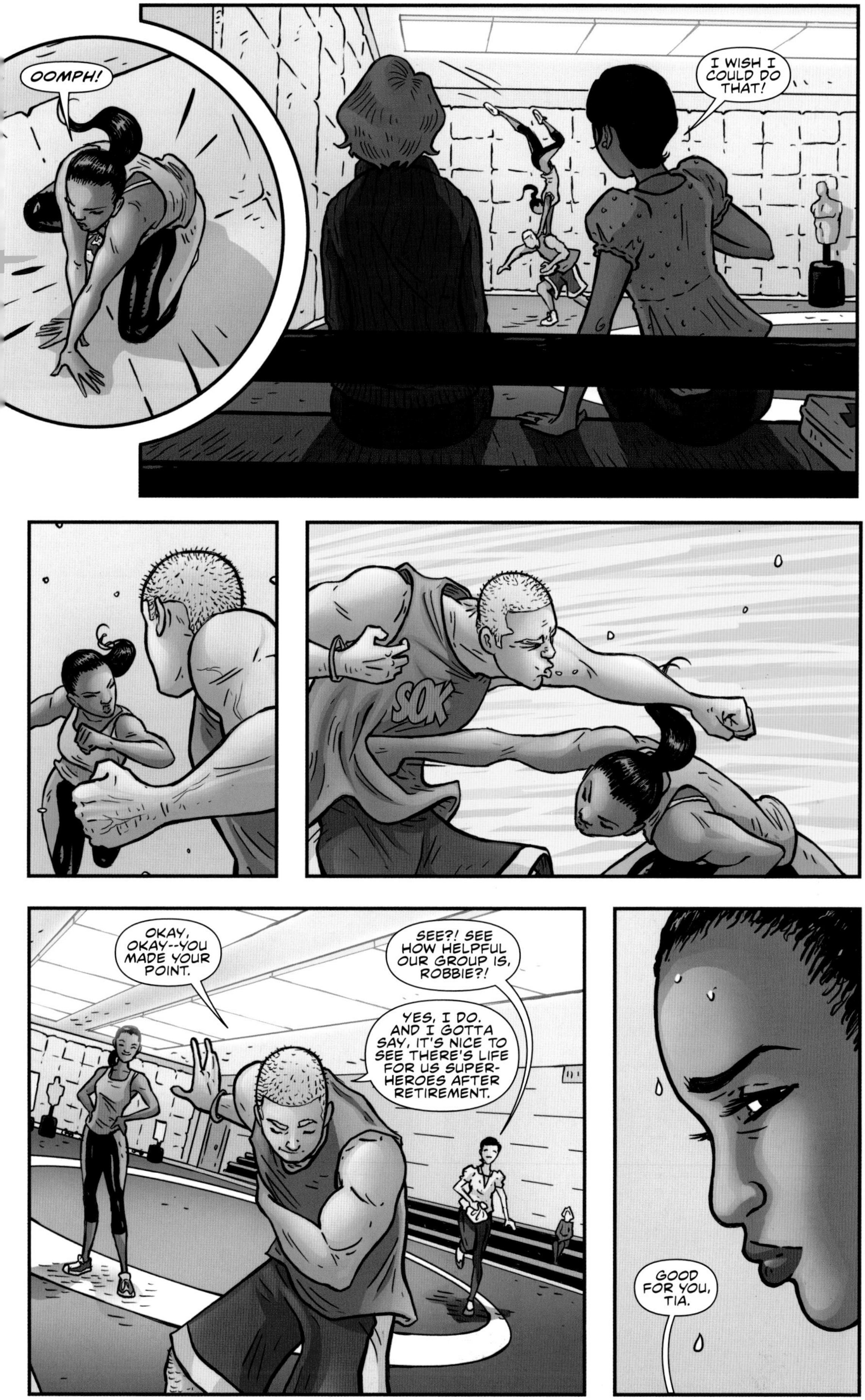
OOMPH!
I WISH I COULD DO THAT!
SOK
OKAY, OKAY--YOU MADE YOUR POINT.
SEE?! SEE HOW HELPFUL OUR GROUP IS, ROBBIE?!
YES, I DO. AND I GOTTA SAY, IT'S NICE TO SEE THERE'S LIFE FOR US SUPER-HEROES AFTER RETIREMENT.
GOOD FOR YOU, TIA.

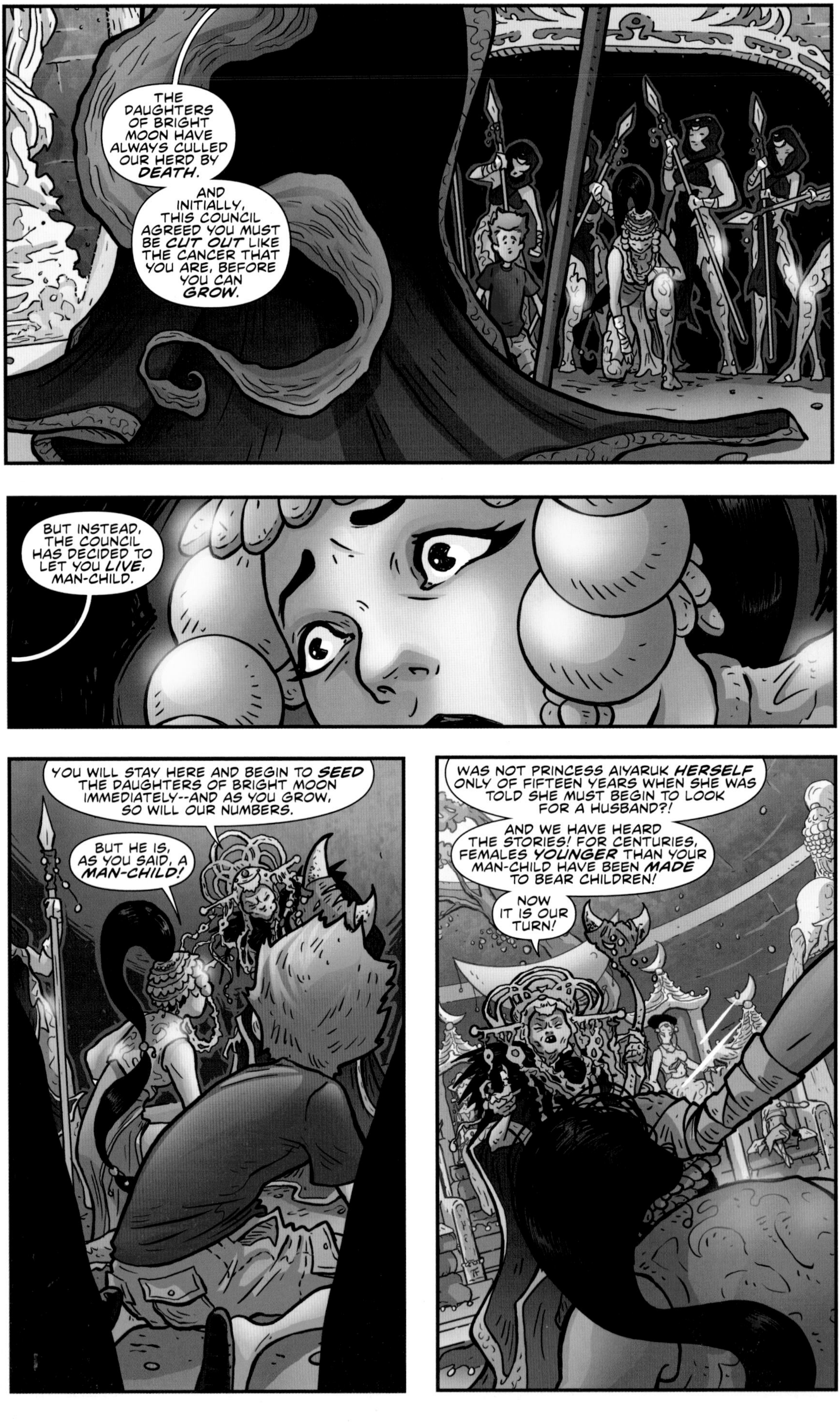
THE DAUGHTERS OF BRIGHT MOON HAVE ALWAYS CULLED OUR HERD BY DEATH.
AND INITIALLY, THIS COUNCIL AGREED YOU MUST BE CUT OUT LIKE THE CANCER THAT YOU ARE, BEFORE YOU CAN GROW.
BUT INSTEAD, THE COUNCIL HAS DECIDED TO LET YOU LIVE, MAN-CHILD.
YOU WILL STAY HERE AND BEGIN TO SEED THE DAUGHTERS OF BRIGHT MOON IMMEDIATELY--AND AS YOU GROW, SO WILL OUR NUMBERS.
BUT HE IS, AS YOU SAID, A MAN-CHILD!
WAS NOT PRINCESS AIYARUK HERSELF ONLY OF FIFTEEN YEARS WHEN SHE WAS TOLD SHE MUST BEGIN TO LOOK FOR A HUSBAND?!
AND WE HAVE HEARD THE STORIES! FOR CENTURIES, FEMALES YOUNGER THAN YOUR MAN-CHILD HAVE BEEN MADE TO BEAR CHILDREN!
NOW IT IS OUR TURN!

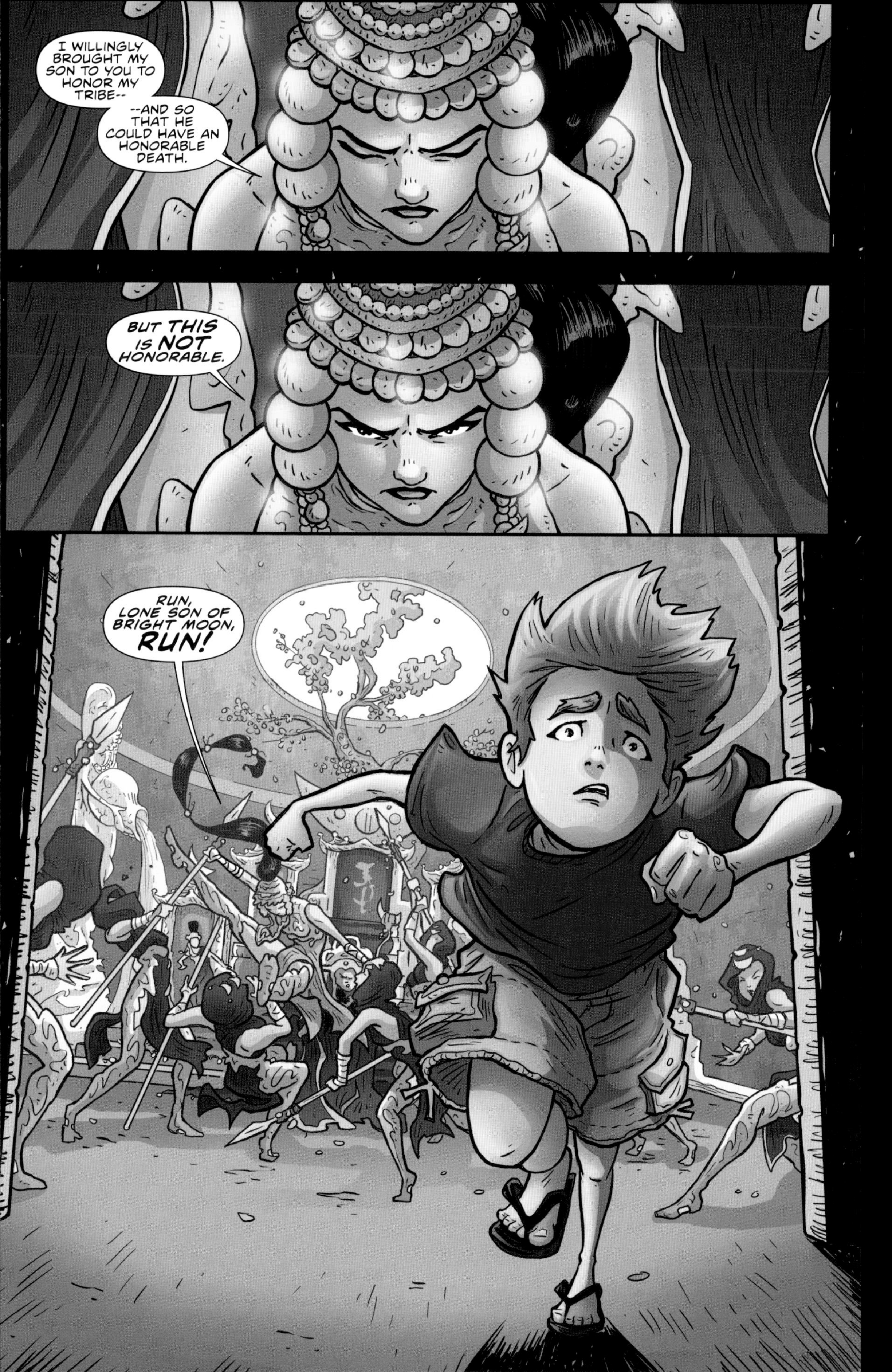
I WILLINGLY BROUGHT MY SON TO YOU TO HONOR MY TRIBE--
--AND SO THAT HE COULD HAVE AN HONORABLE DEATH.
BUT THIS IS NOT HONORABLE.
RUN, LONE SON OF BRIGHT MOON, RUN!

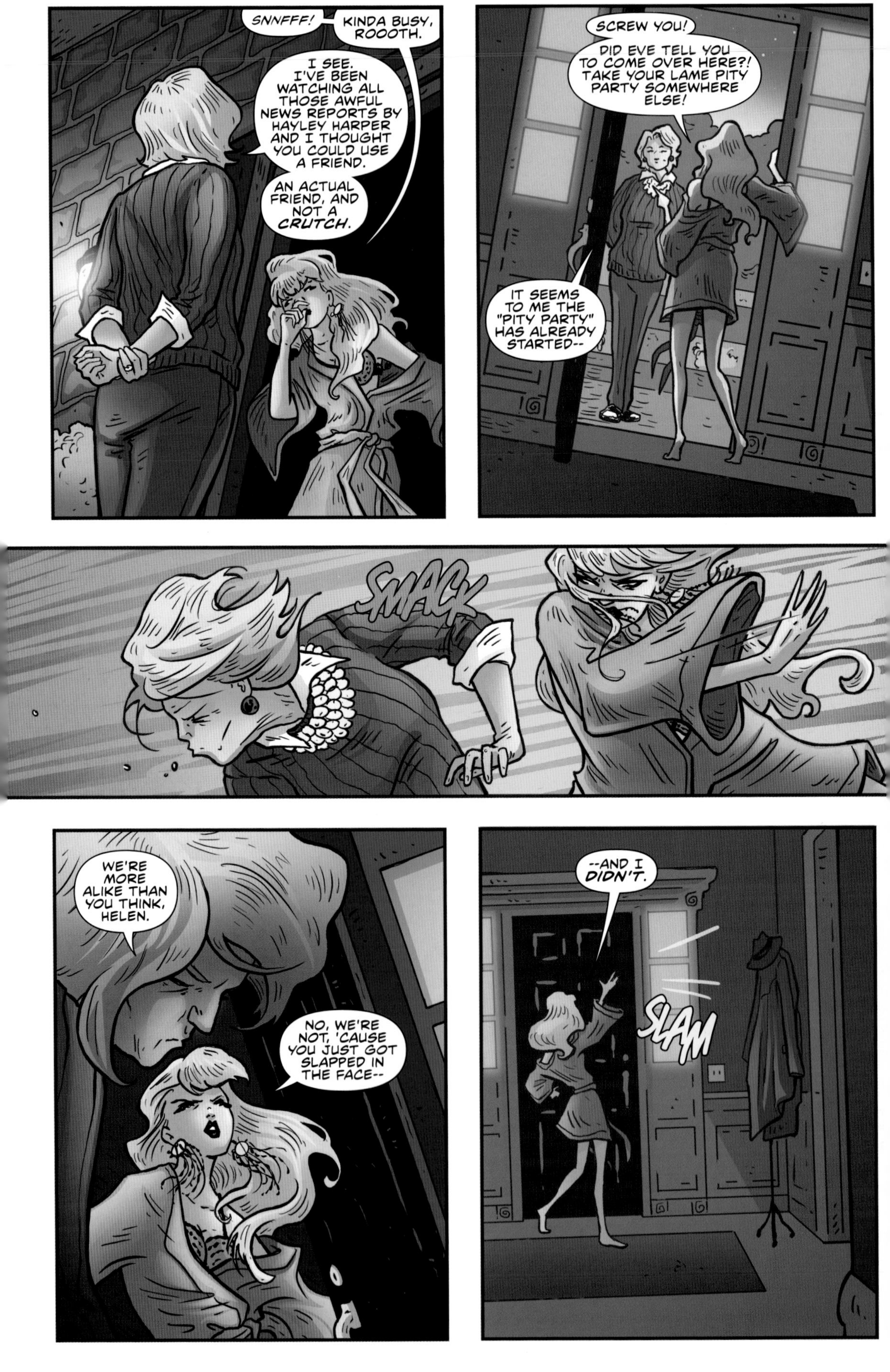
SNNFFF!
KINDA BUSY, ROOOTH.
I SEE. I'VE BEEN WATCHING ALL THOSE AWFUL NEWS REPORTS BY HAYLEY HARPER AND I THOUGHT YOU COULD USE A FRIEND.
AN ACTUAL FRIEND, AND NOT A CRUTCH.
SCREW YOU!
DID EVE TELL YOU TO COME OVER HERE?! TAKE YOUR LAME PITY PARTY SOMEWHERE ELSE!
IT SEEMS TO ME THE "PITY PARTY" HAS ALREADY STARTED--
SMACK
WE'RE MORE ALIKE THAN YOU THINK, HELEN.
NO, WE'RE NOT, 'CAUSE YOU JUST GOT SLAPPED IN THE FACE--
--AND I DIDN'T.
SLAM

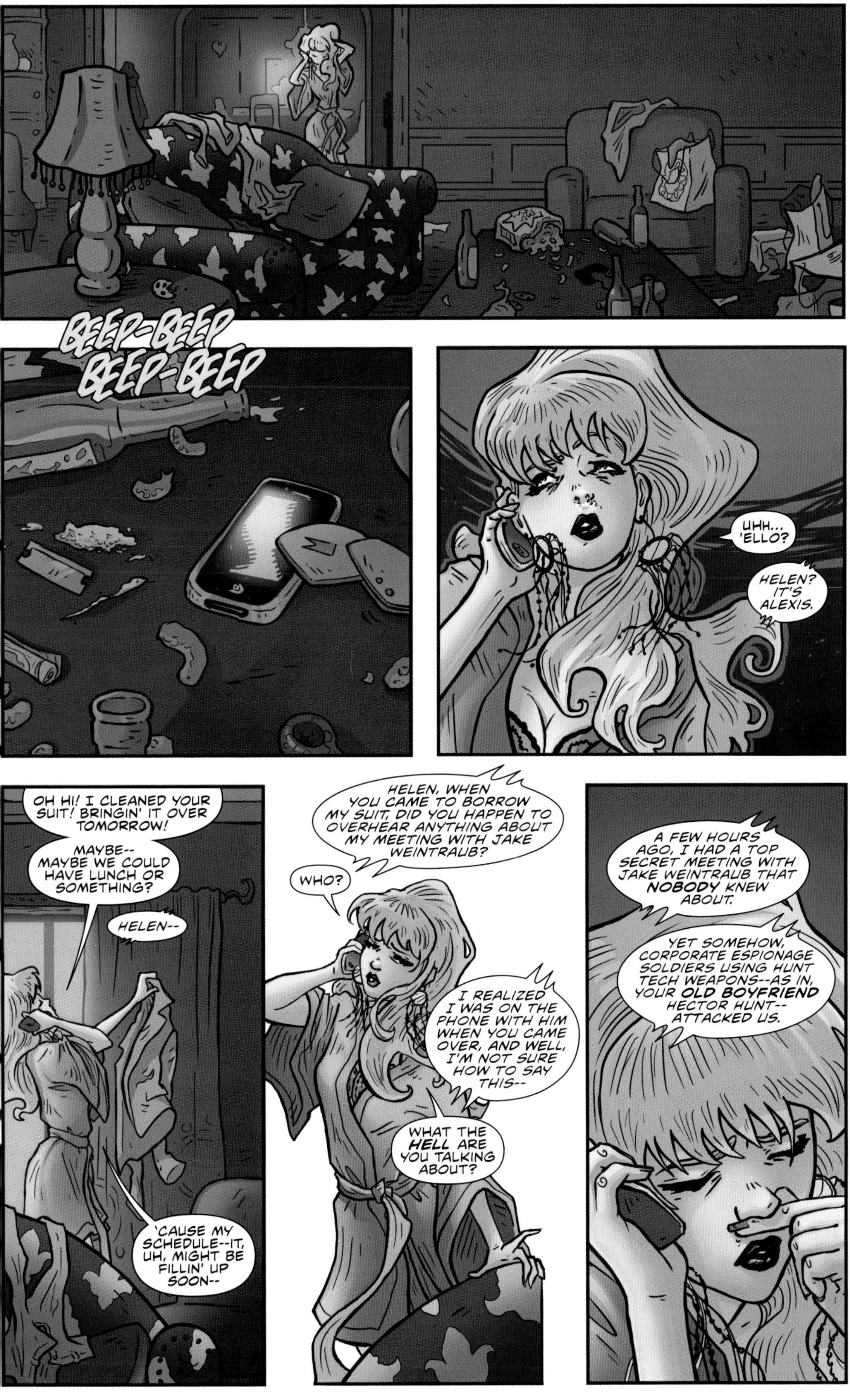
BEEP-BEEP
BEEP-BEEP
UHH... 'ELLO?
HELEN? IT'S ALEXIS.
OH HI! I CLEANED YOUR SUIT! BRINGIN' IT OVER TOMORROW!
MAYBE-- MAYBE WE COULD HAVE LUNCH OR SOMETHING?
HELEN--
'CAUSE MY SCHEDULE--IT, UH, MIGHT BE FILLIN' UP SOON--
HELEN, WHEN YOU CAME TO BORROW MY SUIT, DID YOU HAPPEN TO OVERHEAR ANYTHING ABOUT MY MEETING WITH JAKE WEINTRAUB?
WHO?
I REALIZED I WAS ON THE PHONE WITH HIM WHEN YOU CAME OVER, AND WELL, I'M NOT SURE HOW TO SAY THIS--
WHAT THE HELL ARE YOU TALKING ABOUT?
A FEW HOURS AGO, I HAD A TOP SECRET MEETING WITH JAKE WEINTRAUB THAT NOBODY KNEW ABOUT.
YET SOMEHOW, CORPORATE ESPIONAGE SOLDIERS USING HUNT TECH WEAPONS--AS IN, YOUR OLD BOYFRIEND HECTOR HUNT--ATTACKED US.

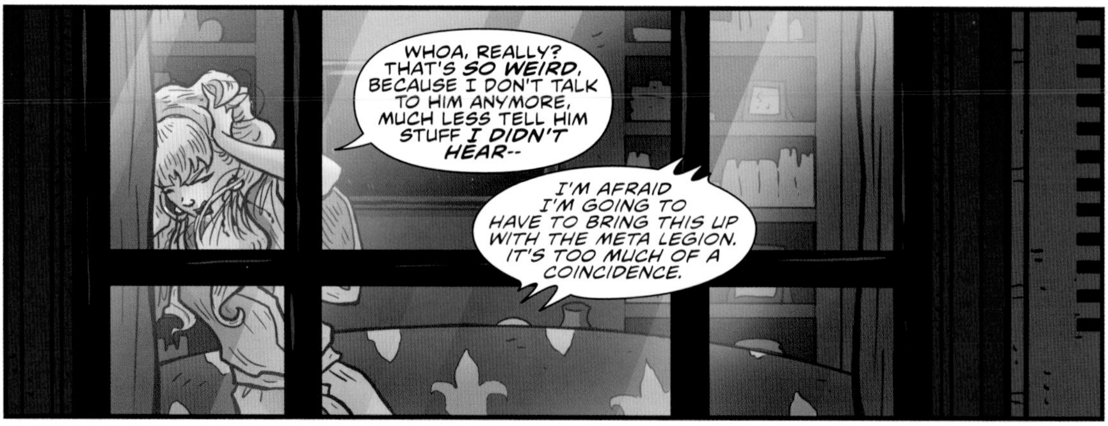
WHOA, REALLY? THAT'S SO WEIRD, BECAUSE I DON'T TALK TO HIM ANYMORE, MUCH LESS TELL HIM STUFF I DIDN'T HEAR--
I'M AFRAID I'M GOING TO HAVE TO BRING THIS UP WITH THE META LEGION. IT'S TOO MUCH OF A COINCIDENCE.

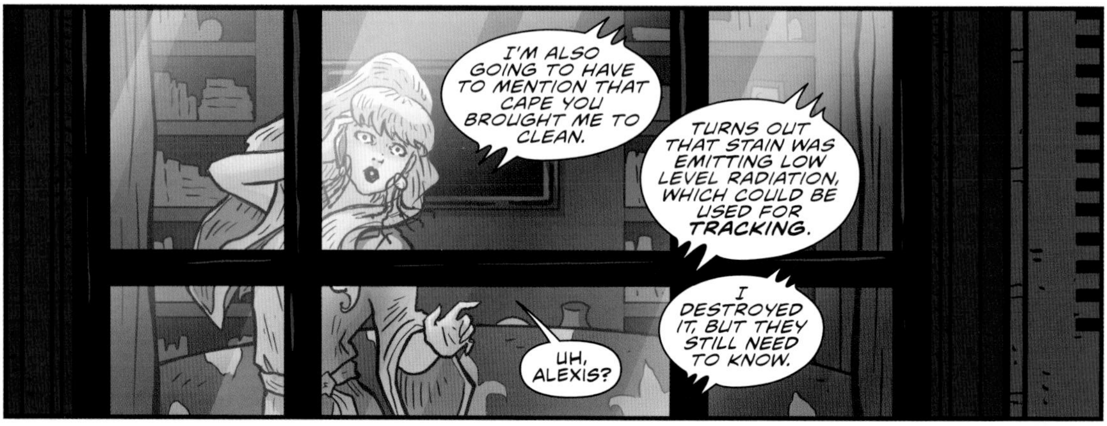
I'M ALSO GOING TO HAVE TO MENTION THAT CAPE YOU BROUGHT ME TO CLEAN.
TURNS OUT THAT STAIN WAS EMITTING LOW LEVEL RADIATION, WHICH COULD BE USED FOR TRACKING.
UH, ALEXIS?
I DESTROYED IT, BUT THEY STILL NEED TO KNOW.

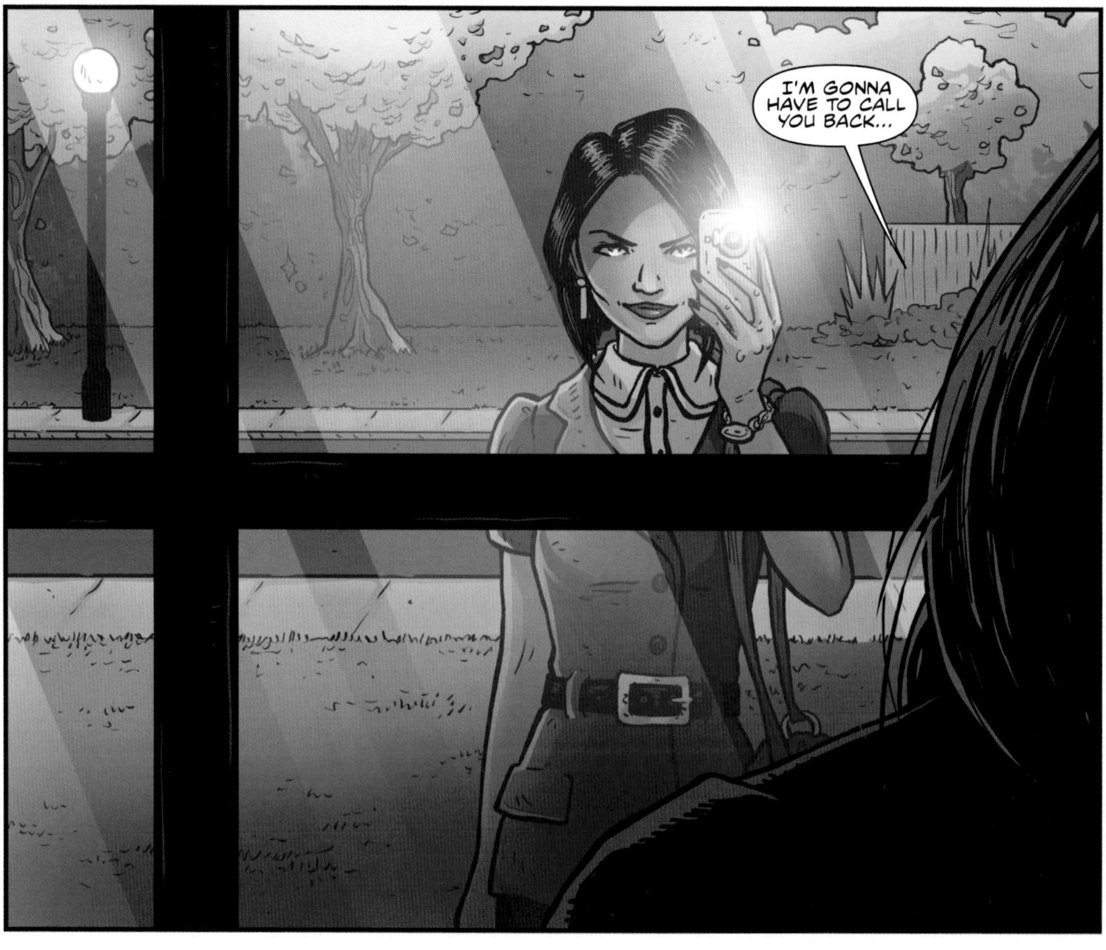
I'M GONNA HAVE TO CALL YOU BACK...

Chapter 3

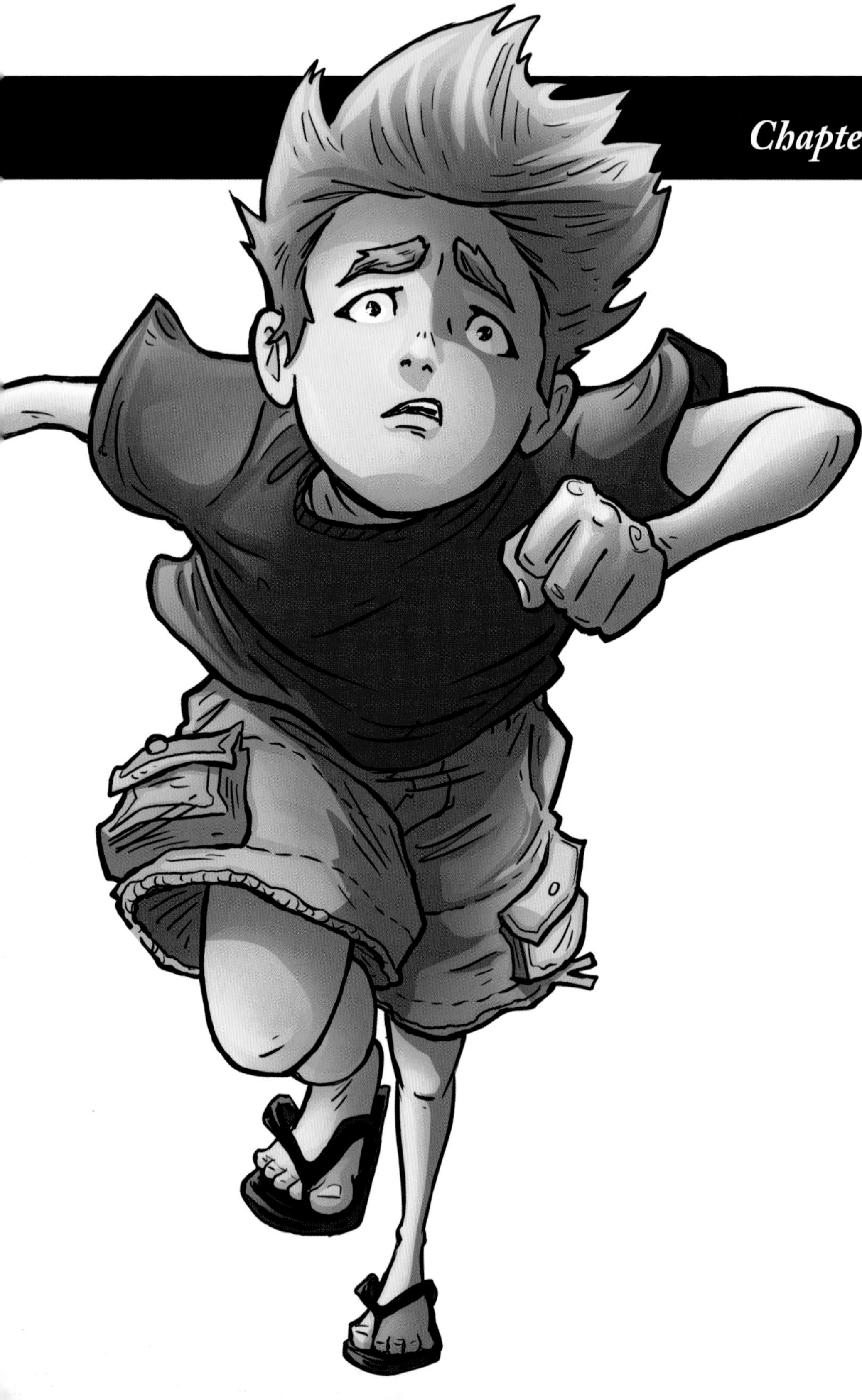

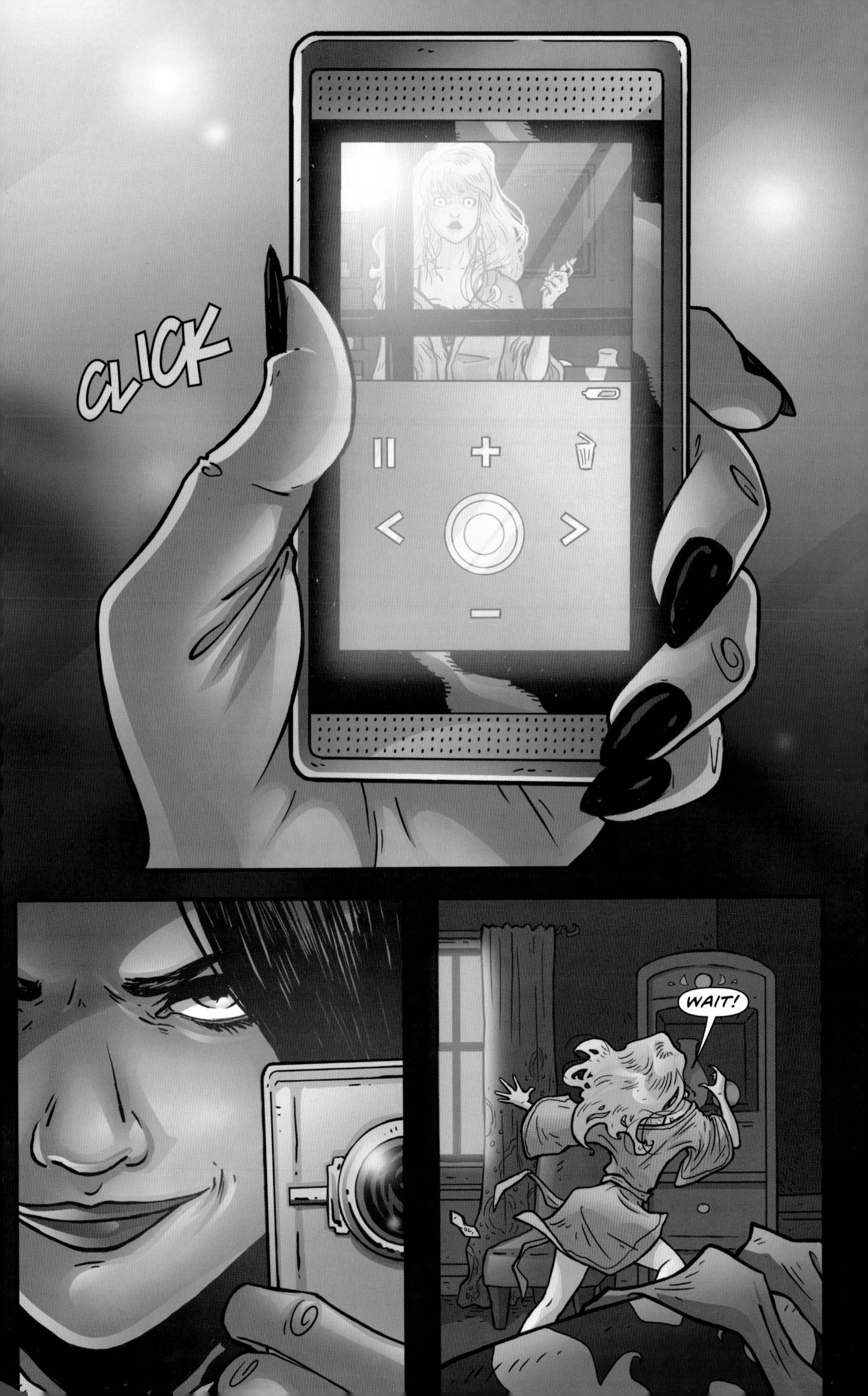
CLICK
WAIT!

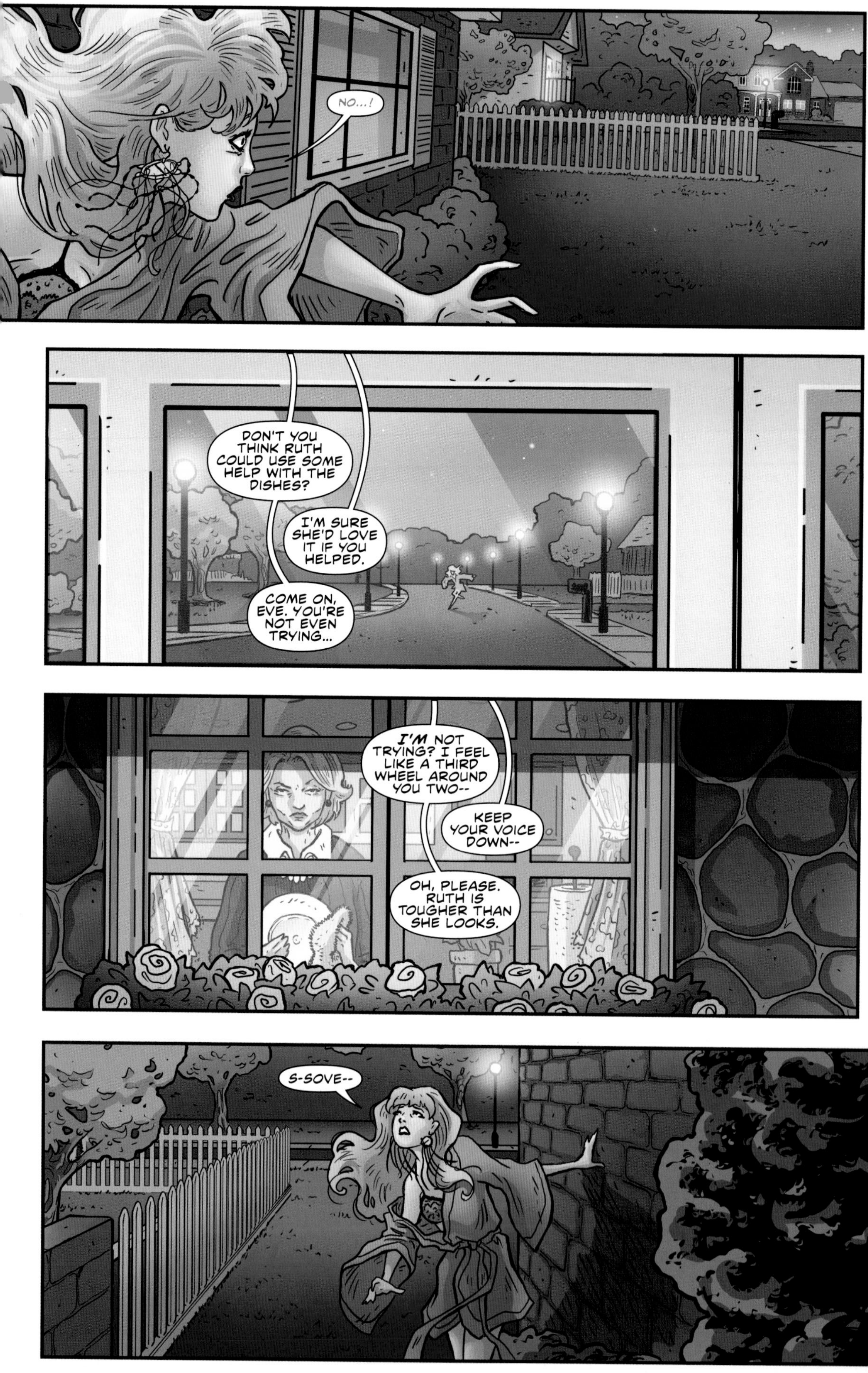
NO...!
DON'T YOU THINK RUTH COULD USE SOME HELP WITH THE DISHES?
I'M SURE SHE'D LOVE IT IF YOU HELPED.
COME ON, EVE. YOU'RE NOT EVEN TRYING...
I'M NOT TRYING? I FEEL LIKE A THIRD WHEEL AROUND YOU TWO--
KEEP YOUR VOICE DOWN--
OH, PLEASE. RUTH IS TOUGHER THAN SHE LOOKS.
S-SOVE--

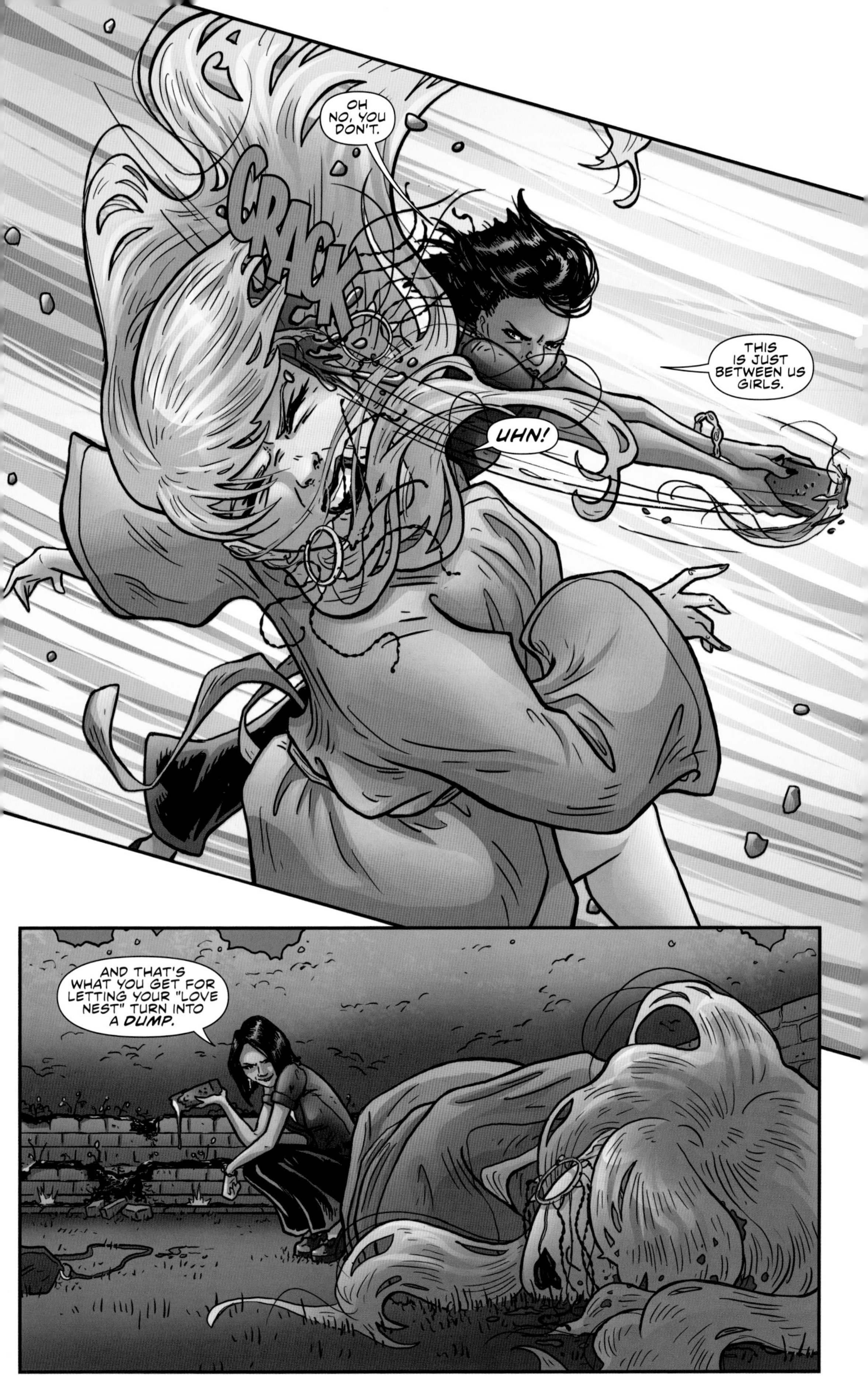
OH NO, YOU DON'T.
CRACK
UHN!
THIS IS JUST BETWEEN US GIRLS.
AND THAT'S WHAT YOU GET FOR LETTING YOUR "LOVE NEST" TURN INTO A *DUMP*.

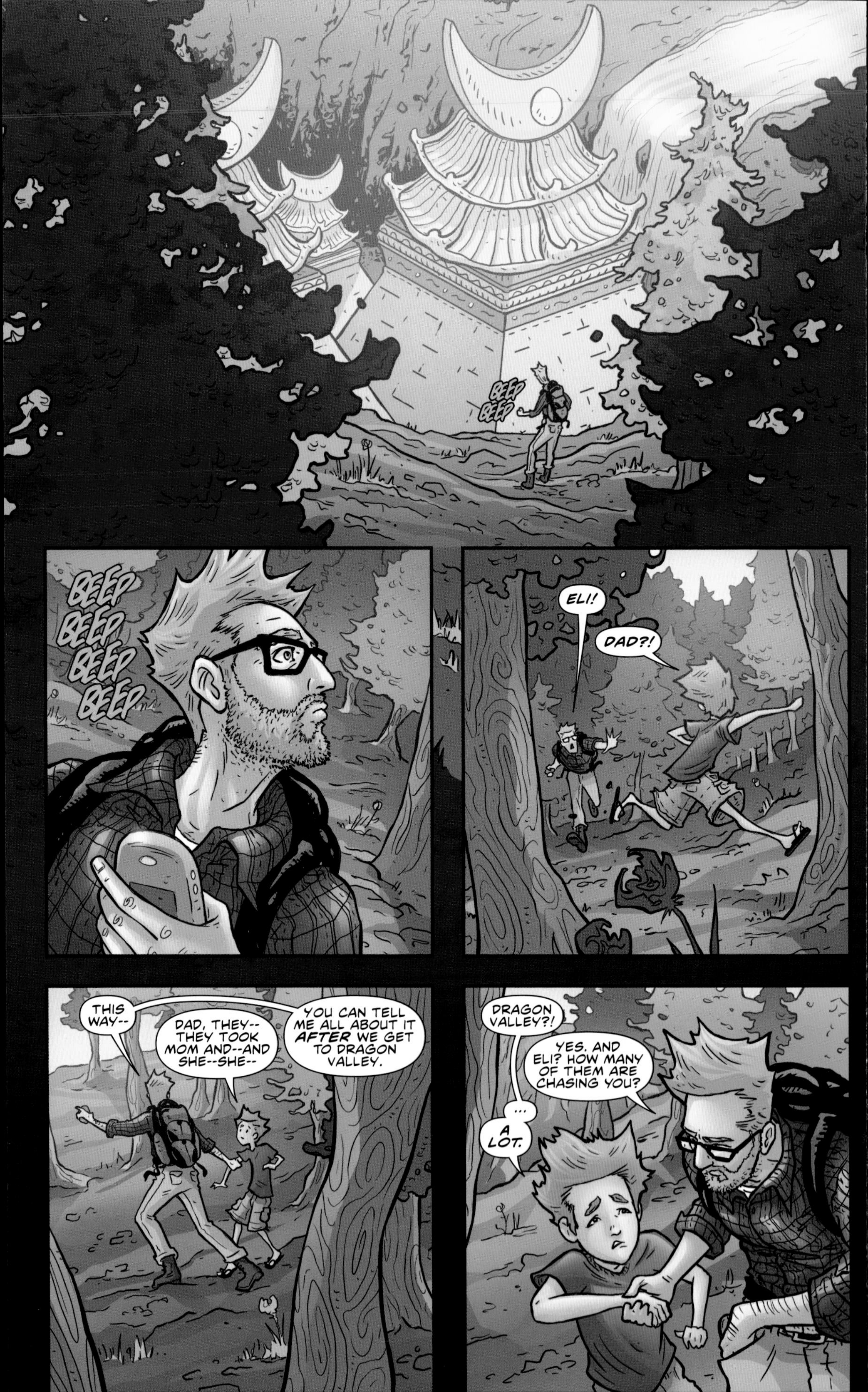
BEEP
BEEP
BEEP
BEEP
BEEP
BEEP
ELI!
DAD?!
THIS WAY--
DAD, THEY-- THEY TOOK MOM AND--AND SHE--SHE--
YOU CAN TELL ME ALL ABOUT IT AFTER WE GET TO DRAGON VALLEY.
DRAGON VALLEY?!
YES. AND ELI? HOW MANY OF THEM ARE CHASING YOU?
...
A LOT.

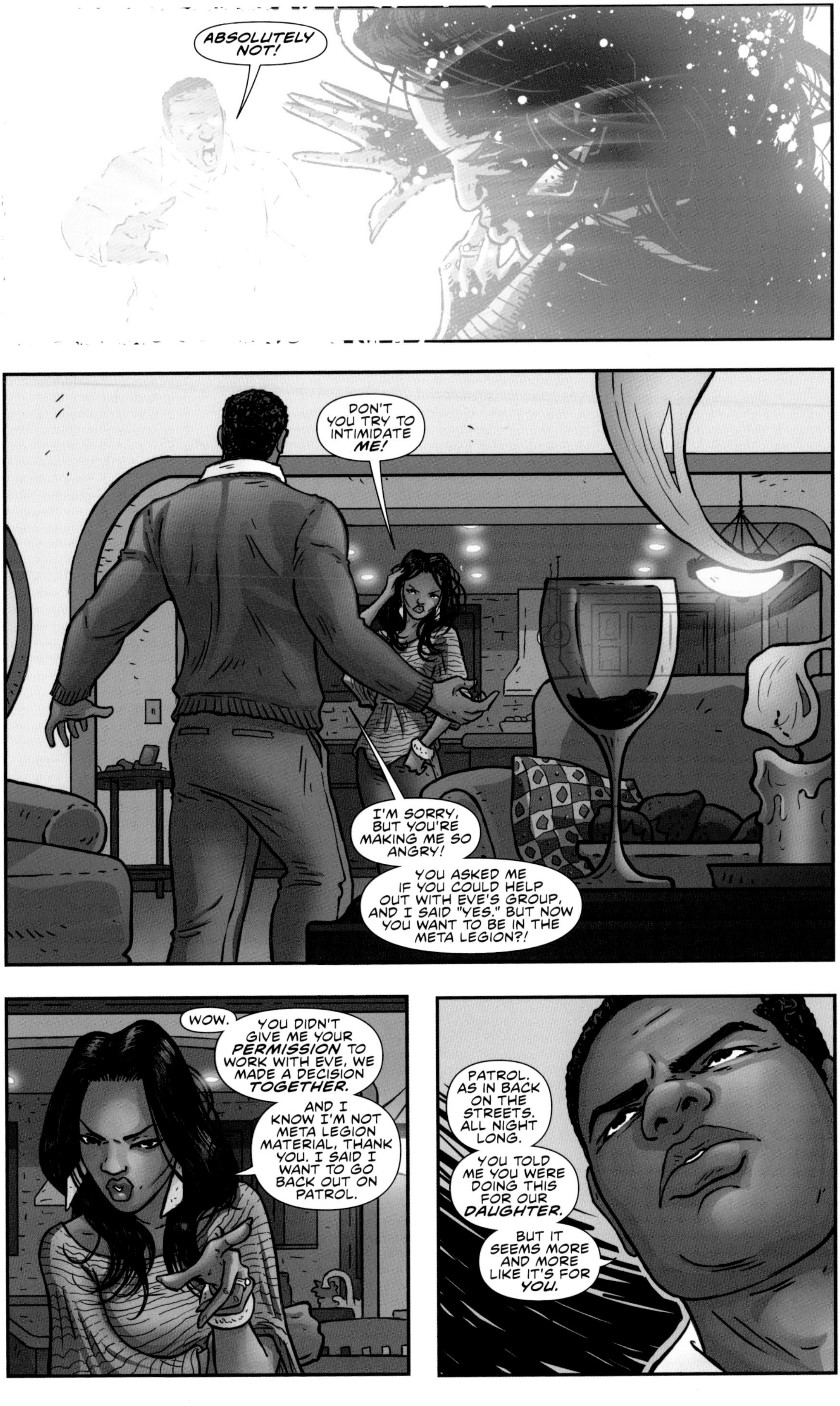
ABSOLUTELY NOT!
DON'T YOU TRY TO INTIMIDATE ME!
I'M SORRY, BUT YOU'RE MAKING ME SO ANGRY!
YOU ASKED ME IF YOU COULD HELP OUT WITH EVE'S GROUP, AND I SAID "YES." BUT NOW YOU WANT TO BE IN THE META LEGION?!
WOW.
YOU DIDN'T GIVE ME YOUR PERMISSION TO WORK WITH EVE, WE MADE A DECISION TOGETHER.
AND I KNOW I'M NOT META LEGION MATERIAL, THANK YOU. I SAID I WANT TO GO BACK OUT ON PATROL.
PATROL. AS IN BACK ON THE STREETS. ALL NIGHT LONG.
YOU TOLD ME YOU WERE DOING THIS FOR OUR DAUGHTER.
BUT IT SEEMS MORE AND MORE LIKE IT'S FOR YOU.

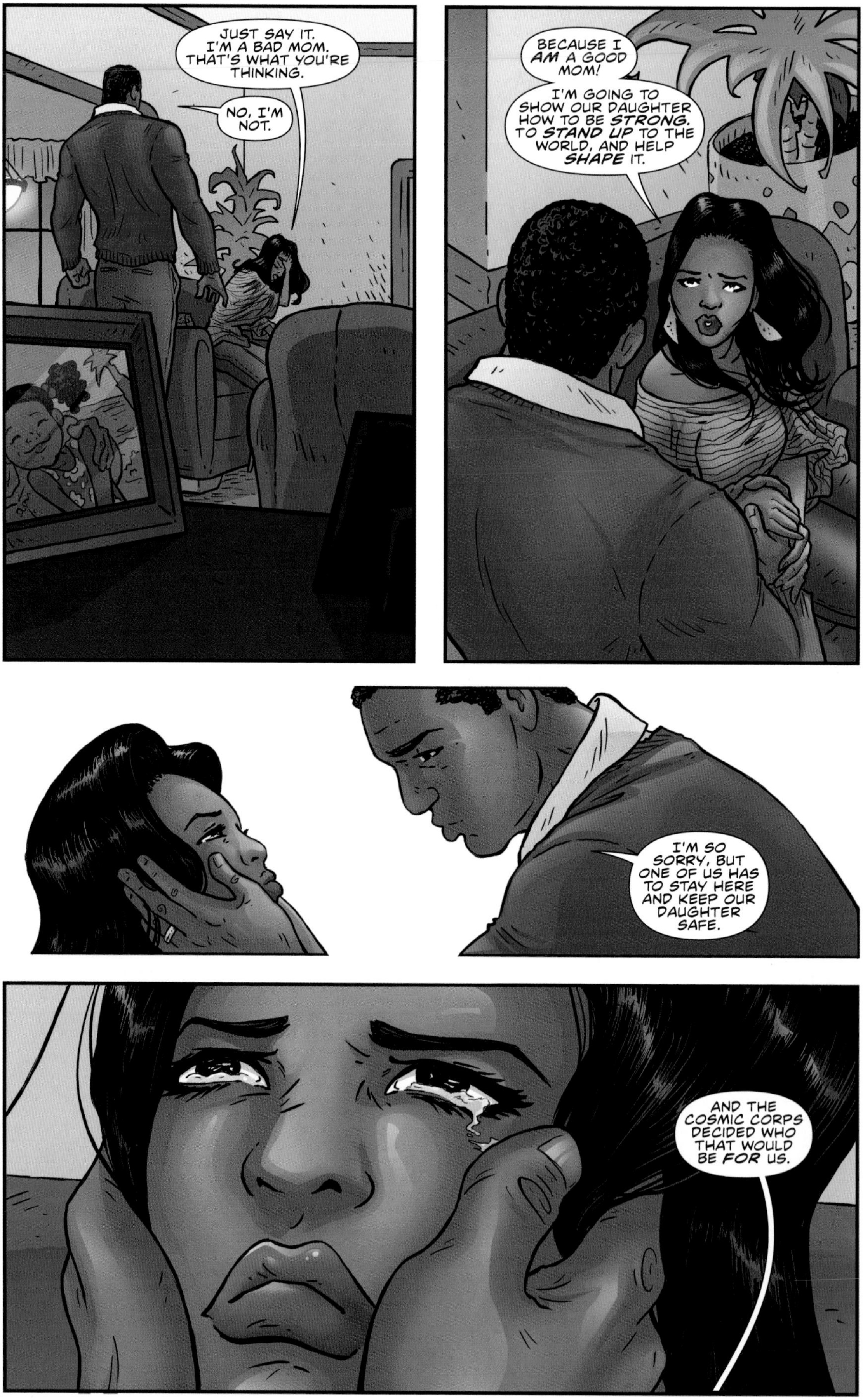
JUST SAY IT. I'M A BAD MOM. THAT'S WHAT YOU'RE THINKING.
NO, I'M NOT.
BECAUSE I *AM* A GOOD MOM!
I'M GOING TO SHOW OUR DAUGHTER HOW TO BE *STRONG*. TO *STAND UP* TO THE WORLD, AND HELP *SHAPE* IT.
I'M SO SORRY, BUT ONE OF US HAS TO STAY HERE AND KEEP OUR DAUGHTER SAFE.
AND THE COSMIC CORPS DECIDED WHO THAT WOULD BE *FOR* US.

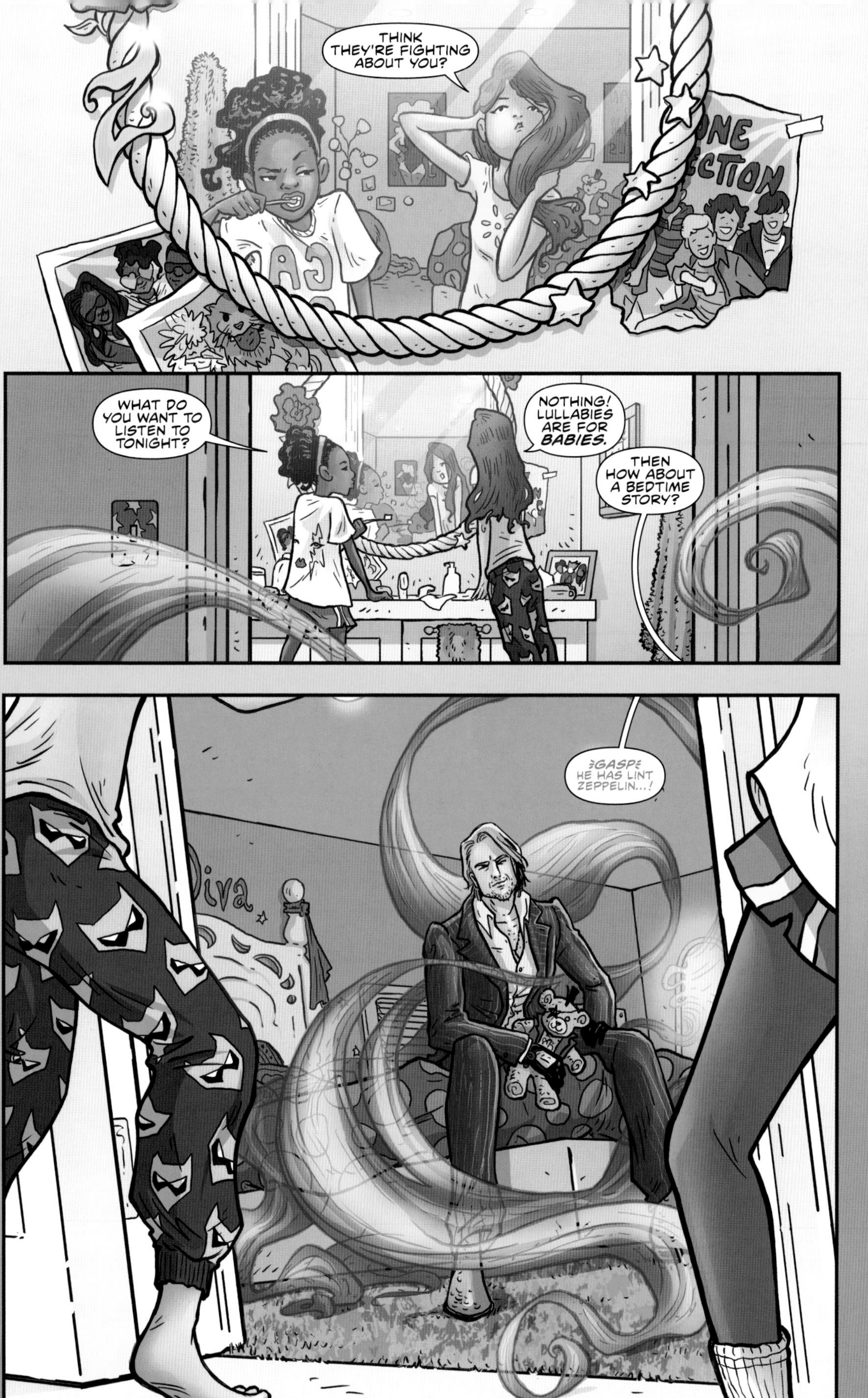
THINK THEY'RE FIGHTING ABOUT YOU?
ONE DIRECTION
WHAT DO YOU WANT TO LISTEN TO TONIGHT?
NOTHING! LULLABIES ARE FOR BABIES.
THEN HOW ABOUT A BEDTIME STORY?
GASP HE HAS LINT ZEPPELIN...!
Diva

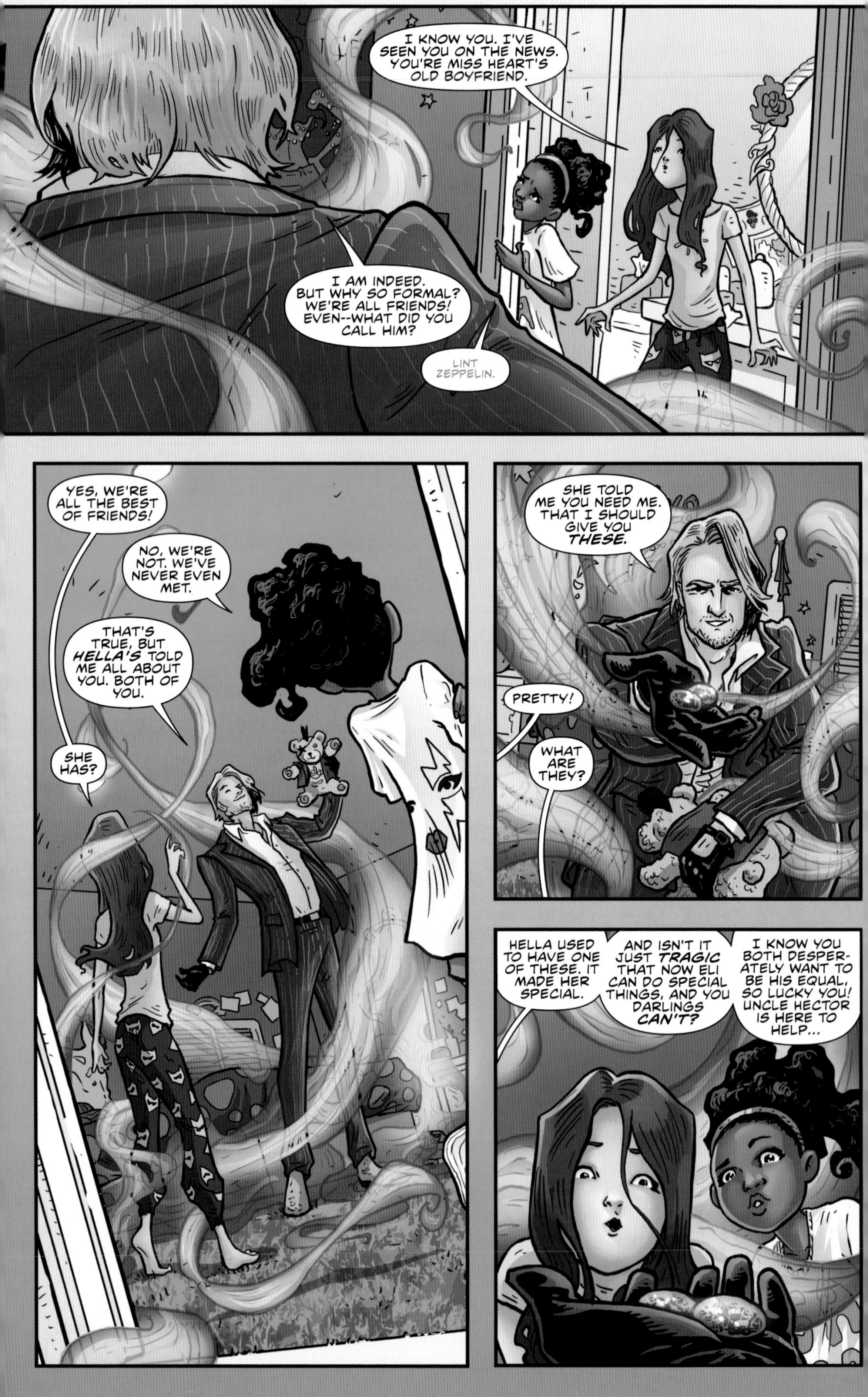

I KNOW YOU. I'VE SEEN YOU ON THE NEWS. YOU'RE MISS HEART'S OLD BOYFRIEND.
I AM INDEED. BUT WHY SO FORMAL? WE'RE ALL FRIENDS! EVEN--WHAT DID YOU CALL HIM?
LINT ZEPPELIN.
YES, WE'RE ALL THE BEST OF FRIENDS!
NO, WE'RE NOT. WE'VE NEVER EVEN MET.
THAT'S TRUE, BUT HELLA'S TOLD ME ALL ABOUT YOU. BOTH OF YOU.
SHE HAS?
SHE TOLD ME YOU NEED ME. THAT I SHOULD GIVE YOU THESE.
PRETTY!
WHAT ARE THEY?
HELLA USED TO HAVE ONE OF THESE. IT MADE HER SPECIAL.
AND ISN'T IT JUST TRAGIC THAT NOW ELI CAN DO SPECIAL THINGS, AND YOU DARLINGS CAN'T?
I KNOW YOU BOTH DESPERATELY WANT TO BE HIS EQUAL, SO LUCKY YOU! UNCLE HECTOR IS HERE TO HELP...

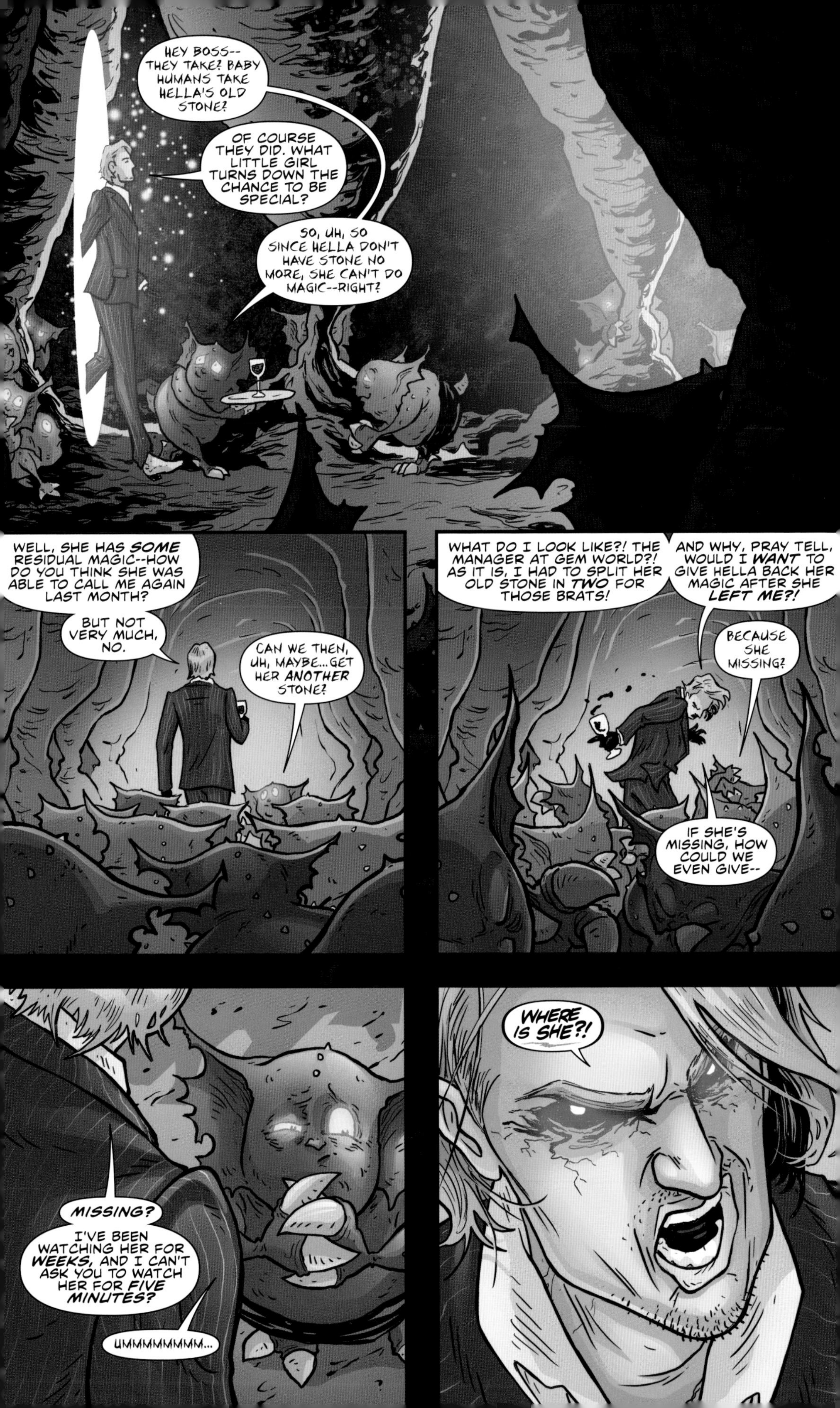
HEY BOSS--THEY TAKE? BABY HUMANS TAKE HELLA'S OLD STONE?
OF COURSE THEY DID. WHAT LITTLE GIRL TURNS DOWN THE CHANCE TO BE SPECIAL?
SO, UH, SO SINCE HELLA DON'T HAVE STONE NO MORE, SHE CAN'T DO MAGIC--RIGHT?
WELL, SHE HAS SOME RESIDUAL MAGIC--HOW DO YOU THINK SHE WAS ABLE TO CALL ME AGAIN LAST MONTH?
BUT NOT VERY MUCH, NO.
CAN WE THEN, UH, MAYBE...GET HER ANOTHER STONE?
WHAT DO I LOOK LIKE?! THE MANAGER AT GEM WORLD?! AS IT IS, I HAD TO SPLIT HER OLD STONE IN TWO FOR THOSE BRATS!
AND WHY, PRAY TELL, WOULD I WANT TO GIVE HELLA BACK HER MAGIC AFTER SHE LEFT ME?!
BECAUSE SHE MISSING?
IF SHE'S MISSING, HOW COULD WE EVEN GIVE--
MISSING?
I'VE BEEN WATCHING HER FOR WEEKS, AND I CAN'T ASK YOU TO WATCH HER FOR FIVE MINUTES?
UMMMMMMMM...
WHERE IS SHE?!

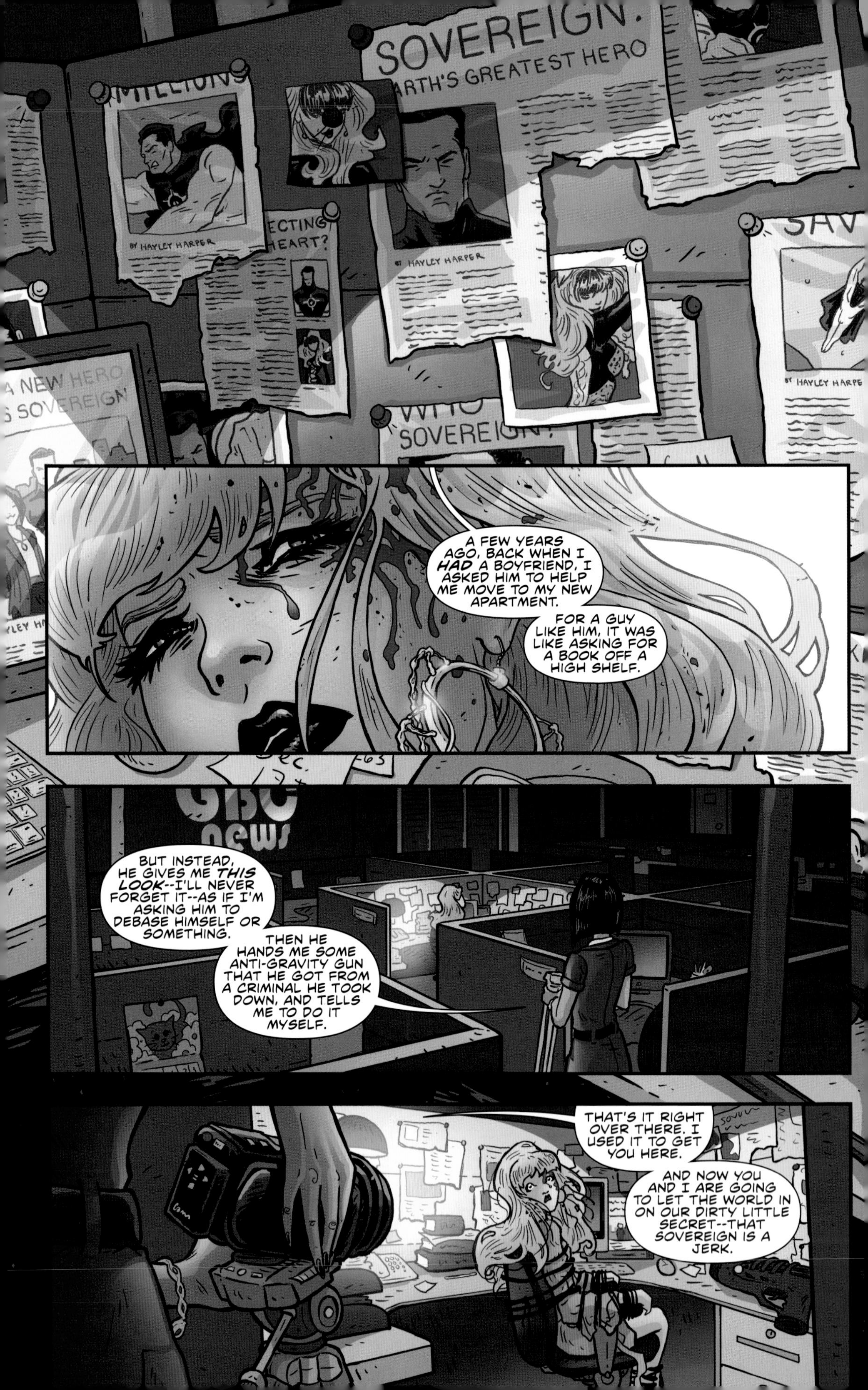
SOVEREIGN:
ARTH'S GREATEST HERO
BY HAYLEY HARPER
BY HAYLEY HARPER
A NEW HERO
S SOVEREIGN
SOVEREIGN
A FEW YEARS AGO, BACK WHEN I *HAD* A BOYFRIEND, I ASKED HIM TO HELP ME MOVE TO MY NEW APARTMENT.
FOR A GUY LIKE HIM, IT WAS LIKE ASKING FOR A BOOK OFF A HIGH SHELF.
BUT INSTEAD, HE GIVES ME ***THIS LOOK***--I'LL NEVER FORGET IT--AS IF I'M ASKING HIM TO DEBASE HIMSELF OR SOMETHING.
THEN HE HANDS ME SOME ANTI-GRAVITY GUN THAT HE GOT FROM A CRIMINAL HE TOOK DOWN, AND TELLS ME TO DO IT MYSELF.
THAT'S IT RIGHT OVER THERE. I USED IT TO GET YOU HERE.
AND NOW YOU AND I ARE GOING TO LET THE WORLD IN ON OUR DIRTY LITTLE SECRET--THAT SOVEREIGN IS A JERK.

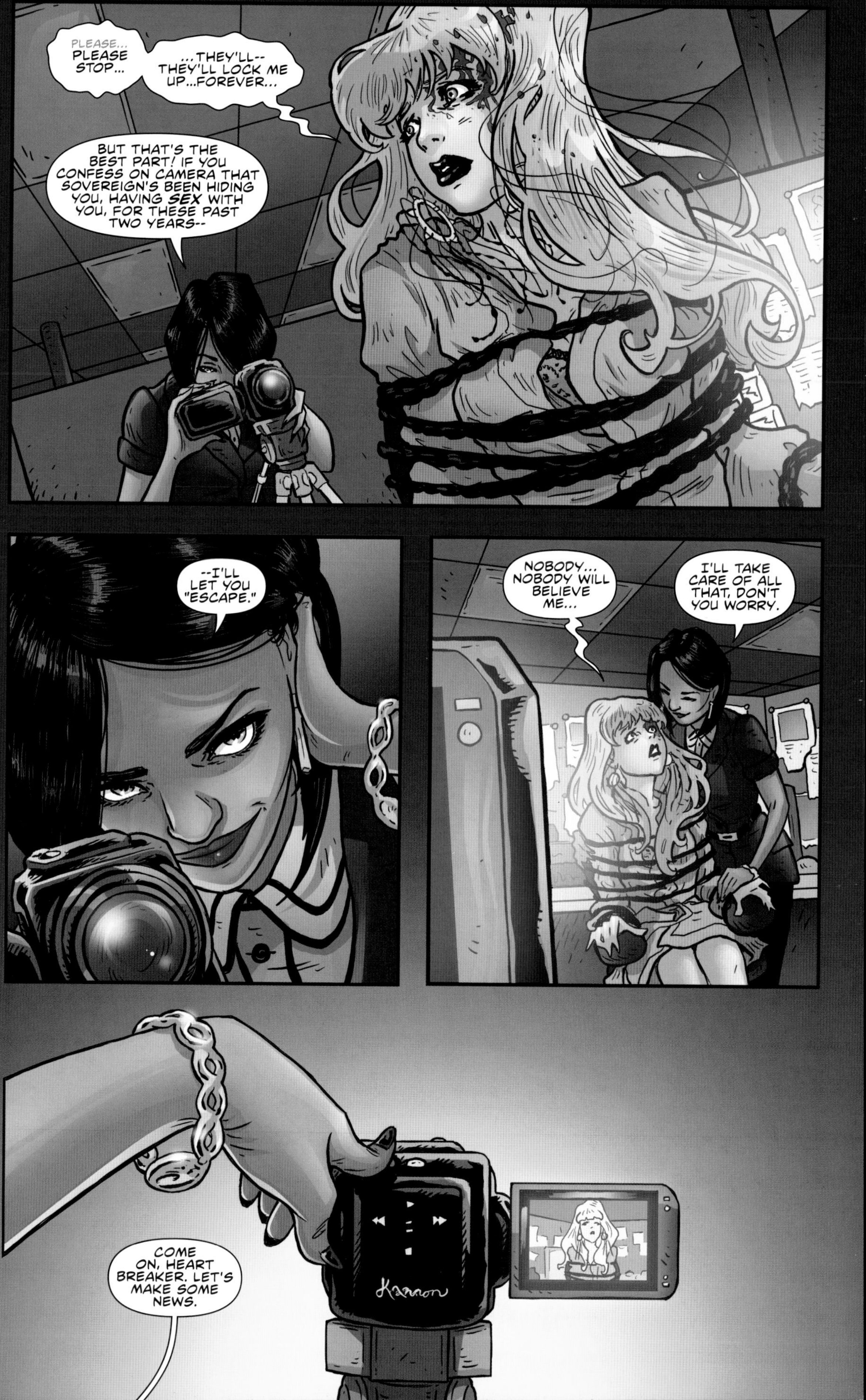

PLEASE... PLEASE STOP...
...THEY'LL-- THEY'LL LOCK ME UP...FOREVER...
BUT THAT'S THE BEST PART! IF YOU CONFESS ON CAMERA THAT SOVEREIGN'S BEEN HIDING YOU, HAVING SEX WITH YOU, FOR THESE PAST TWO YEARS--
--I'LL LET YOU "ESCAPE."
NOBODY... NOBODY WILL BELIEVE ME...
I'LL TAKE CARE OF ALL THAT, DON'T YOU WORRY.
COME ON, HEART BREAKER. LET'S MAKE SOME NEWS.
Kannon

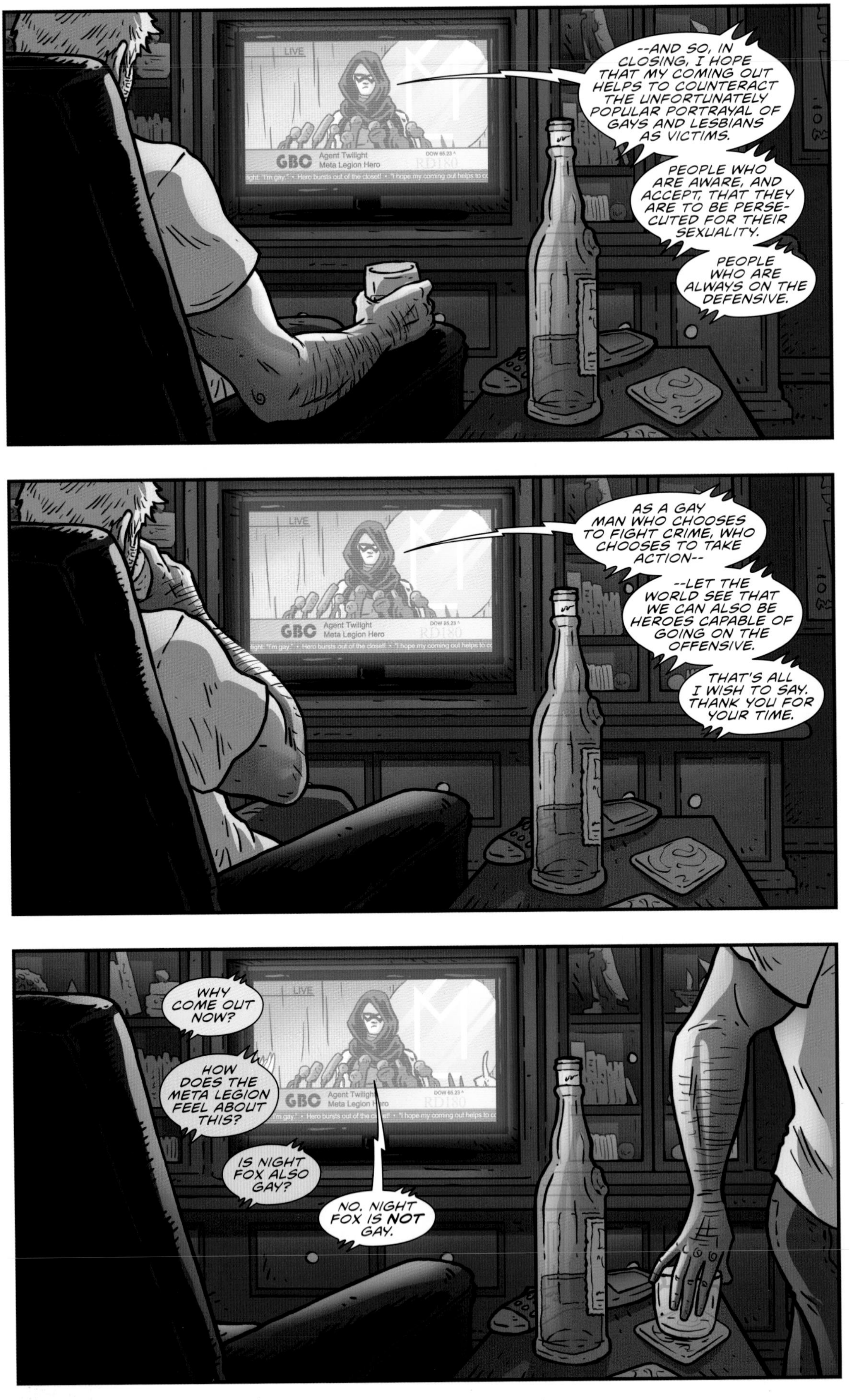
LIVE
GBC Agent Twilight Meta Legion Hero
DOW 65.23
RD180
light: "I'm gay." • Hero bursts out of the closet! • "I hope my coming out helps to c
--AND SO, IN CLOSING, I HOPE THAT MY COMING OUT HELPS TO COUNTERACT THE UNFORTUNATELY POPULAR PORTRAYAL OF GAYS AND LESBIANS AS VICTIMS.
PEOPLE WHO ARE AWARE, AND ACCEPT, THAT THEY ARE TO BE PERSE-CUTED FOR THEIR SEXUALITY.
PEOPLE WHO ARE ALWAYS ON THE DEFENSIVE.
AS A GAY MAN WHO CHOOSES TO FIGHT CRIME, WHO CHOOSES TO TAKE ACTION--
--LET THE WORLD SEE THAT WE CAN ALSO BE HEROES CAPABLE OF GOING ON THE OFFENSIVE.
THAT'S ALL I WISH TO SAY. THANK YOU FOR YOUR TIME.
WHY COME OUT NOW?
HOW DOES THE META LEGION FEEL ABOUT THIS?
IS NIGHT FOX ALSO GAY?
NO. NIGHT FOX IS **NOT** GAY.

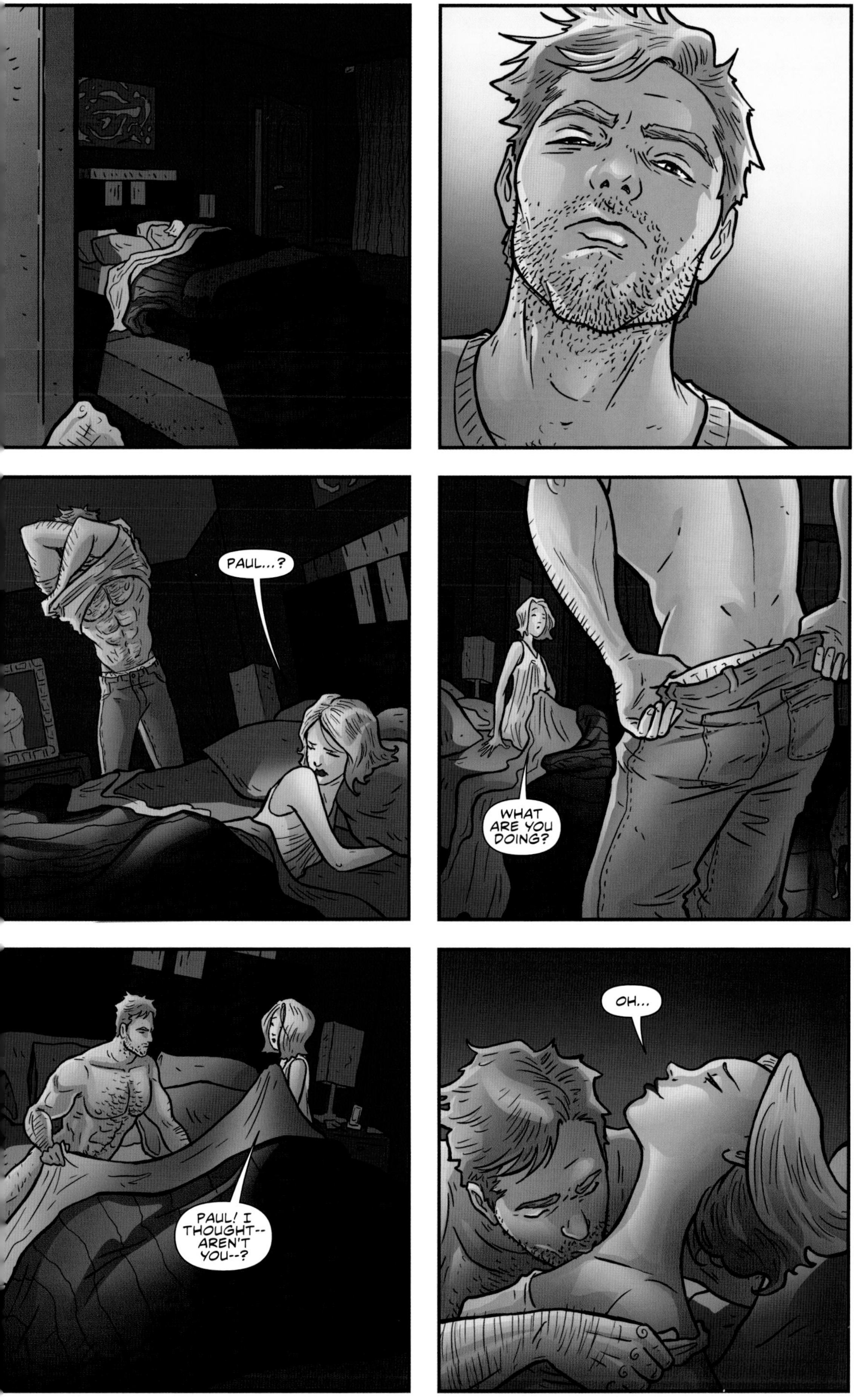
PAUL...?
WHAT ARE YOU DOING?
PAUL! I THOUGHT-- AREN'T YOU--?
OH...

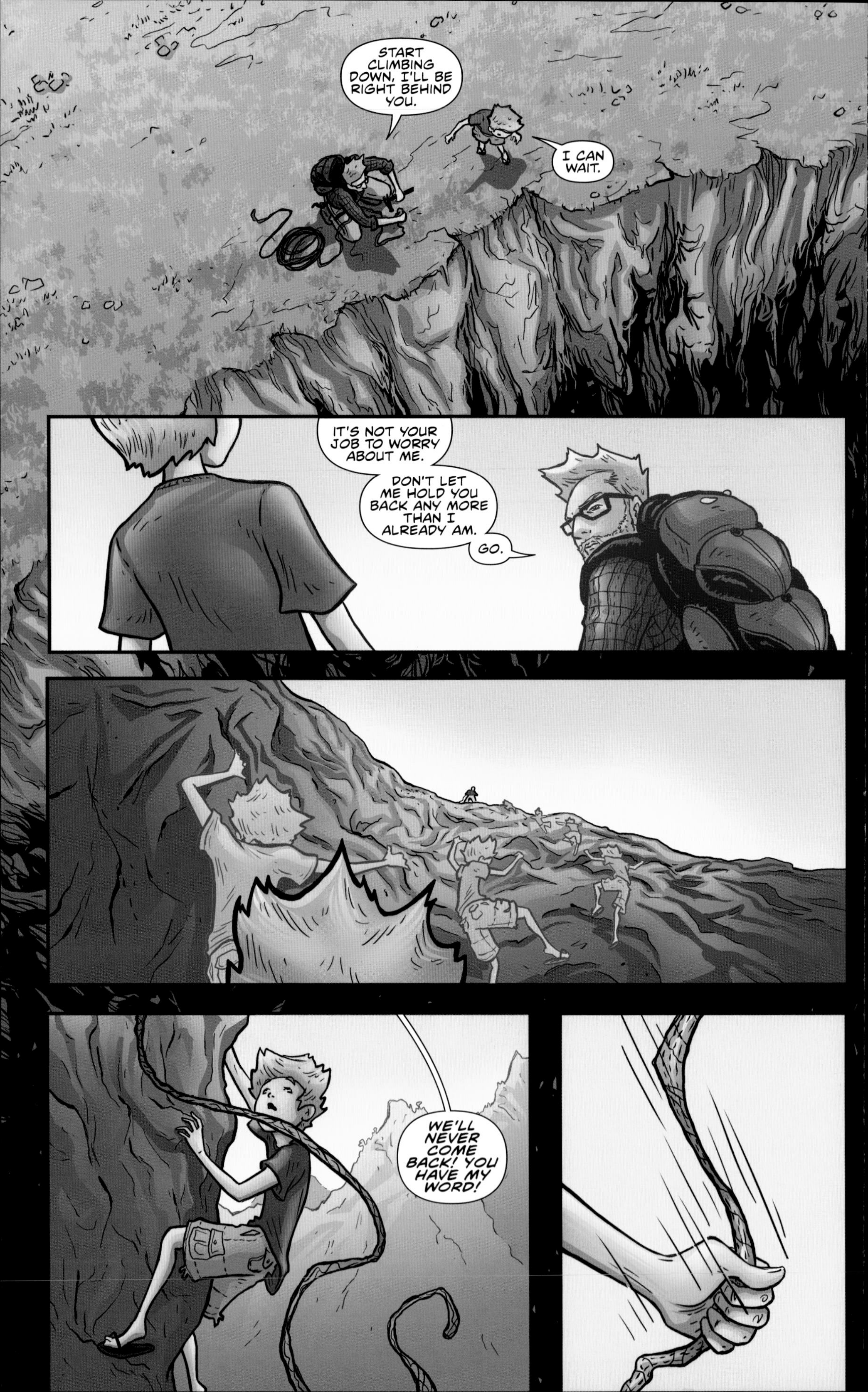
START CLIMBING DOWN, I'LL BE RIGHT BEHIND YOU.
I CAN WAIT.
IT'S NOT YOUR JOB TO WORRY ABOUT ME.
DON'T LET ME HOLD YOU BACK ANY MORE THAN I ALREADY AM.
GO.
WE'LL NEVER COME BACK! YOU HAVE MY WORD!

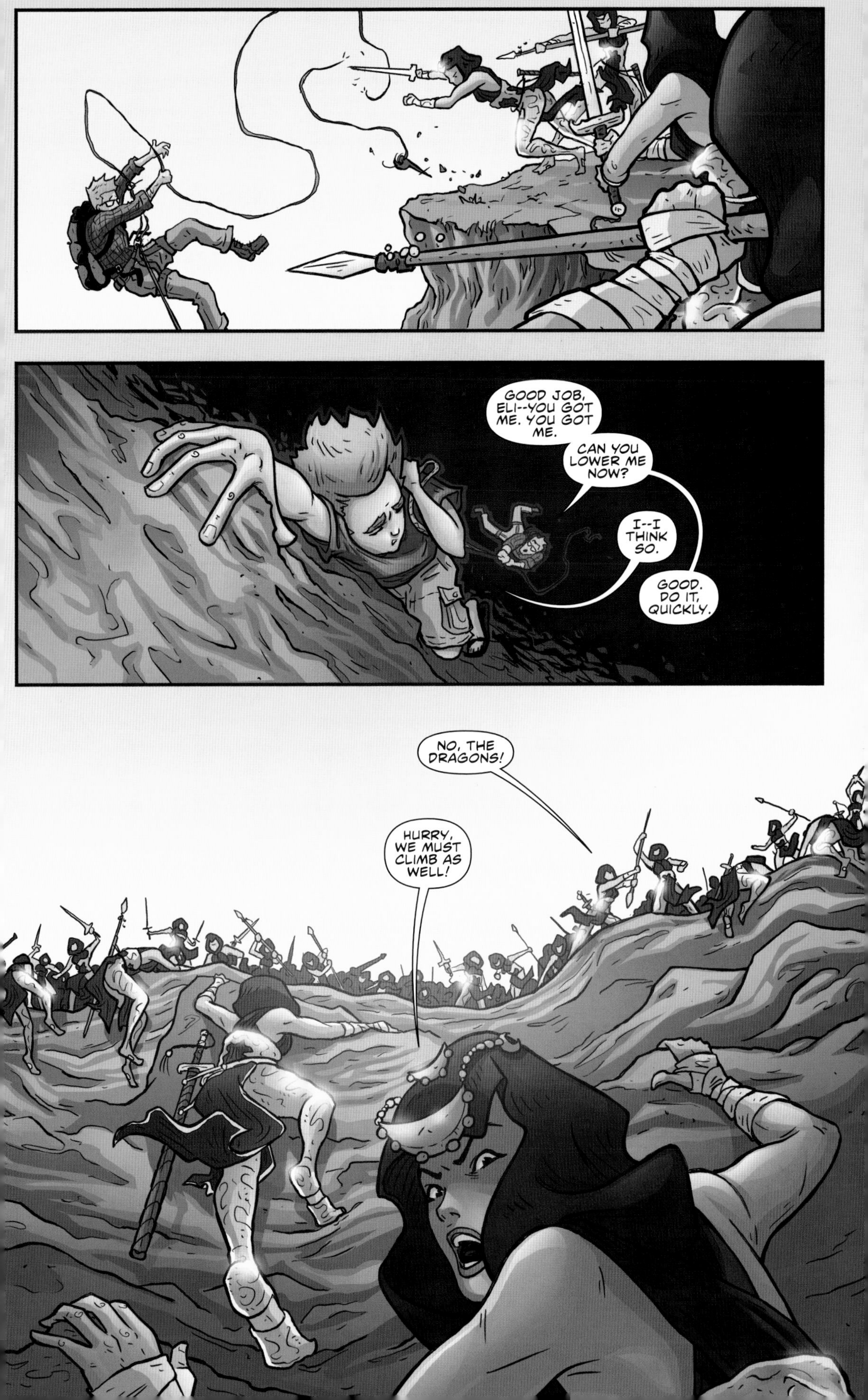
GOOD JOB, ELI--YOU GOT ME. YOU GOT ME.
CAN YOU LOWER ME NOW?
I--I THINK SO.
GOOD. DO IT, QUICKLY.
NO, THE DRAGONS!
HURRY, WE MUST CLIMB AS WELL!

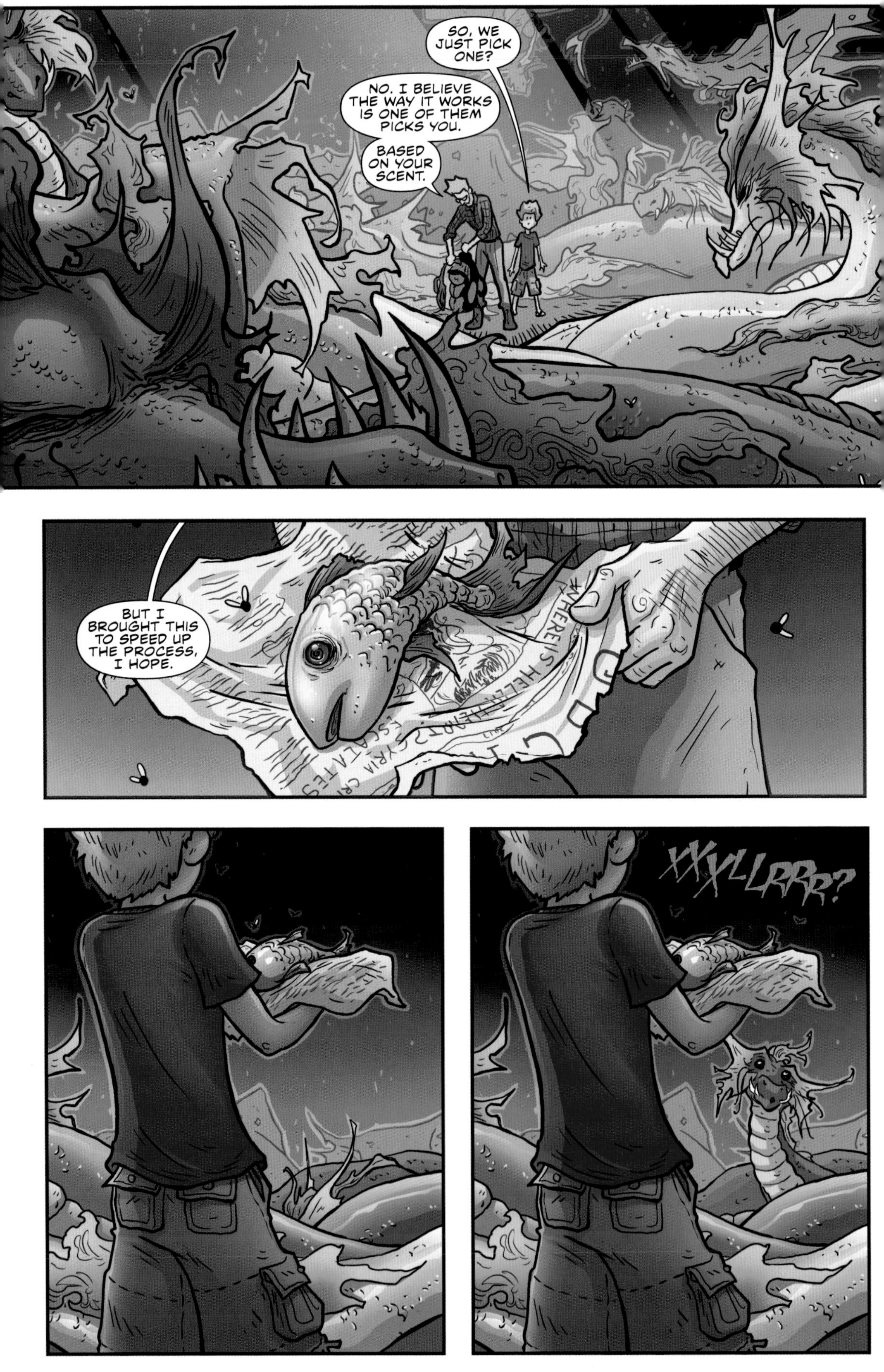
SO, WE JUST PICK ONE?
NO. I BELIEVE THE WAY IT WORKS IS ONE OF THEM PICKS YOU.
BASED ON YOUR SCENT.
BUT I BROUGHT THIS TO SPEED UP THE PROCESS, I HOPE.
XXXLLRRR?

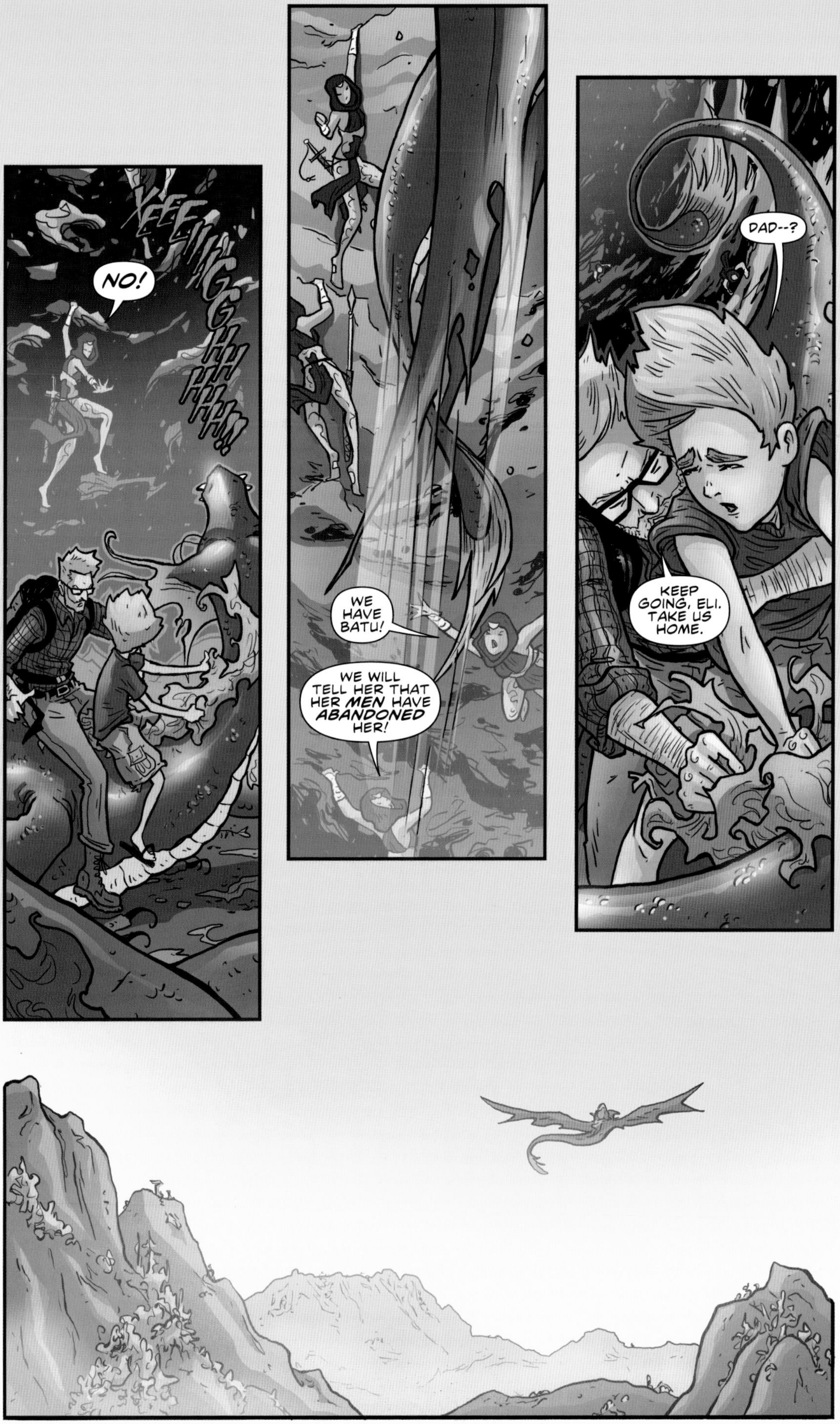
YEEEAAGGHHHHH!!
NO!
WE HAVE BATU!
WE WILL TELL HER THAT HER MEN HAVE ABANDONED HER!
DAD--?
KEEP GOING, ELI. TAKE US HOME.

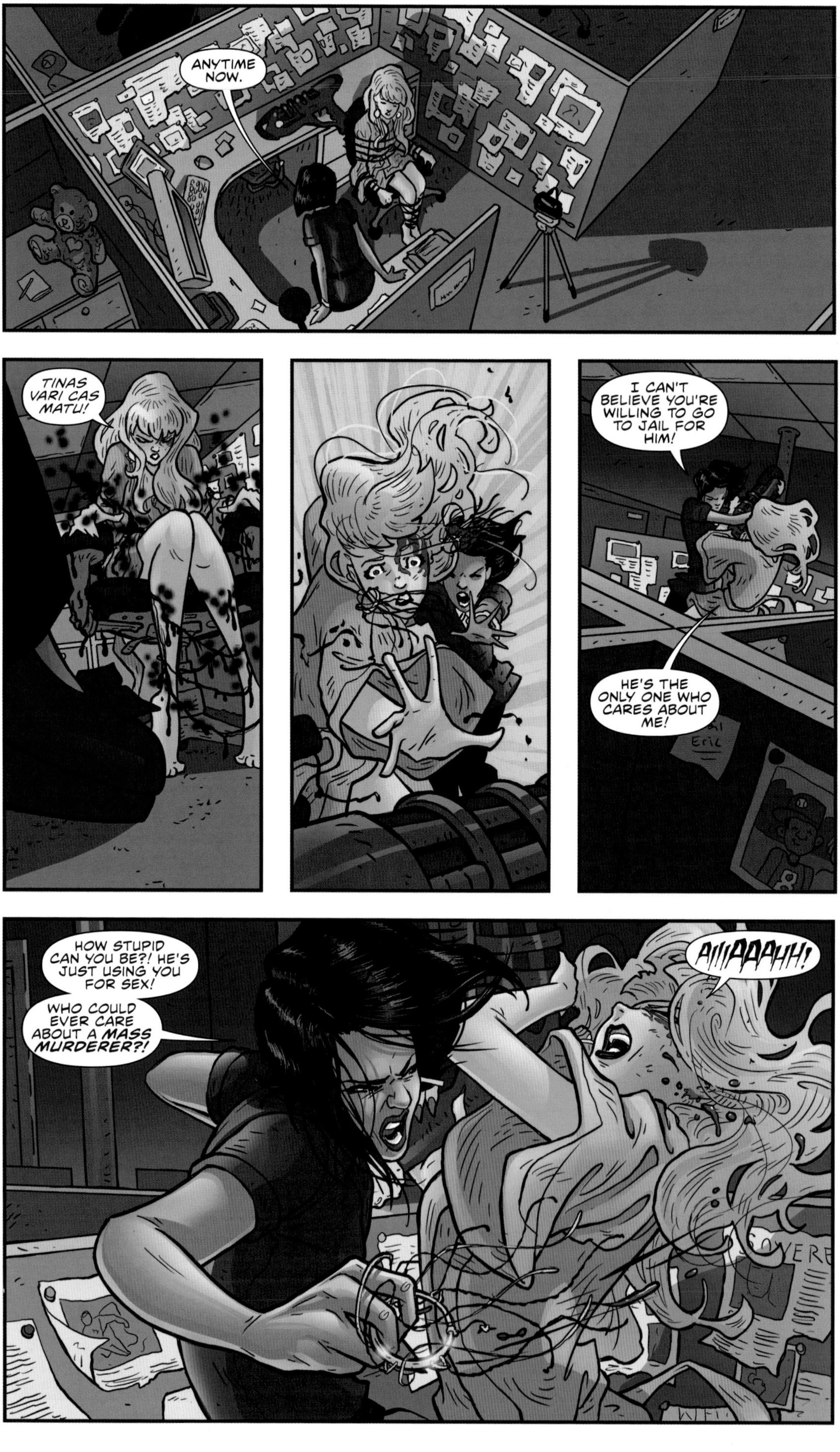

ANYTIME NOW.
TINAS VARI CAS MATU!
I CAN'T BELIEVE YOU'RE WILLING TO GO TO JAIL FOR HIM!
HE'S THE ONLY ONE WHO CARES ABOUT ME!
HOW STUPID CAN YOU BE?! HE'S JUST USING YOU FOR SEX!
WHO COULD EVER CARE ABOUT A *MASS MURDERER?!*
AIIIAAAHH!

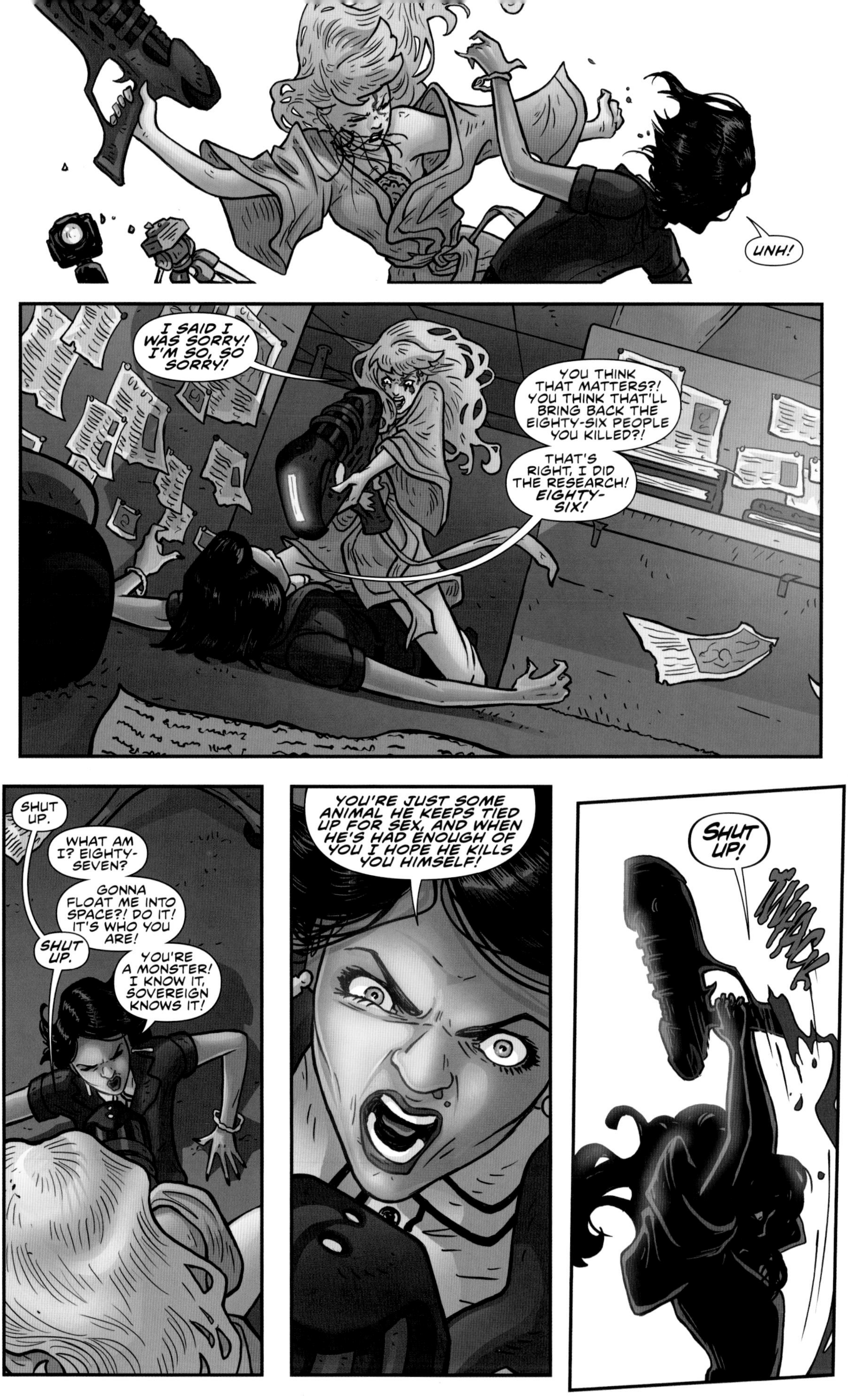
UNH!
I SAID I WAS SORRY! I'M SO, SO SORRY!
YOU THINK THAT MATTERS?! YOU THINK THAT'LL BRING BACK THE EIGHTY-SIX PEOPLE YOU KILLED?!
THAT'S RIGHT, I DID THE RESEARCH! EIGHTY-SIX!
SHUT UP.
WHAT AM I? EIGHTY-SEVEN?
GONNA FLOAT ME INTO SPACE?! DO IT! IT'S WHO YOU ARE!
SHUT UP.
YOU'RE A MONSTER! I KNOW IT, SOVEREIGN KNOWS IT!
YOU'RE JUST SOME ANIMAL HE KEEPS TIED UP FOR SEX, AND WHEN HE'S HAD ENOUGH OF YOU I HOPE HE KILLS YOU HIMSELF!
SHUT UP!
THWACK

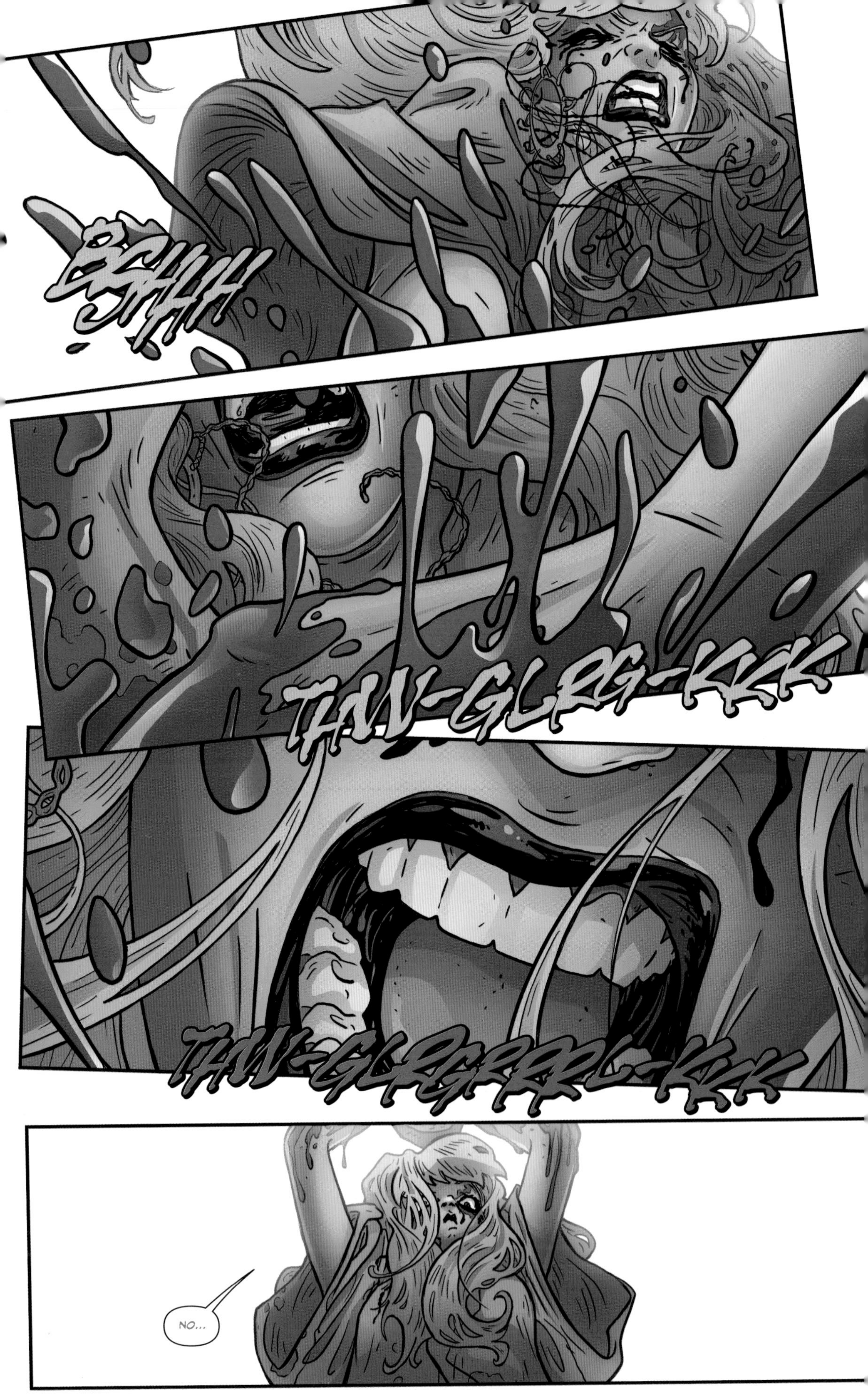
BGHHH
THW-GLRG-KKK
THW-GLRGRRRG-KKK
NO...

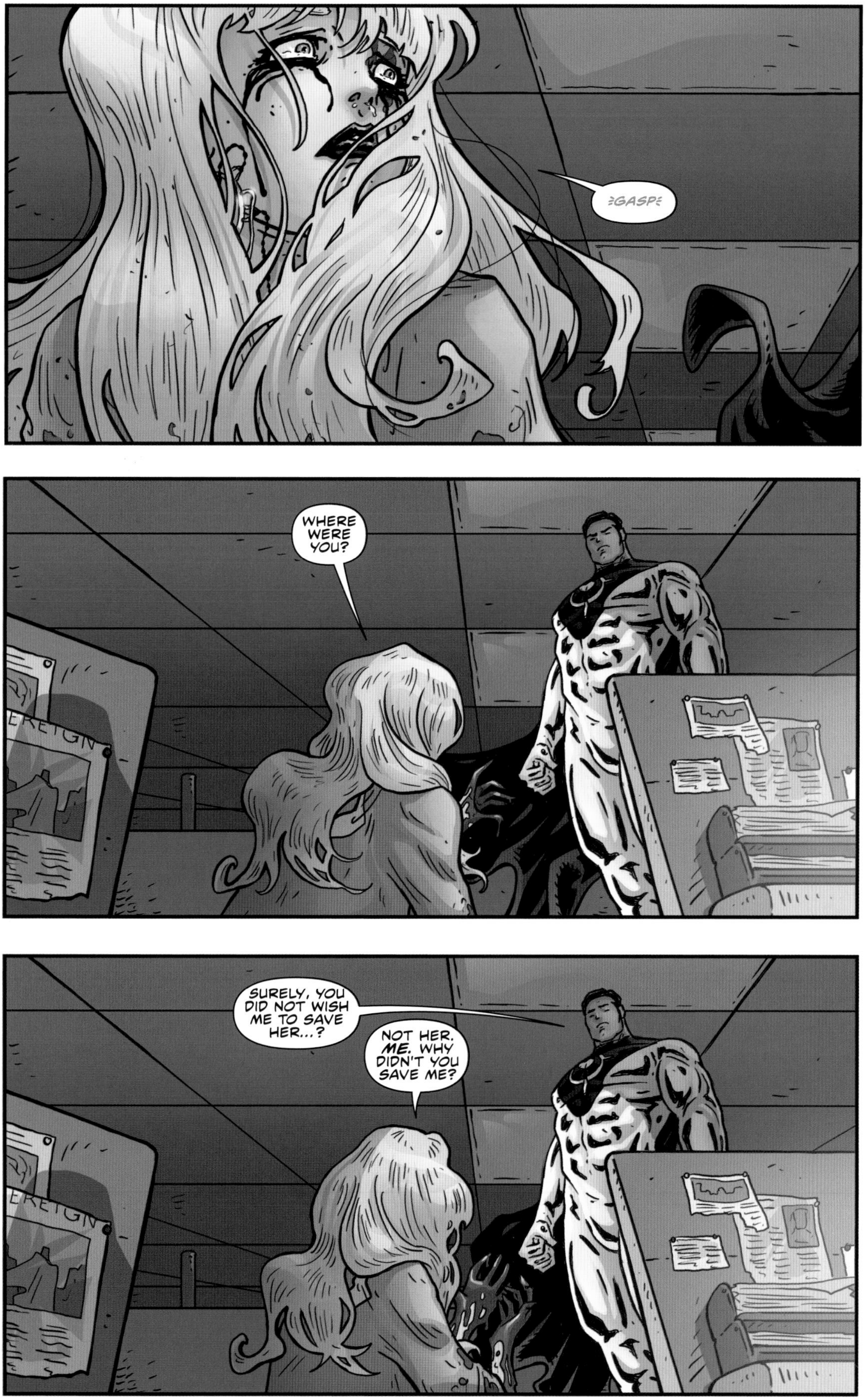
GASP
WHERE WERE YOU?
SURELY, YOU DID NOT WISH ME TO SAVE HER...?
NOT HER. ***ME.*** WHY DIDN'T YOU SAVE ME?

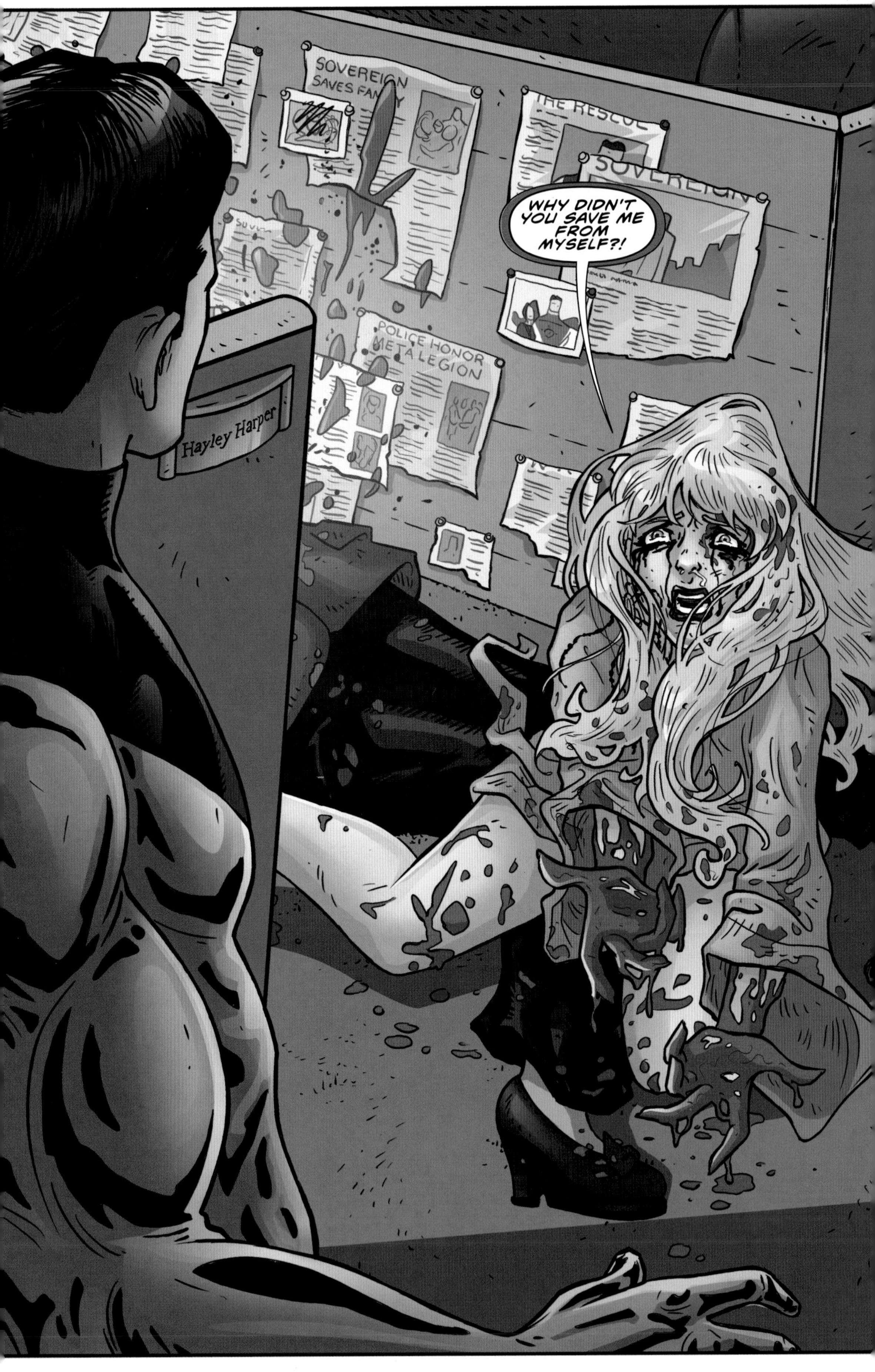
WHY DIDN'T YOU SAVE ME FROM MYSELF?!
SOVEREIGN
POLICE HONOR META LEGION
Hayley Harper

Chapter 4

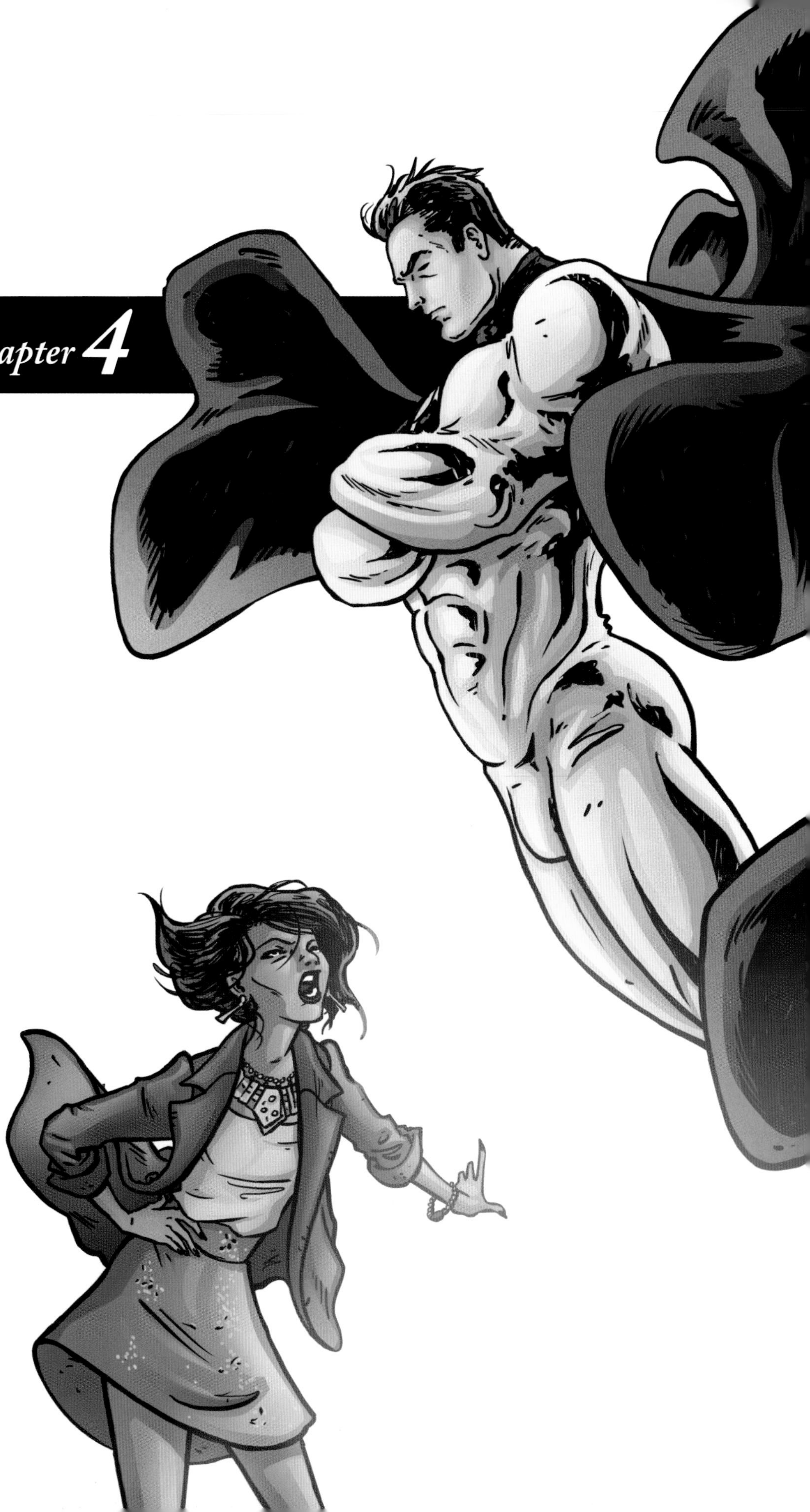

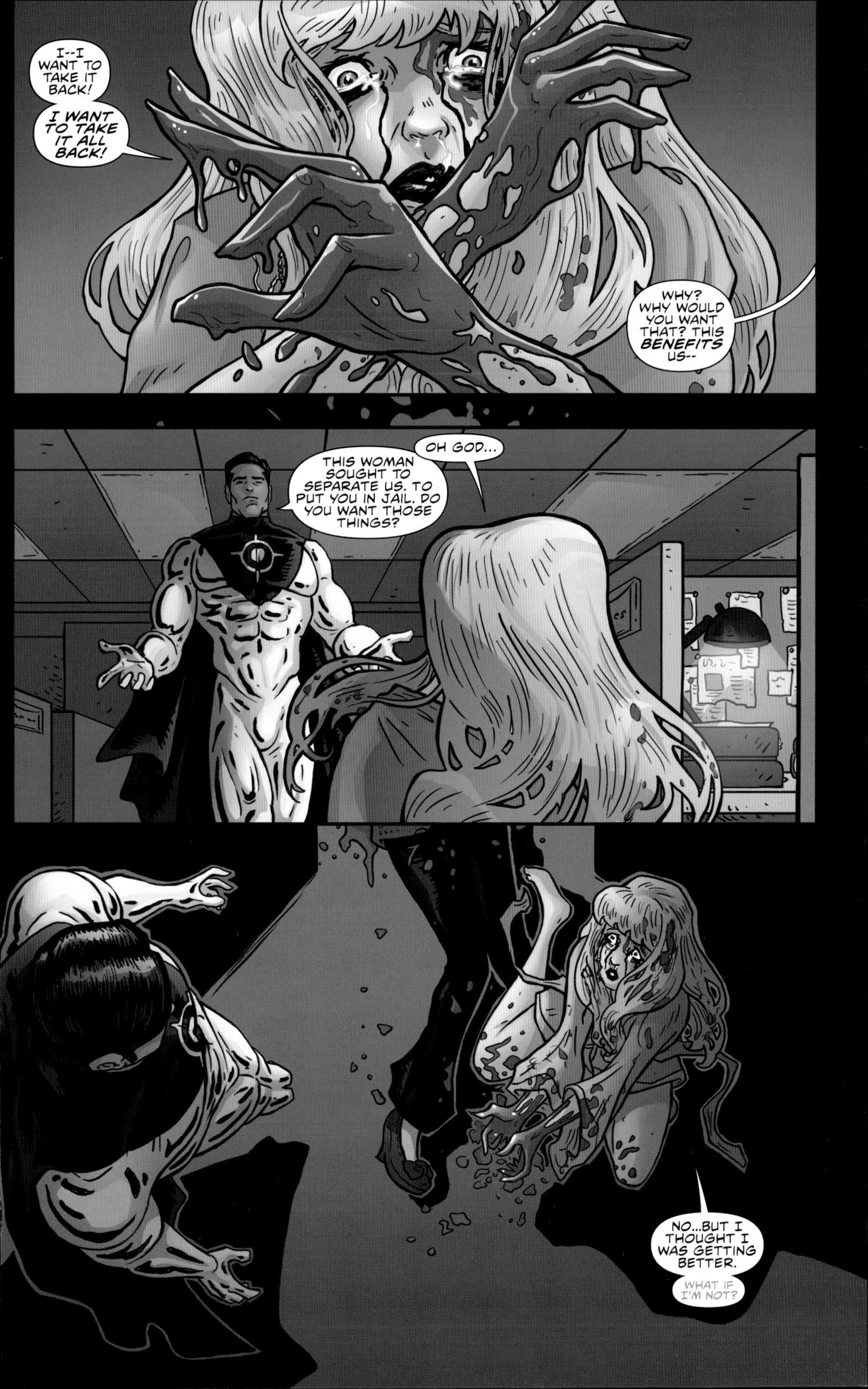
I--I WANT TO TAKE IT BACK!
I WANT TO TAKE IT ALL BACK!
WHY? WHY WOULD YOU WANT THAT? THIS BENEFITS US--
THIS WOMAN SOUGHT TO SEPARATE US. TO PUT YOU IN JAIL. DO YOU WANT THOSE THINGS?
OH GOD...
NO...BUT I THOUGHT I WAS GETTING BETTER.
WHAT IF I'M NOT?

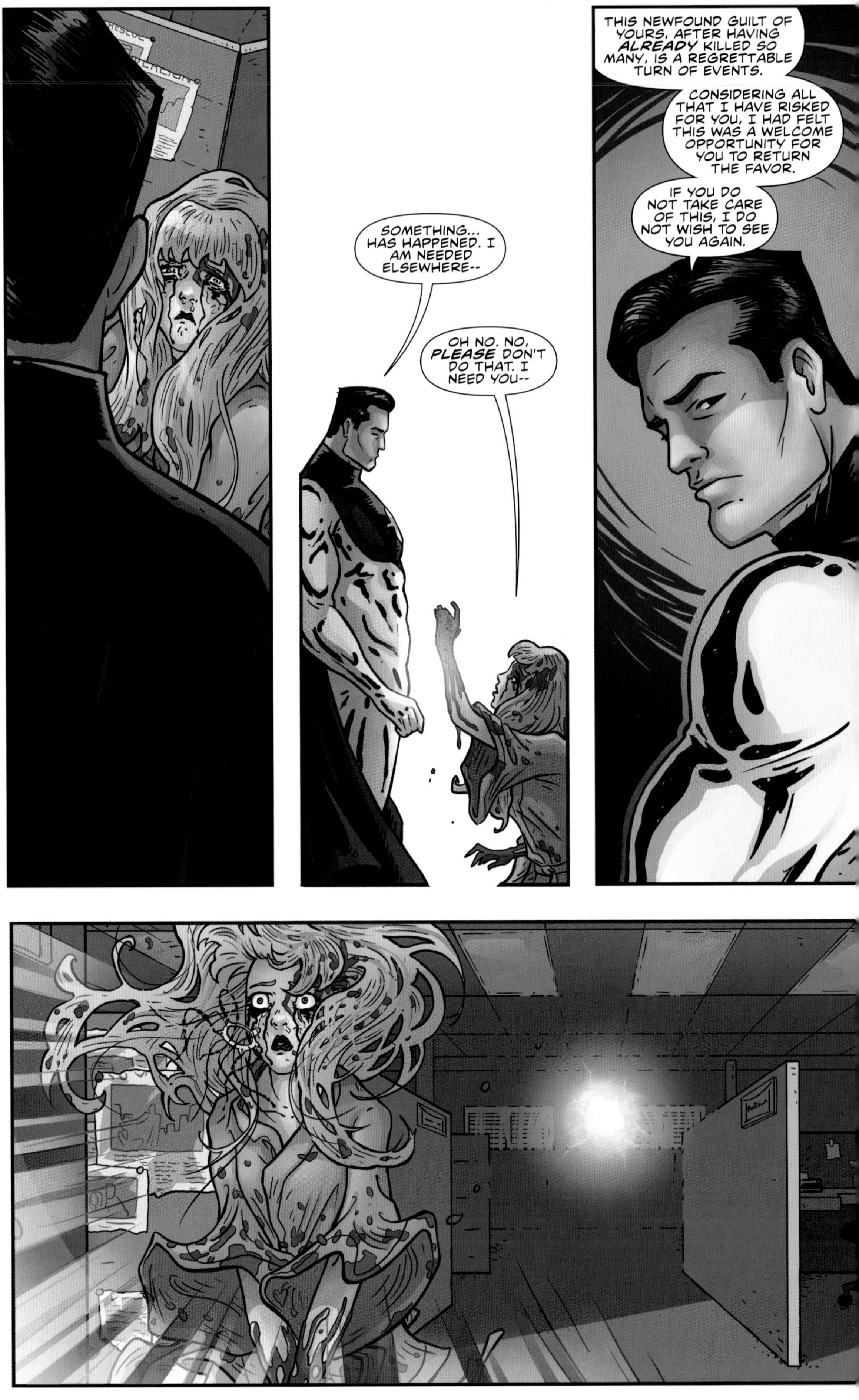
SOMETHING... HAS HAPPENED. I AM NEEDED ELSEWHERE--
OH NO. NO, PLEASE DON'T DO THAT. I NEED YOU--
THIS NEWFOUND GUILT OF YOURS, AFTER HAVING ALREADY KILLED SO MANY, IS A REGRETTABLE TURN OF EVENTS.
CONSIDERING ALL THAT I HAVE RISKED FOR YOU, I HAD FELT THIS WAS A WELCOME OPPORTUNITY FOR YOU TO RETURN THE FAVOR.
IF YOU DO NOT TAKE CARE OF THIS, I DO NOT WISH TO SEE YOU AGAIN.

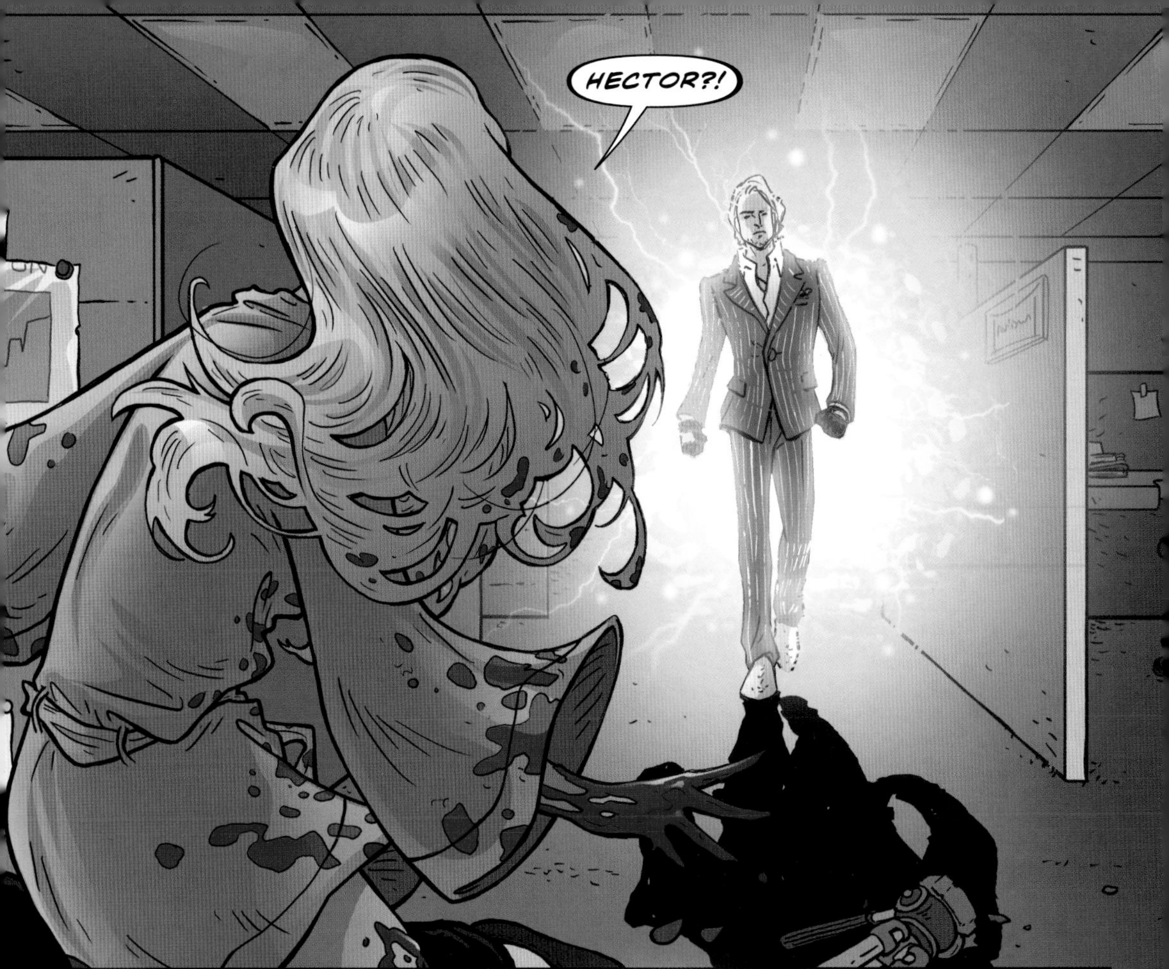
HECTOR?!

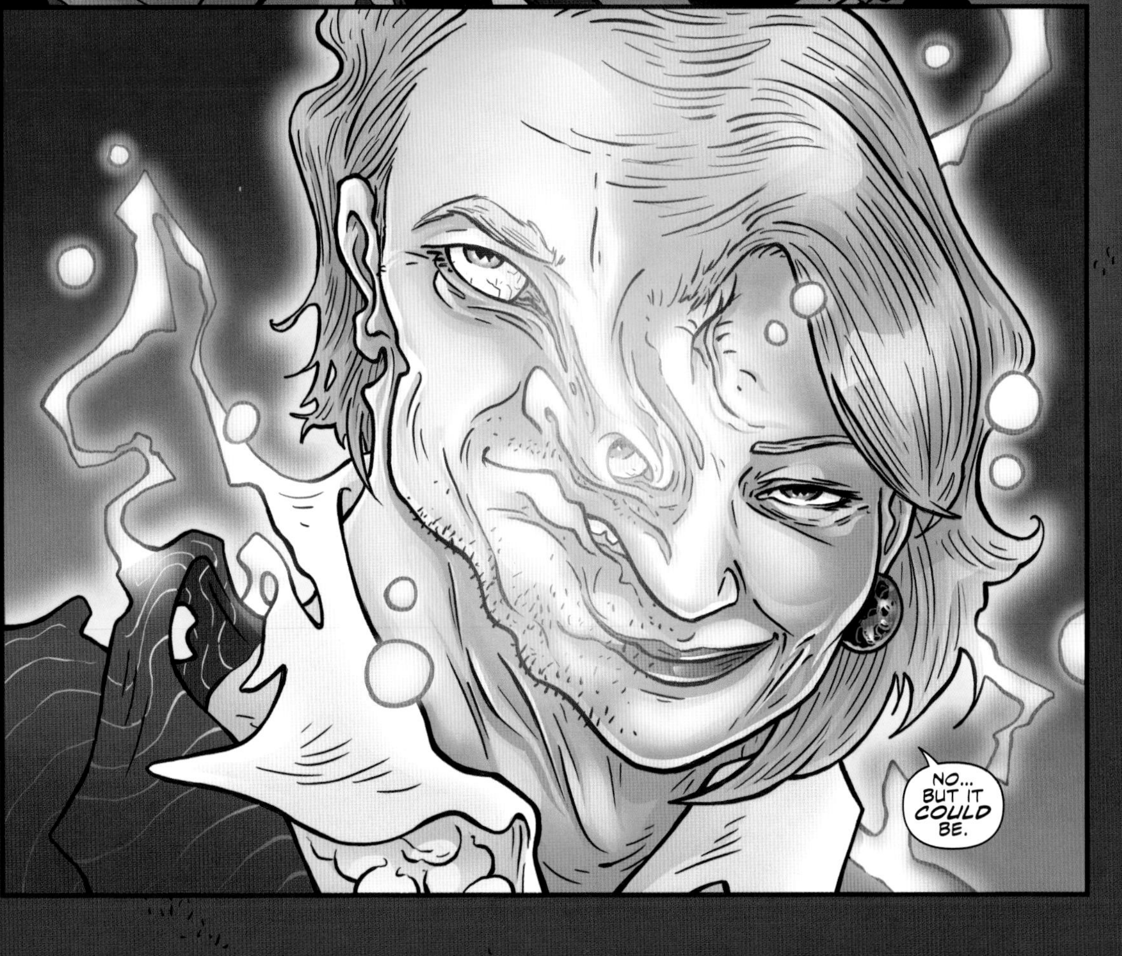
NO... BUT IT COULD BE.

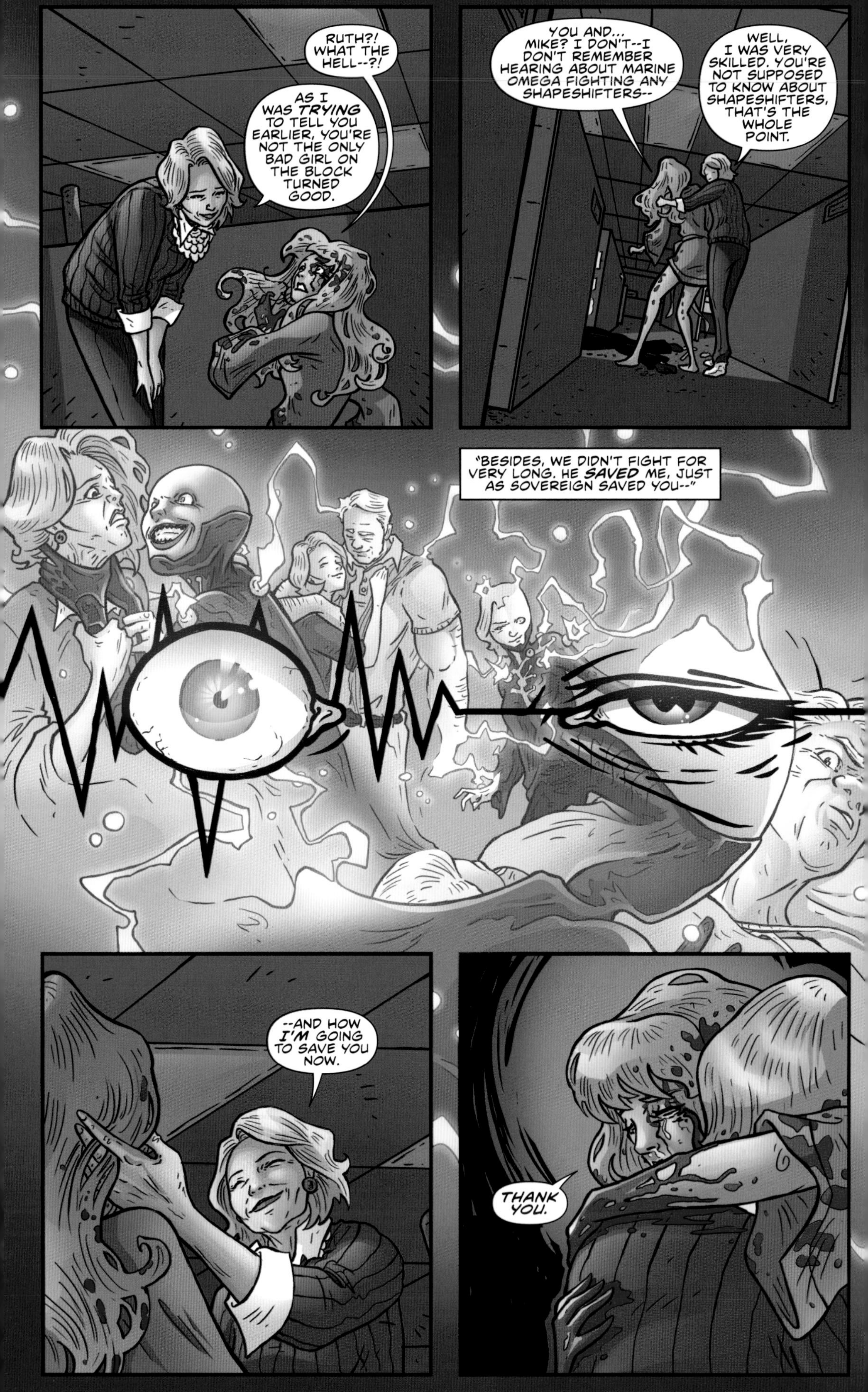
RUTH?! WHAT THE HELL--?!
AS I WAS TRYING TO TELL YOU EARLIER, YOU'RE NOT THE ONLY BAD GIRL ON THE BLOCK TURNED GOOD.
YOU AND... MIKE? I DON'T--I DON'T REMEMBER HEARING ABOUT MARINE OMEGA FIGHTING ANY SHAPESHIFTERS--
WELL, I WAS VERY SKILLED. YOU'RE NOT SUPPOSED TO KNOW ABOUT SHAPESHIFTERS, THAT'S THE WHOLE POINT.
"BESIDES, WE DIDN'T FIGHT FOR VERY LONG. HE SAVED ME, JUST AS SOVEREIGN SAVED YOU--"
--AND HOW I'M GOING TO SAVE YOU NOW.
THANK YOU.

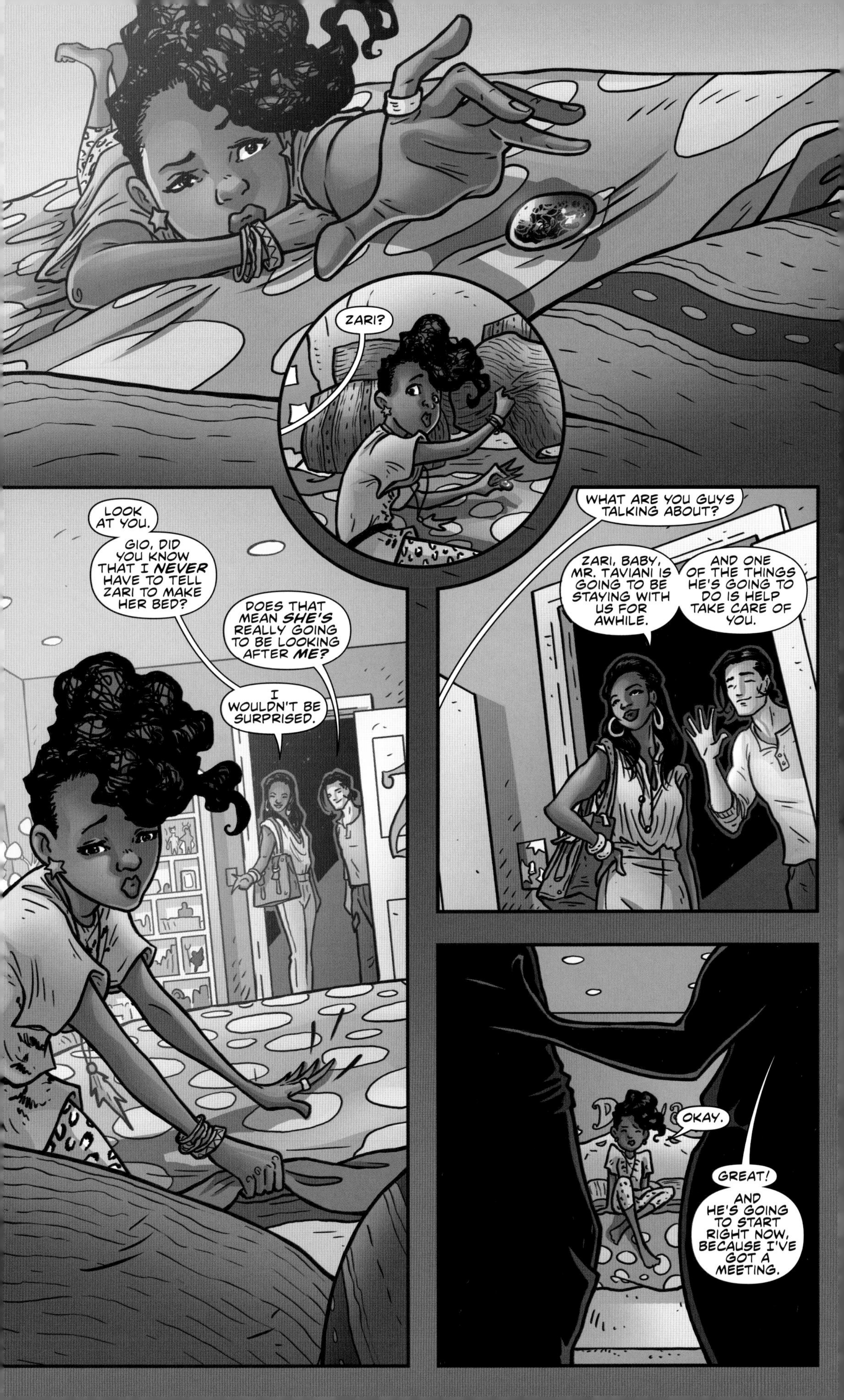
ZARI?
LOOK AT YOU.
GIO, DID YOU KNOW THAT I NEVER HAVE TO TELL ZARI TO MAKE HER BED?
DOES THAT MEAN SHE'S REALLY GOING TO BE LOOKING AFTER ME?
I WOULDN'T BE SURPRISED.
WHAT ARE YOU GUYS TALKING ABOUT?
ZARI, BABY, MR. TAVIANI IS GOING TO BE STAYING WITH US FOR AWHILE.
AND ONE OF THE THINGS HE'S GOING TO DO IS HELP TAKE CARE OF YOU.
OKAY.
GREAT!
AND HE'S GOING TO START RIGHT NOW, BECAUSE I'VE GOT A MEETING.

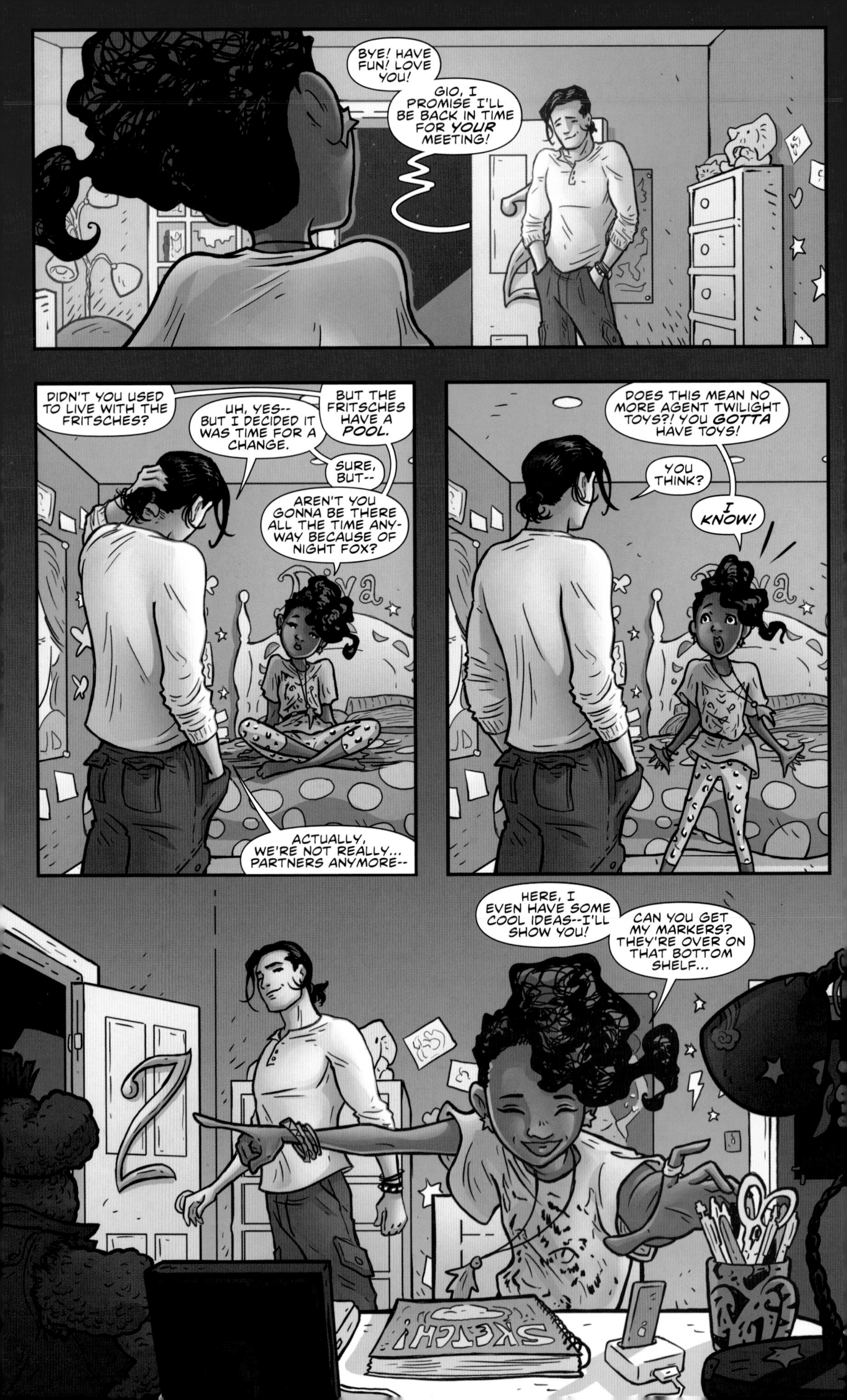
BYE! HAVE FUN! LOVE YOU!
GIO, I PROMISE I'LL BE BACK IN TIME FOR YOUR MEETING!
DIDN'T YOU USED TO LIVE WITH THE FRITSCHES?
UH, YES-- BUT I DECIDED IT WAS TIME FOR A CHANGE.
BUT THE FRITSCHES HAVE A POOL.
SURE, BUT--
AREN'T YOU GONNA BE THERE ALL THE TIME ANYWAY BECAUSE OF NIGHT FOX?
ACTUALLY, WE'RE NOT REALLY... PARTNERS ANYMORE--
DOES THIS MEAN NO MORE AGENT TWILIGHT TOYS?! YOU GOTTA HAVE TOYS!
YOU THINK?
I KNOW!
HERE, I EVEN HAVE SOME COOL IDEAS--I'LL SHOW YOU!
CAN YOU GET MY MARKERS? THEY'RE OVER ON THAT BOTTOM SHELF...
SKETCH!

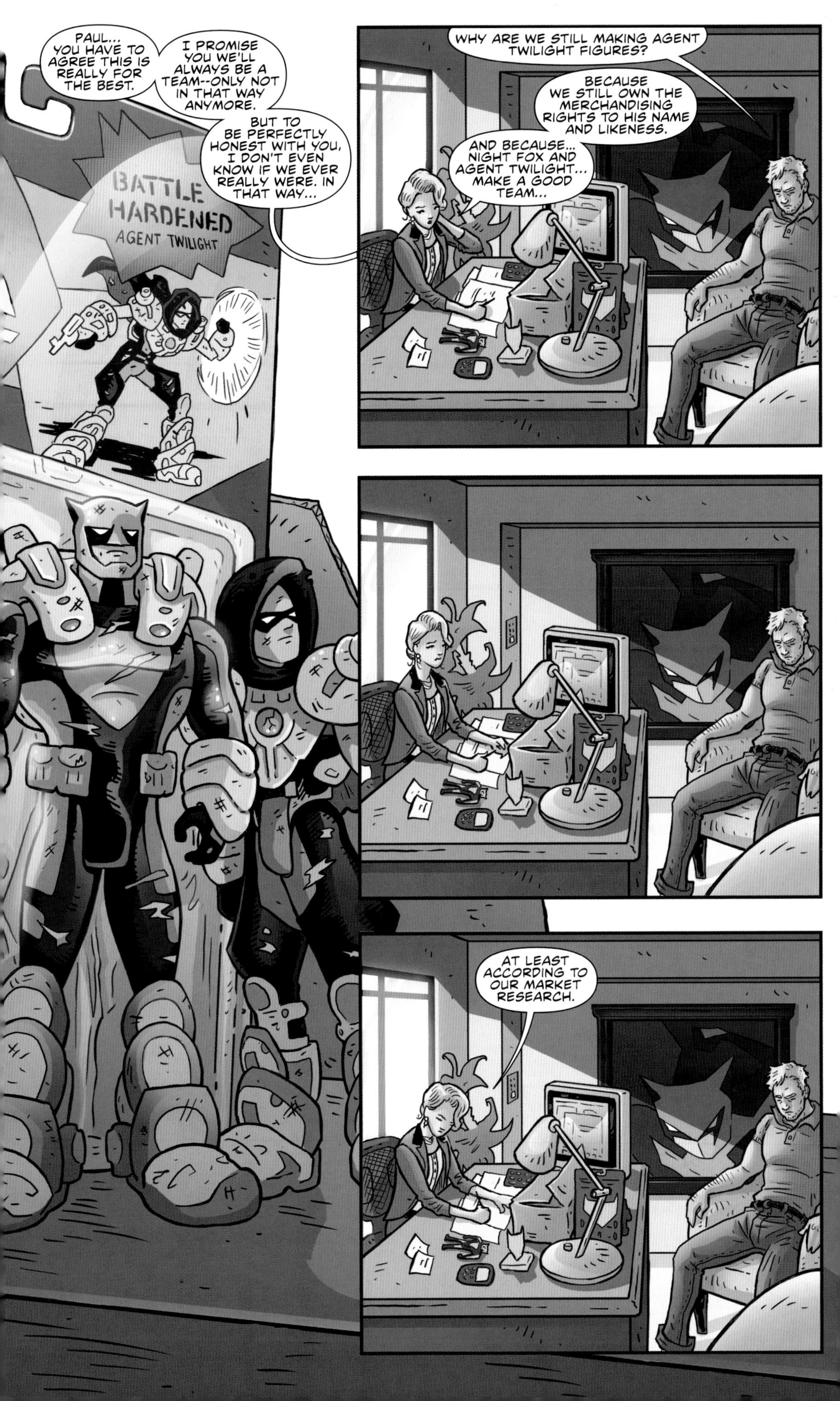
PAUL... YOU HAVE TO AGREE THIS IS REALLY FOR THE BEST.
I PROMISE YOU WE'LL ALWAYS BE A TEAM--ONLY NOT IN THAT WAY ANYMORE.
BUT TO BE PERFECTLY HONEST WITH YOU, I DON'T EVEN KNOW IF WE EVER REALLY WERE. IN THAT WAY...
BATTLE HARDENED
AGENT TWILIGHT
WHY ARE WE STILL MAKING AGENT TWILIGHT FIGURES?
BECAUSE WE STILL OWN THE MERCHANDISING RIGHTS TO HIS NAME AND LIKENESS.
AND BECAUSE... NIGHT FOX AND AGENT TWILIGHT... MAKE A GOOD TEAM...
AT LEAST ACCORDING TO OUR MARKET RESEARCH.

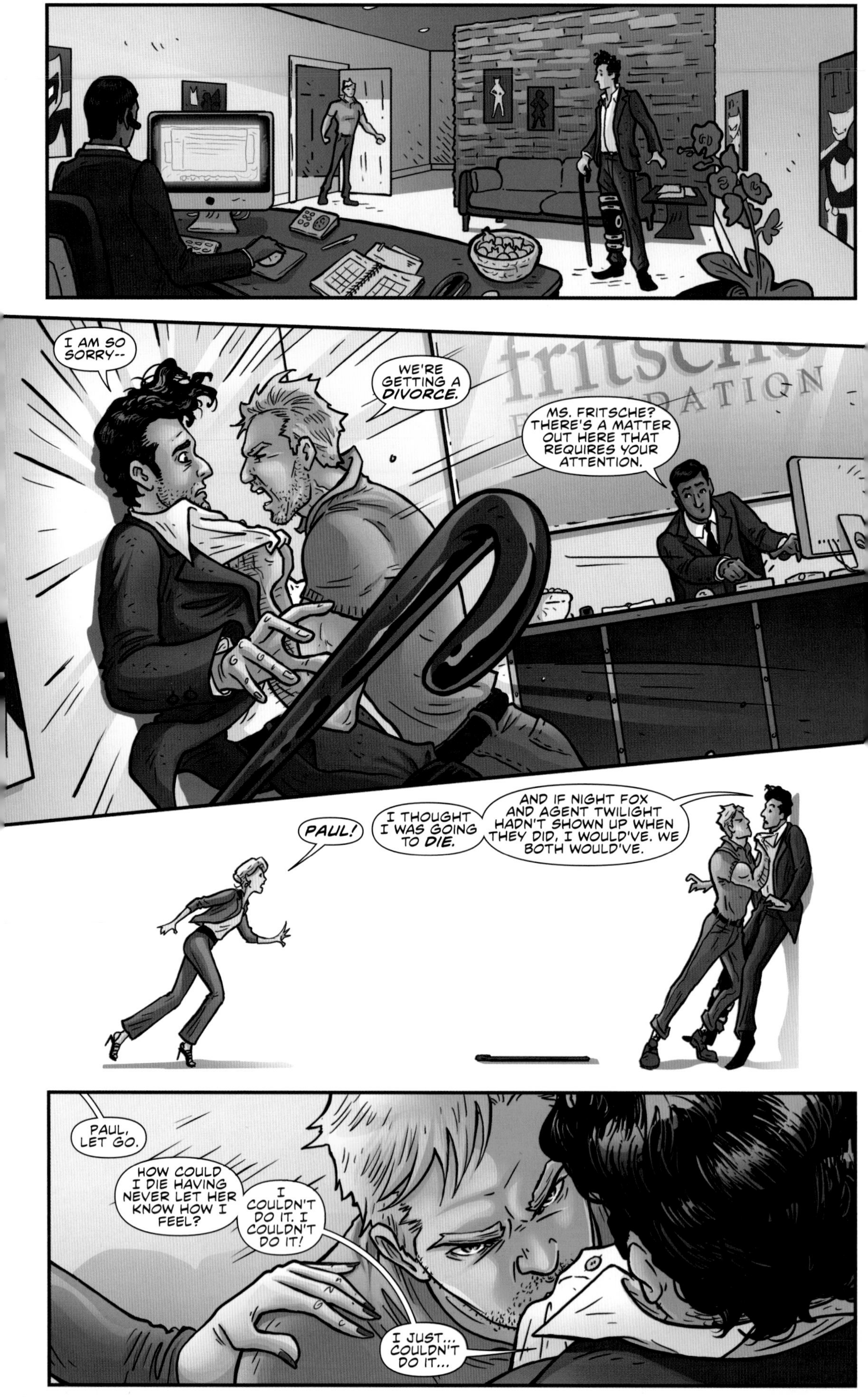
I AM SO SORRY--
WE'RE GETTING A DIVORCE.
fritsche FOUNDATION
MS. FRITSCHE? THERE'S A MATTER OUT HERE THAT REQUIRES YOUR ATTENTION.
PAUL!
I THOUGHT I WAS GOING TO DIE.
AND IF NIGHT FOX AND AGENT TWILIGHT HADN'T SHOWN UP WHEN THEY DID, I WOULD'VE. WE BOTH WOULD'VE.
PAUL, LET GO.
HOW COULD I DIE HAVING NEVER LET HER KNOW HOW I FEEL?
I COULDN'T DO IT. I COULDN'T DO IT!
I JUST... COULDN'T DO IT...

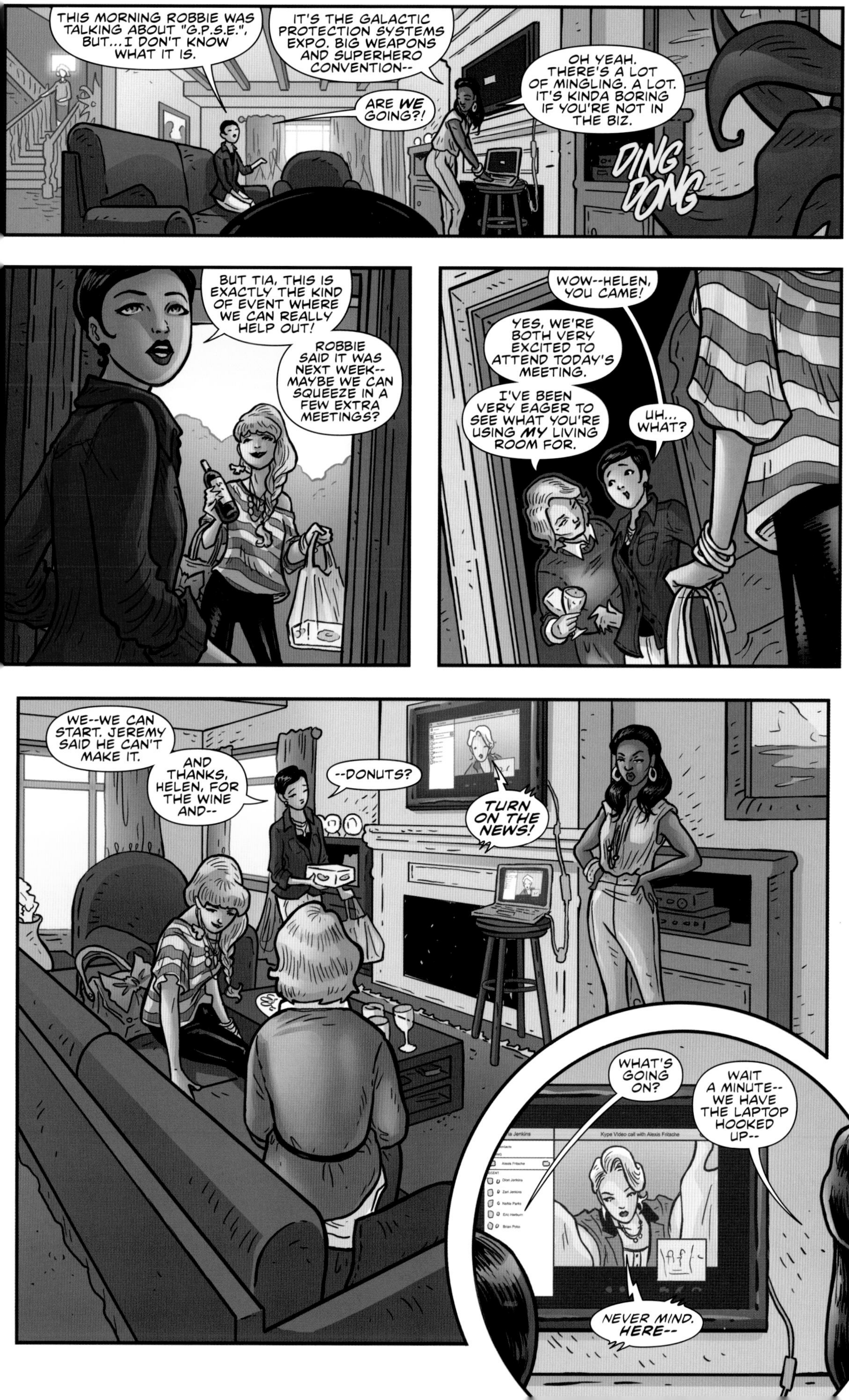
THIS MORNING ROBBIE WAS TALKING ABOUT "G.P.S.E.", BUT... I DON'T KNOW WHAT IT IS.
IT'S THE GALACTIC PROTECTION SYSTEMS EXPO. BIG WEAPONS AND SUPERHERO CONVENTION--
ARE *WE* GOING?!
OH YEAH. THERE'S A LOT OF MINGLING. A LOT. IT'S KINDA BORING IF YOU'RE NOT IN THE BIZ.
DING DONG
BUT TIA, THIS IS EXACTLY THE KIND OF EVENT WHERE WE CAN REALLY HELP OUT!
ROBBIE SAID IT WAS NEXT WEEK-- MAYBE WE CAN SQUEEZE IN A FEW EXTRA MEETINGS?
WOW--HELEN, YOU CAME!
YES, WE'RE BOTH VERY EXCITED TO ATTEND TODAY'S MEETING.
I'VE BEEN VERY EAGER TO SEE WHAT YOU'RE USING *MY* LIVING ROOM FOR.
UH... WHAT?
WE--WE CAN START. JEREMY SAID HE CAN'T MAKE IT.
AND THANKS, HELEN, FOR THE WINE AND--
--DONUTS?
TURN ON THE NEWS!
WHAT'S GOING ON?
WAIT A MINUTE-- WE HAVE THE LAPTOP HOOKED UP--
NEVER MIND. *HERE--*

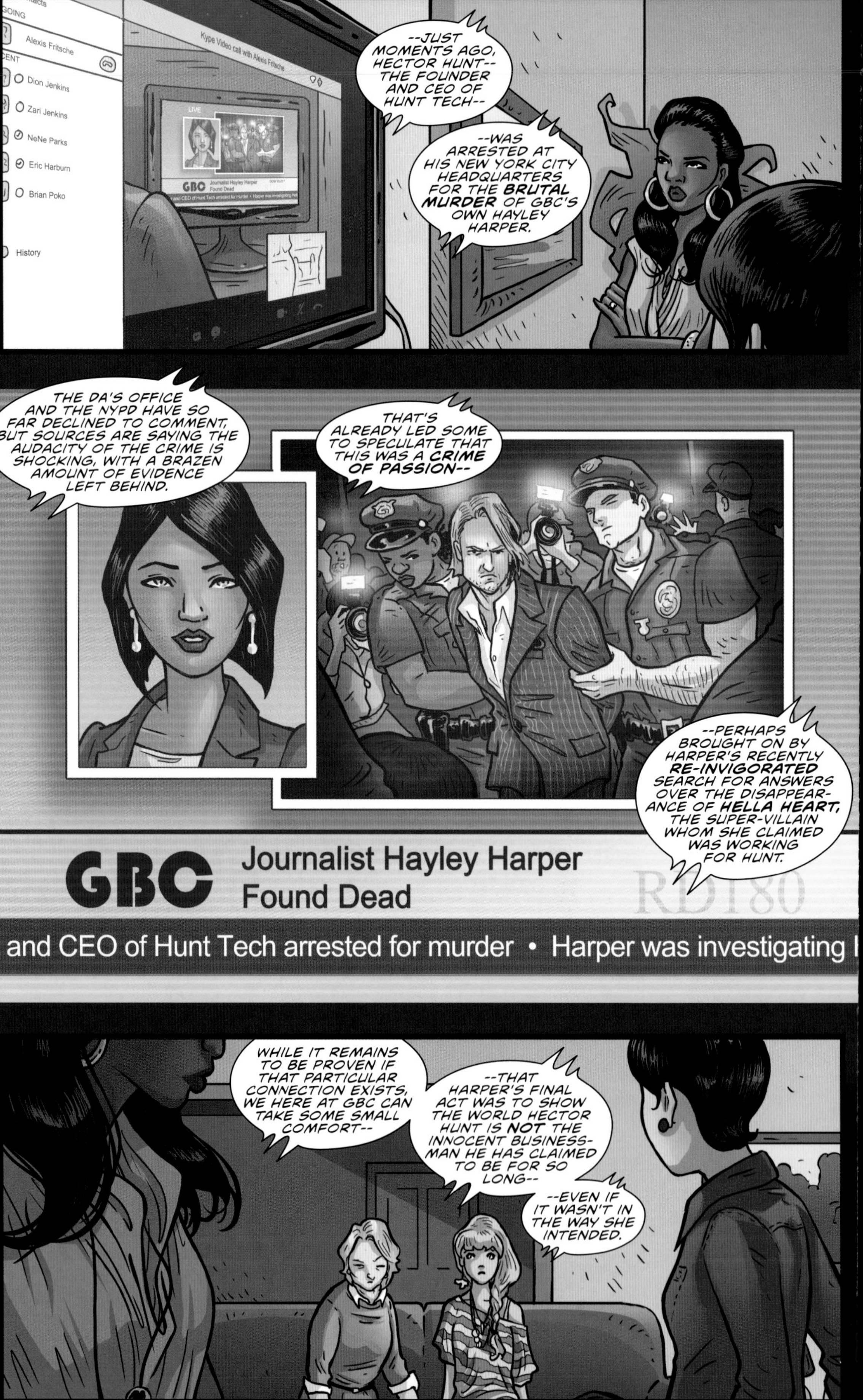
GOING
Alexis Fritsche
Kype Video call with Alexis Fritsche
Dion Jenkins
Zari Jenkins
NeNe Parks
Eric Harburn
Brian Poko
History
--JUST MOMENTS AGO, HECTOR HUNT-- THE FOUNDER AND CEO OF HUNT TECH--
--WAS ARRESTED AT HIS NEW YORK CITY HEADQUARTERS FOR THE BRUTAL MURDER OF GBC'S OWN HAYLEY HARPER.
THE DA'S OFFICE AND THE NYPD HAVE SO FAR DECLINED TO COMMENT, BUT SOURCES ARE SAYING THE AUDACITY OF THE CRIME IS SHOCKING, WITH A BRAZEN AMOUNT OF EVIDENCE LEFT BEHIND.
THAT'S ALREADY LED SOME TO SPECULATE THAT THIS WAS A CRIME OF PASSION--
--PERHAPS BROUGHT ON BY HARPER'S RECENTLY RE-INVIGORATED SEARCH FOR ANSWERS OVER THE DISAPPEAR-ANCE OF HELLA HEART, THE SUPER-VILLAIN WHOM SHE CLAIMED WAS WORKING FOR HUNT.
GBC
Journalist Hayley Harper Found Dead
RD180
der and CEO of Hunt Tech arrested for murder • Harper was investigating
WHILE IT REMAINS TO BE PROVEN IF THAT PARTICULAR CONNECTION EXISTS, WE HERE AT GBC CAN TAKE SOME SMALL COMFORT--
--THAT HARPER'S FINAL ACT WAS TO SHOW THE WORLD HECTOR HUNT IS NOT THE INNOCENT BUSINESS-MAN HE HAS CLAIMED TO BE FOR SO LONG--
--EVEN IF IT WASN'T IN THE WAY SHE INTENDED.

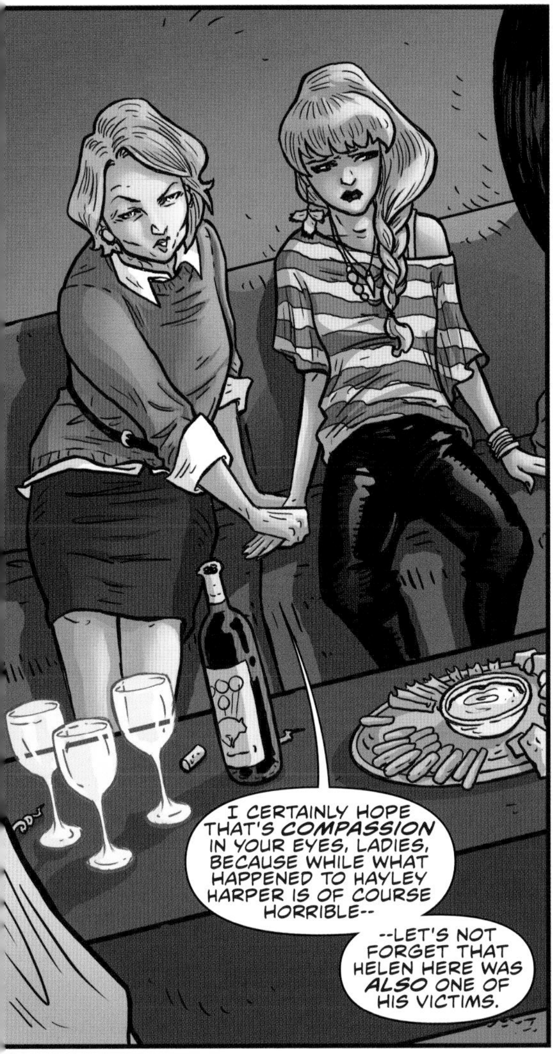
I CERTAINLY HOPE THAT'S COMPASSION IN YOUR EYES, LADIES, BECAUSE WHILE WHAT HAPPENED TO HAYLEY HARPER IS OF COURSE HORRIBLE--
--LET'S NOT FORGET THAT HELEN HERE WAS ALSO ONE OF HIS VICTIMS.

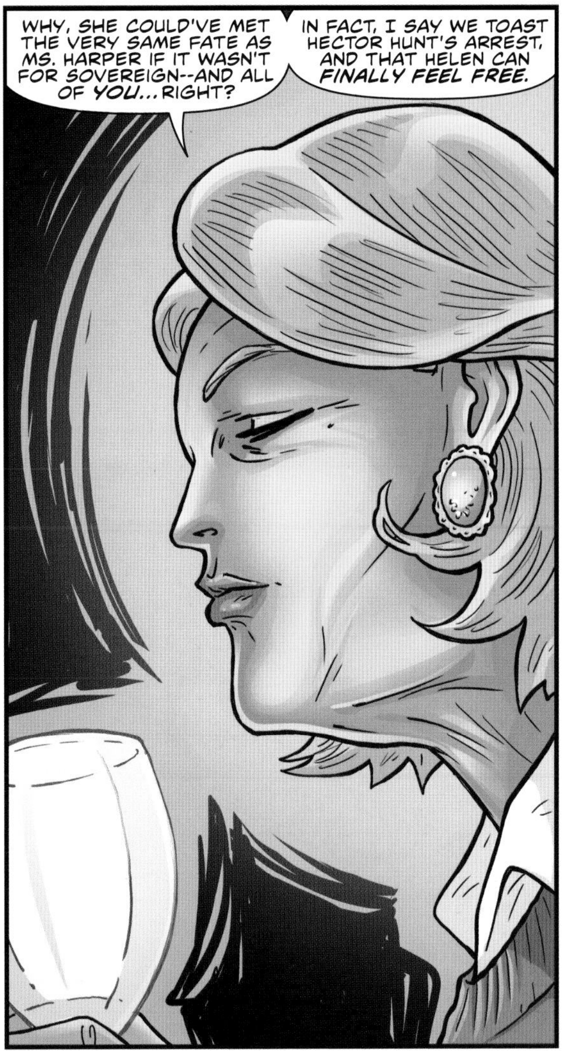
WHY, SHE COULD'VE MET THE VERY SAME FATE AS MS. HARPER IF IT WASN'T FOR SOVEREIGN--AND ALL OF YOU... RIGHT?
IN FACT, I SAY WE TOAST HECTOR HUNT'S ARREST, AND THAT HELEN CAN FINALLY FEEL FREE.

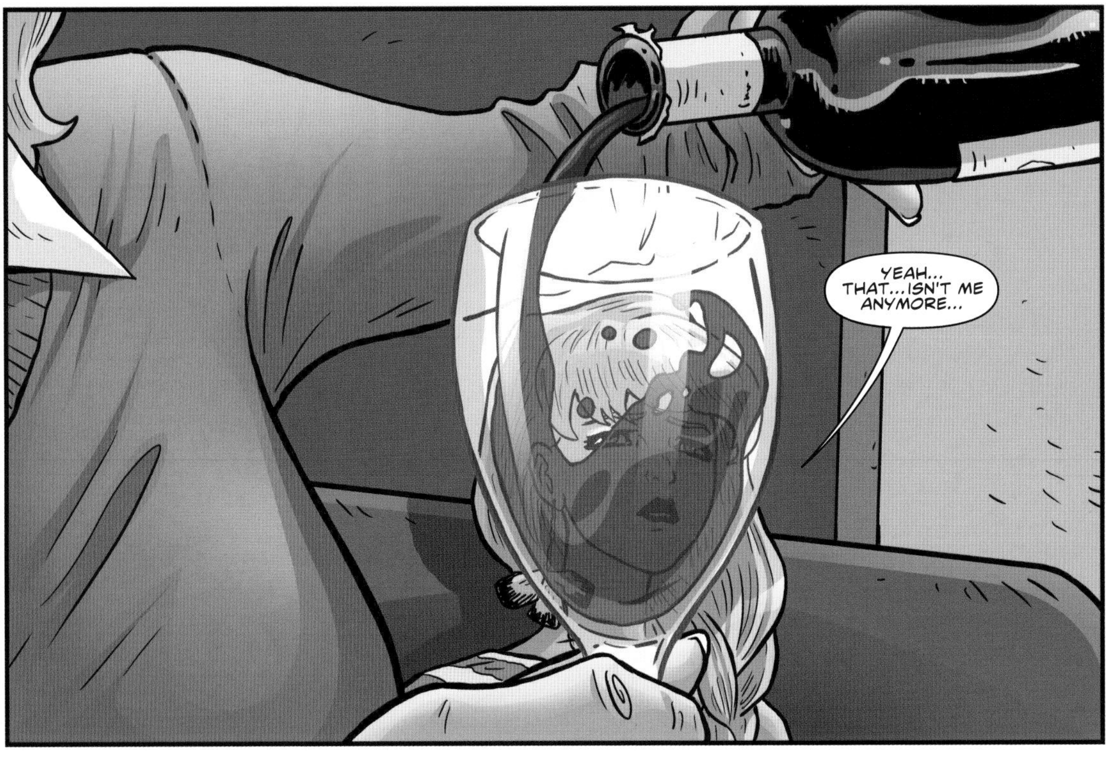
YEAH... THAT...ISN'T ME ANYMORE...

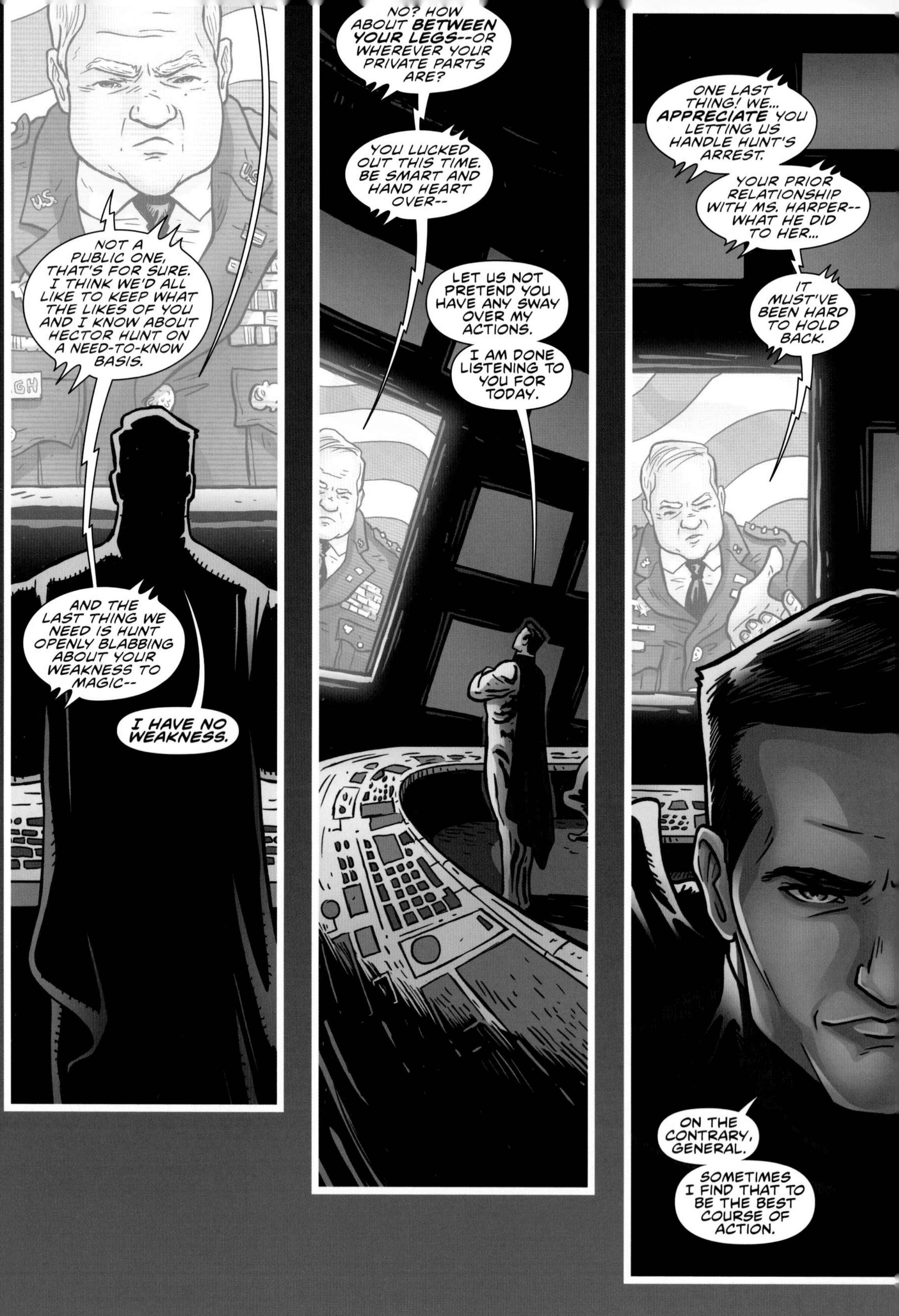
NOT A PUBLIC ONE, THAT'S FOR SURE. I THINK WE'D ALL LIKE TO KEEP WHAT THE LIKES OF YOU AND I KNOW ABOUT HECTOR HUNT ON A NEED-TO-KNOW BASIS.
AND THE LAST THING WE NEED IS HUNT OPENLY BLABBING ABOUT YOUR WEAKNESS TO MAGIC--
I HAVE NO WEAKNESS.
NO? HOW ABOUT BETWEEN YOUR LEGS--OR WHEREVER YOUR PRIVATE PARTS ARE?
YOU LUCKED OUT THIS TIME. BE SMART AND HAND HEART OVER--
LET US NOT PRETEND YOU HAVE ANY SWAY OVER MY ACTIONS.
I AM DONE LISTENING TO YOU FOR TODAY.
ONE LAST THING! WE... APPRECIATE YOU LETTING US HANDLE HUNT'S ARREST.
YOUR PRIOR RELATIONSHIP WITH MS. HARPER-- WHAT HE DID TO HER...
IT MUST'VE BEEN HARD TO HOLD BACK.
ON THE CONTRARY, GENERAL.
SOMETIMES I FIND THAT TO BE THE BEST COURSE OF ACTION.

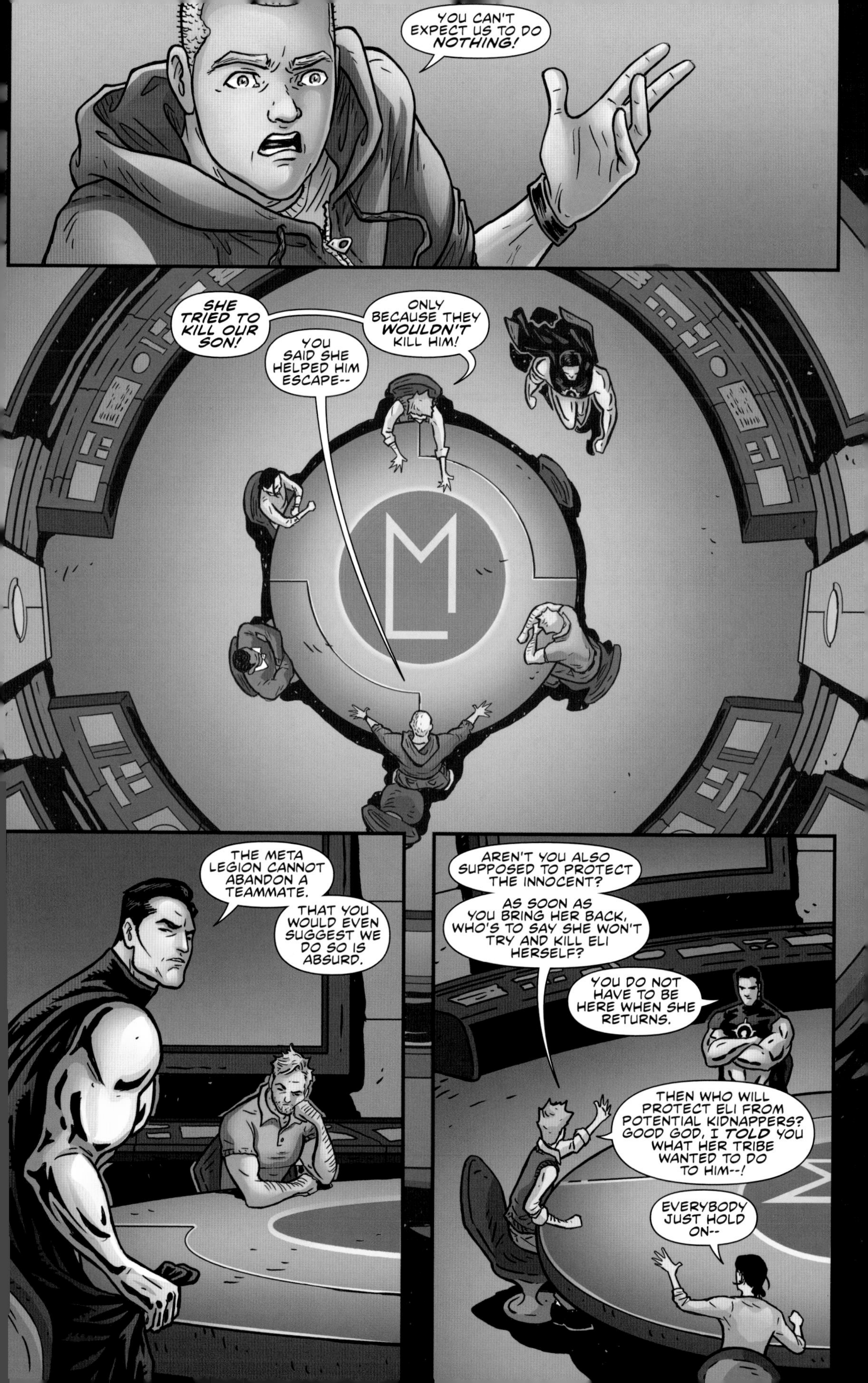
YOU CAN'T EXPECT US TO DO NOTHING!
SHE TRIED TO KILL OUR SON!
ONLY BECAUSE THEY WOULDN'T KILL HIM!
YOU SAID SHE HELPED HIM ESCAPE--
THE META LEGION CANNOT ABANDON A TEAMMATE.
THAT YOU WOULD EVEN SUGGEST WE DO SO IS ABSURD.
AREN'T YOU ALSO SUPPOSED TO PROTECT THE INNOCENT?
AS SOON AS YOU BRING HER BACK, WHO'S TO SAY SHE WON'T TRY AND KILL ELI HERSELF?
YOU DO NOT HAVE TO BE HERE WHEN SHE RETURNS.
THEN WHO WILL PROTECT ELI FROM POTENTIAL KIDNAPPERS? GOOD GOD, I TOLD YOU WHAT HER TRIBE WANTED TO DO TO HIM--!
EVERYBODY JUST HOLD ON--

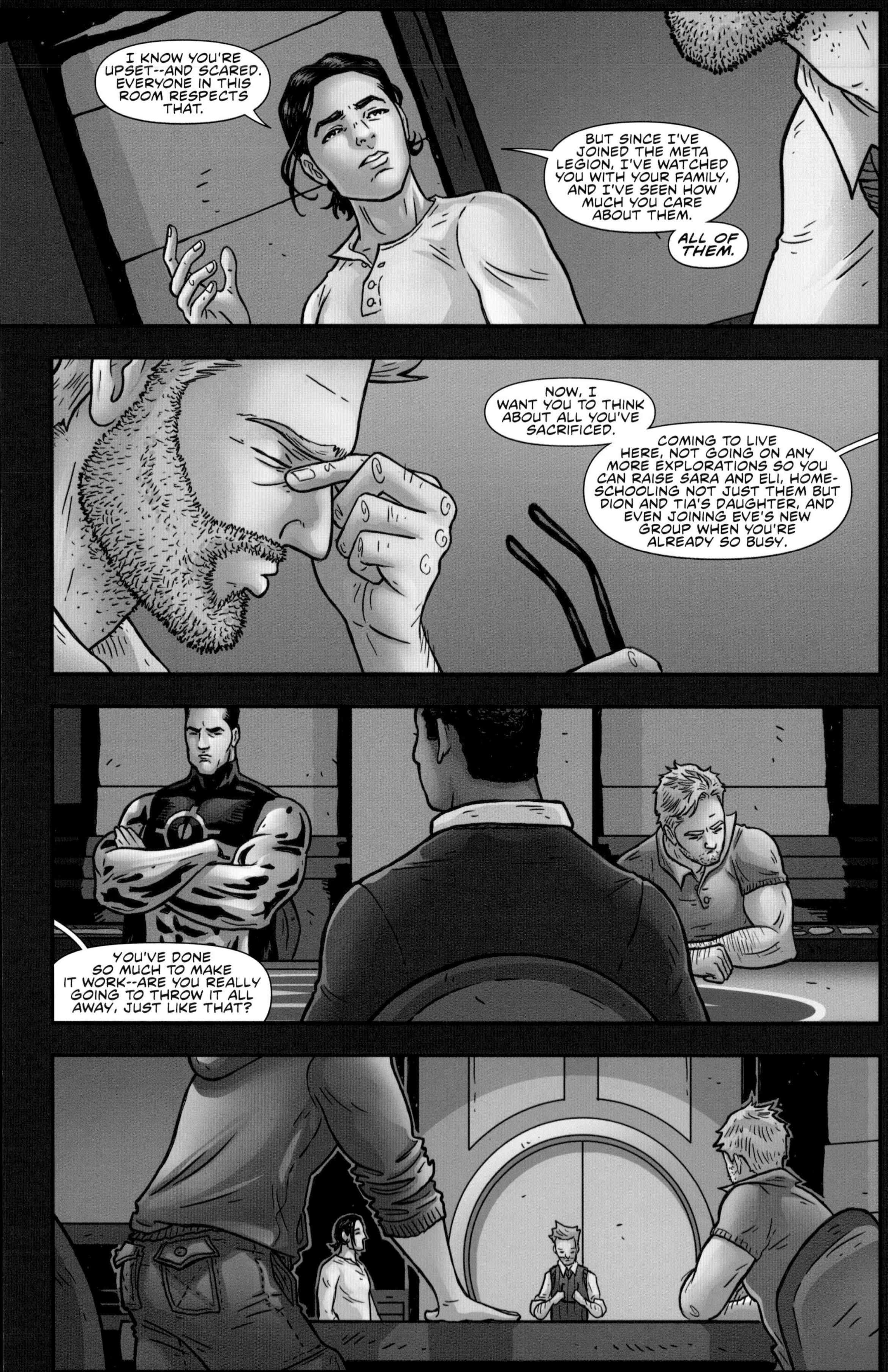
I KNOW YOU'RE UPSET--AND SCARED. EVERYONE IN THIS ROOM RESPECTS THAT.
BUT SINCE I'VE JOINED THE META LEGION, I'VE WATCHED YOU WITH YOUR FAMILY, AND I'VE SEEN HOW MUCH YOU CARE ABOUT THEM.
ALL OF THEM.
NOW, I WANT YOU TO THINK ABOUT ALL YOU'VE SACRIFICED.
COMING TO LIVE HERE, NOT GOING ON ANY MORE EXPLORATIONS SO YOU CAN RAISE SARA AND ELI, HOME-SCHOOLING NOT JUST THEM BUT DION AND TIA'S DAUGHTER, AND EVEN JOINING EVE'S NEW GROUP WHEN YOU'RE ALREADY SO BUSY.
YOU'VE DONE SO MUCH TO MAKE IT WORK--ARE YOU REALLY GOING TO THROW IT ALL AWAY, JUST LIKE THAT?

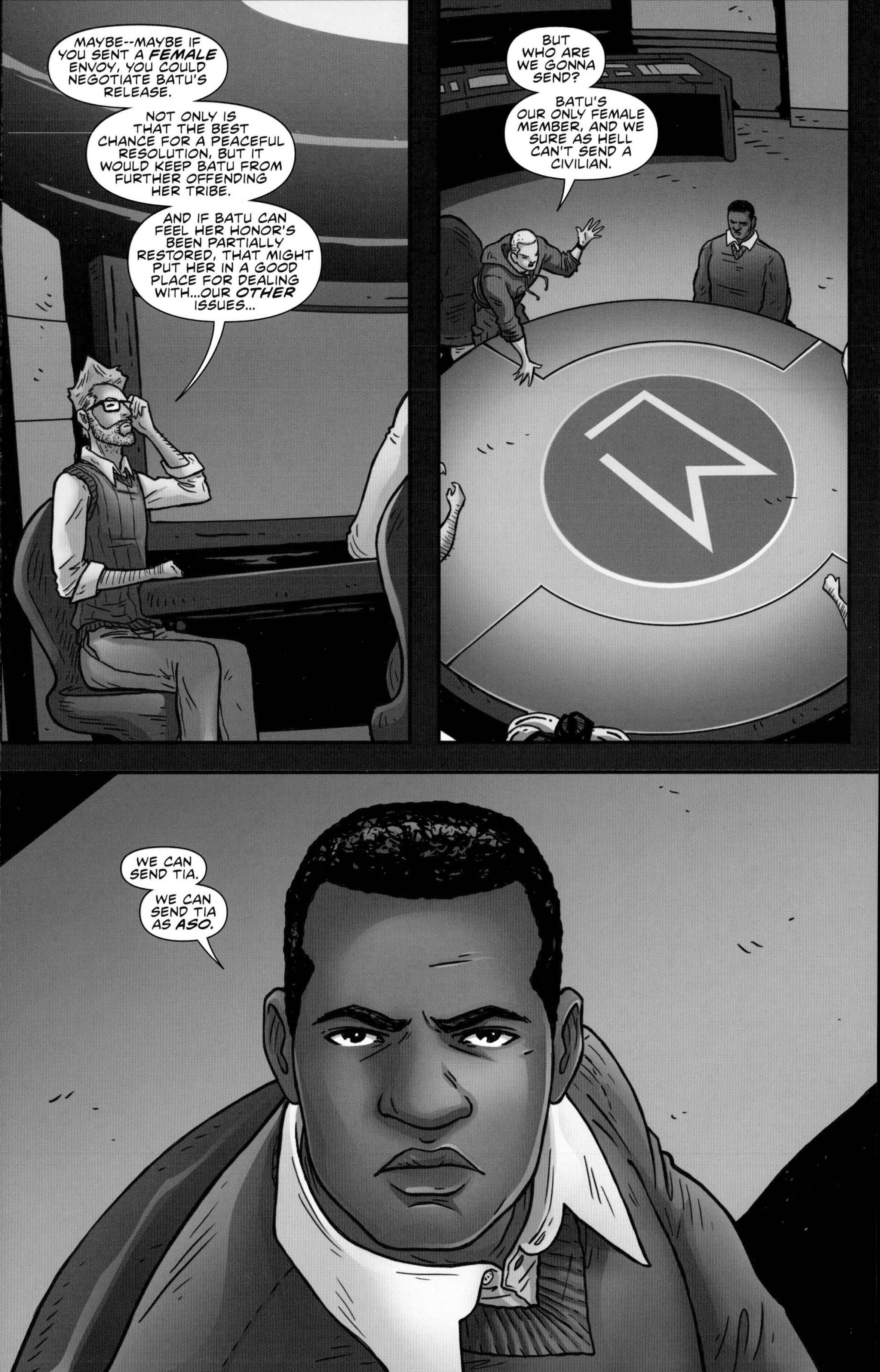
MAYBE--MAYBE IF YOU SENT A FEMALE ENVOY, YOU COULD NEGOTIATE BATU'S RELEASE.
NOT ONLY IS THAT THE BEST CHANCE FOR A PEACEFUL RESOLUTION, BUT IT WOULD KEEP BATU FROM FURTHER OFFENDING HER TRIBE.
AND IF BATU CAN FEEL HER HONOR'S BEEN PARTIALLY RESTORED, THAT MIGHT PUT HER IN A GOOD PLACE FOR DEALING WITH...OUR OTHER ISSUES...
BUT WHO ARE WE GONNA SEND?
BATU'S OUR ONLY FEMALE MEMBER, AND WE SURE AS HELL CAN'T SEND A CIVILIAN.
WE CAN SEND TIA.
WE CAN SEND TIA AS ASO.

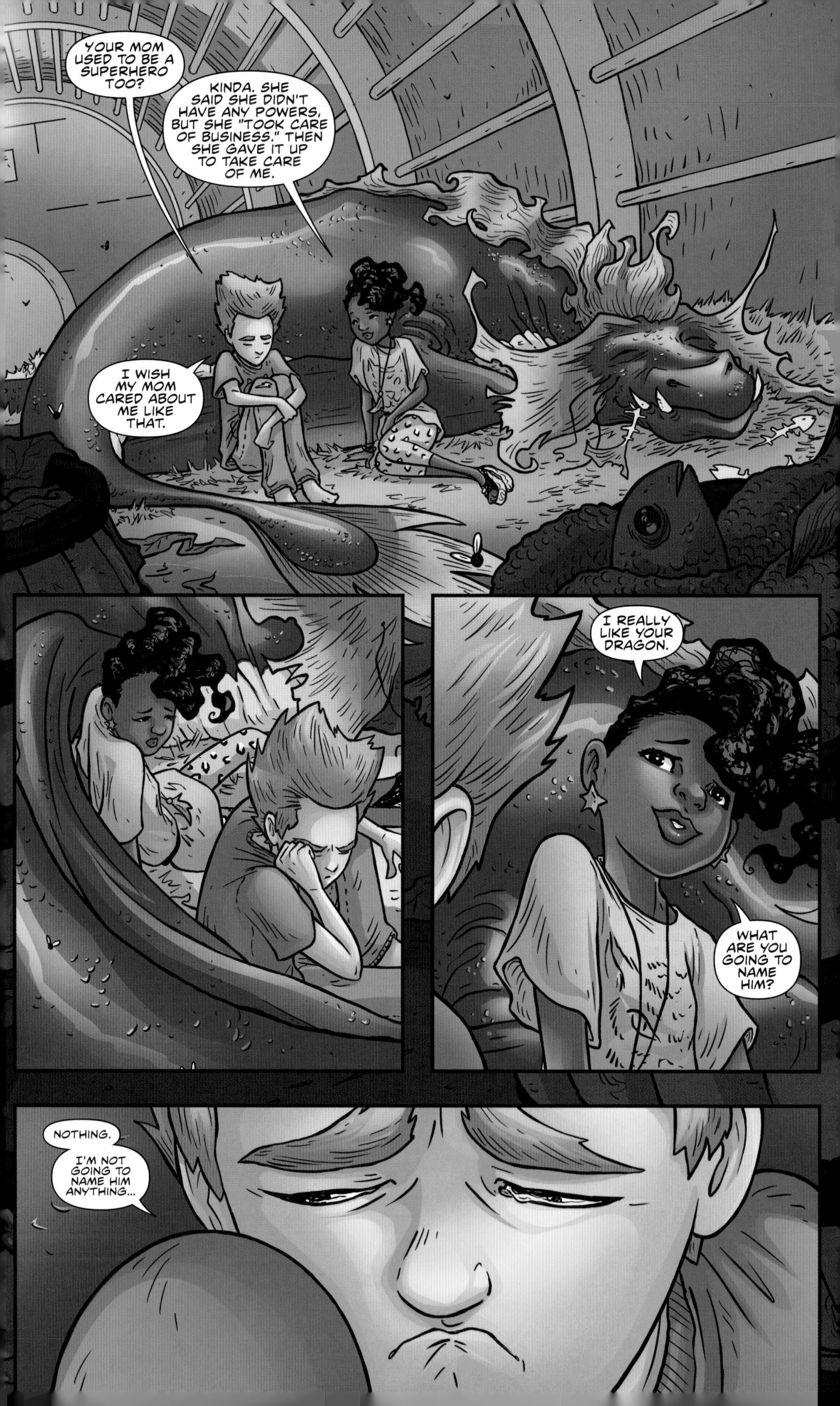

YOUR MOM USED TO BE A SUPERHERO TOO?
KINDA. SHE SAID SHE DIDN'T HAVE ANY POWERS, BUT SHE "TOOK CARE OF BUSINESS." THEN SHE GAVE IT UP TO TAKE CARE OF ME.
I WISH MY MOM CARED ABOUT ME LIKE THAT.
I REALLY LIKE YOUR DRAGON.
WHAT ARE YOU GOING TO NAME HIM?
NOTHING.
I'M NOT GOING TO NAME HIM ANYTHING...

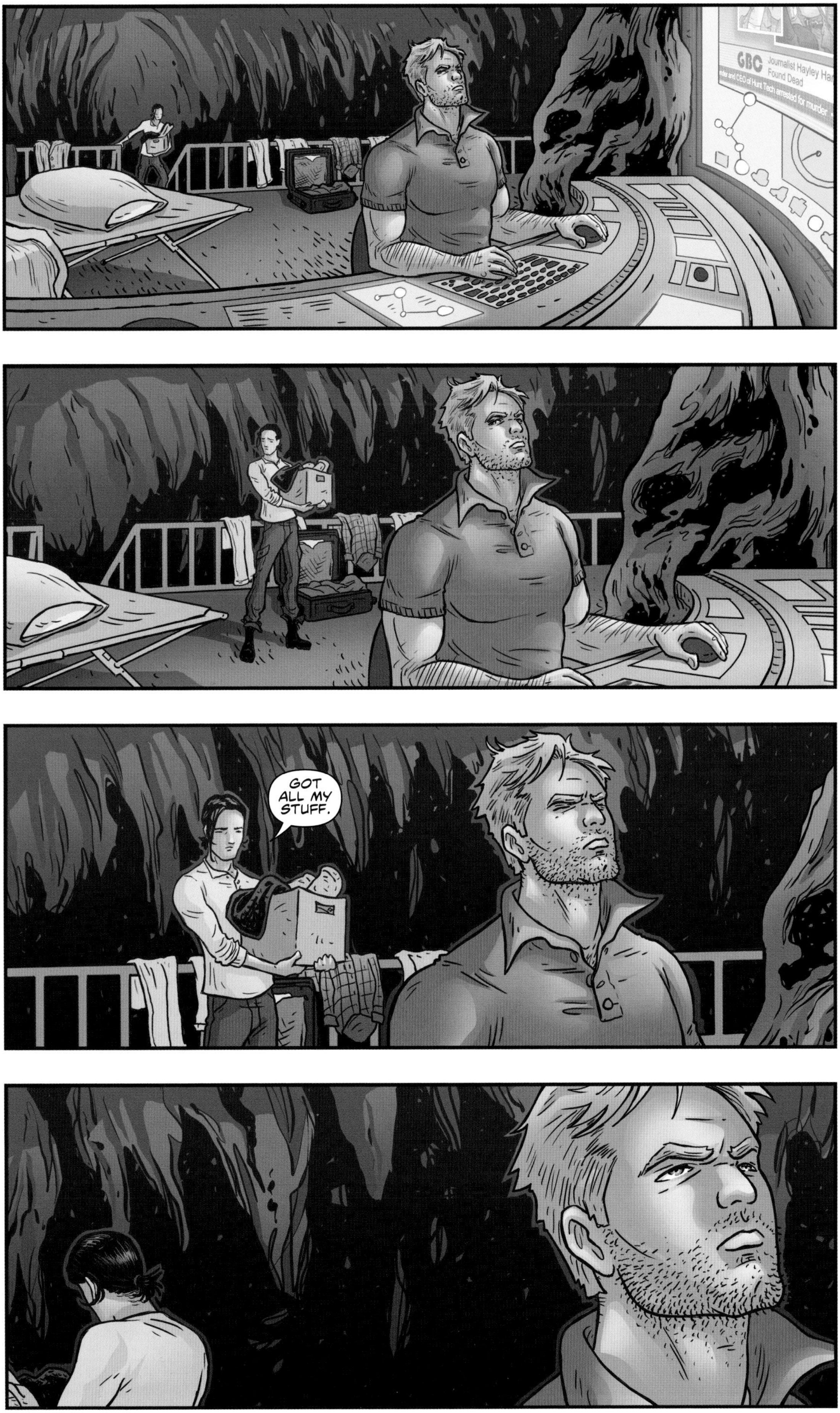
GBC
Journalist Hayley
Found Dead
CEO of Hunt Tech arrested for murder
GOT ALL MY STUFF.

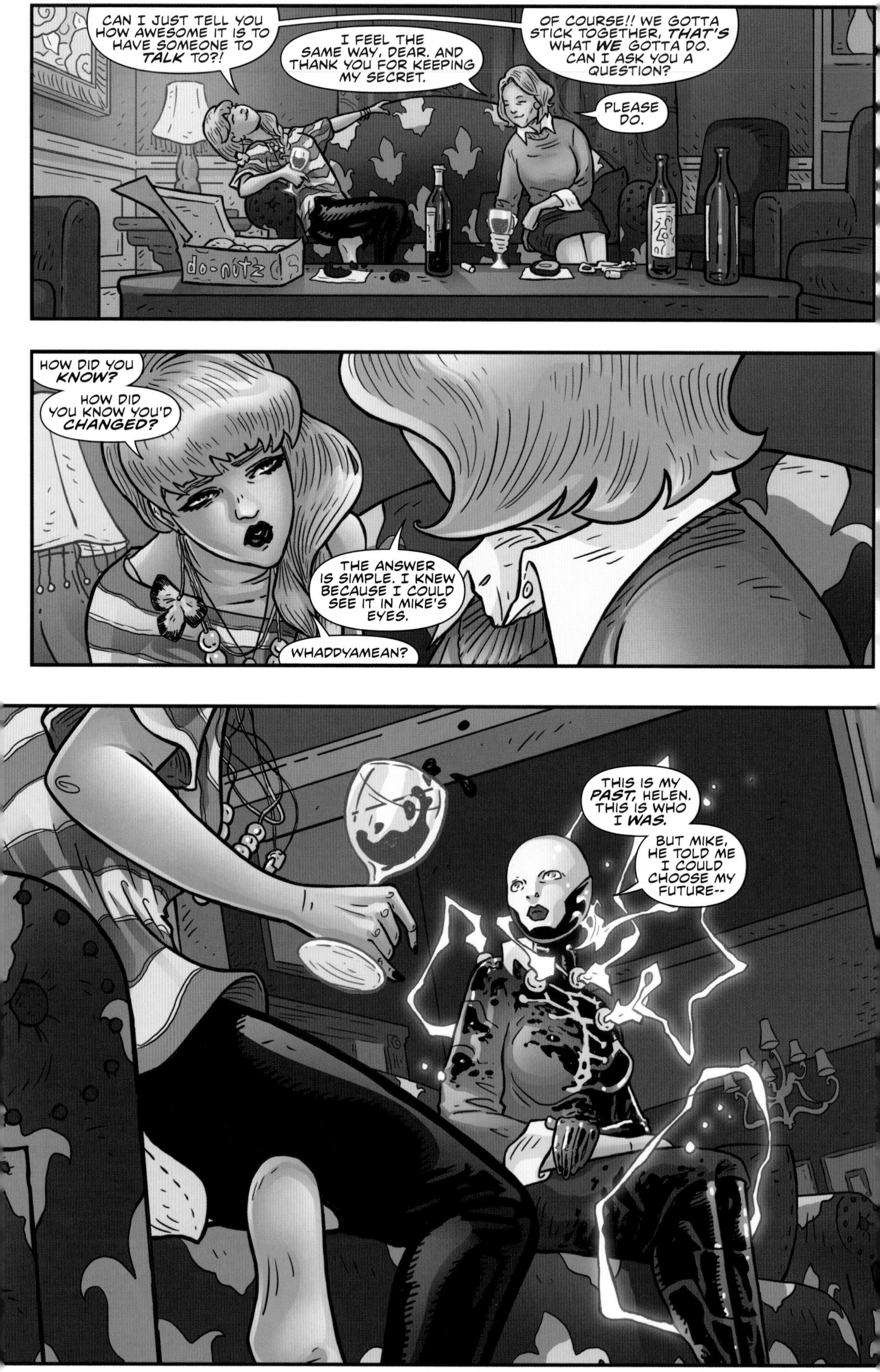

CAN I JUST TELL YOU HOW AWESOME IT IS TO HAVE SOMEONE TO TALK TO?!
I FEEL THE SAME WAY, DEAR. AND THANK YOU FOR KEEPING MY SECRET.
OF COURSE!! WE GOTTA STICK TOGETHER, THAT'S WHAT WE GOTTA DO. CAN I ASK YOU A QUESTION?
PLEASE DO.
do-nutz
HOW DID YOU KNOW?
HOW DID YOU KNOW YOU'D CHANGED?
THE ANSWER IS SIMPLE. I KNEW BECAUSE I COULD SEE IT IN MIKE'S EYES.
WHADDYAMEAN?
THIS IS MY PAST, HELEN. THIS IS WHO I WAS.
BUT MIKE, HE TOLD ME I COULD CHOOSE MY FUTURE--

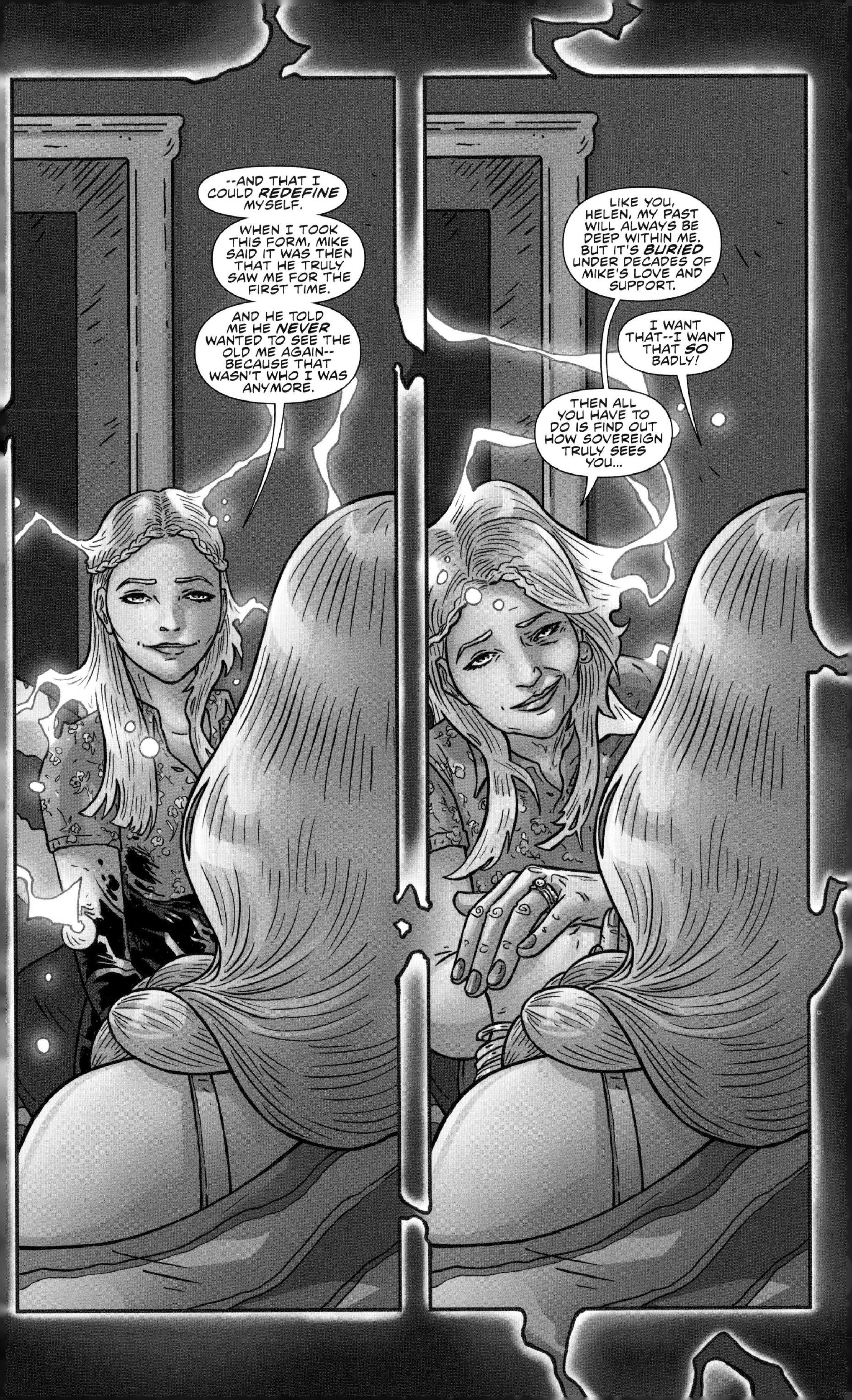
--AND THAT I COULD REDEFINE MYSELF.
WHEN I TOOK THIS FORM, MIKE SAID IT WAS THEN THAT HE TRULY SAW ME FOR THE FIRST TIME.
AND HE TOLD ME HE NEVER WANTED TO SEE THE OLD ME AGAIN--BECAUSE THAT WASN'T WHO I WAS ANYMORE.
LIKE YOU, HELEN, MY PAST WILL ALWAYS BE DEEP WITHIN ME. BUT IT'S BURIED UNDER DECADES OF MIKE'S LOVE AND SUPPORT.
I WANT THAT--I WANT THAT SO BADLY!
THEN ALL YOU HAVE TO DO IS FIND OUT HOW SOVEREIGN TRULY SEES YOU...

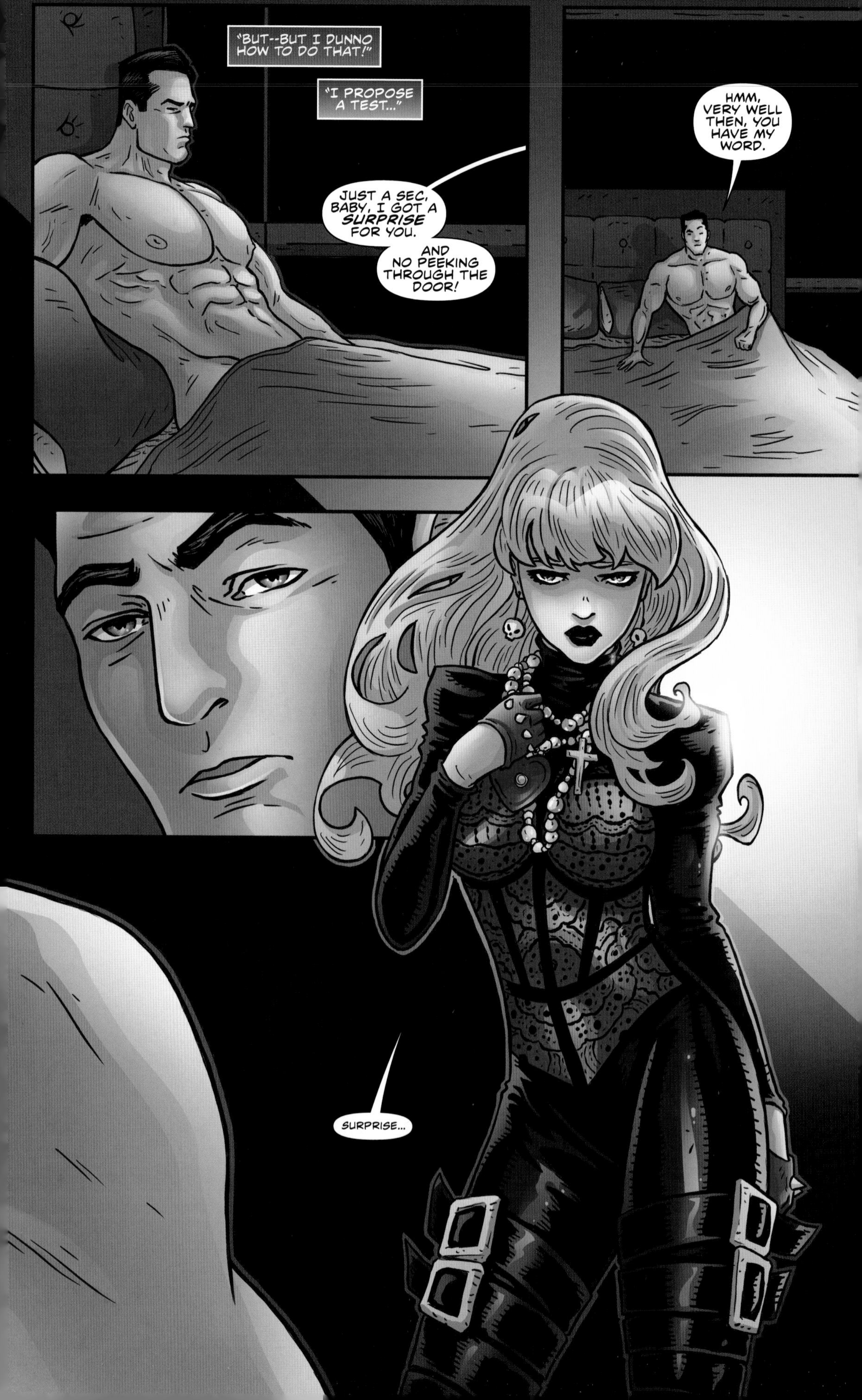
"BUT--BUT I DUNNO HOW TO DO THAT!"
"I PROPOSE A TEST..."
JUST A SEC, BABY, I GOT A SURPRISE FOR YOU.
AND NO PEEKING THROUGH THE DOOR!
HMM, VERY WELL THEN, YOU HAVE MY WORD.
SURPRISE...

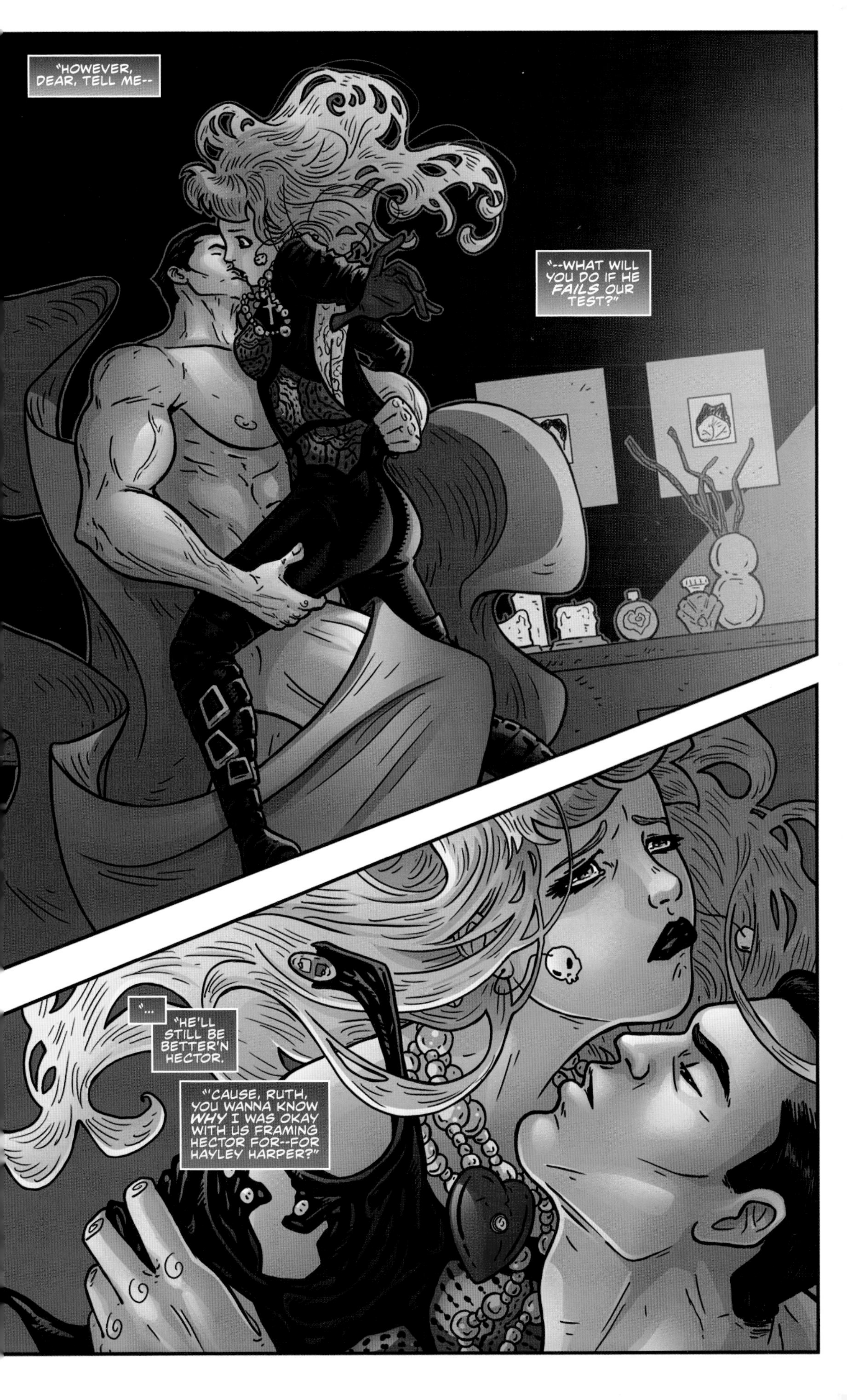
"HOWEVER, DEAR, TELL ME--
"--WHAT WILL YOU DO IF HE FAILS OUR TEST?"
"...
"HE'LL STILL BE BETTER'N HECTOR.
"'CAUSE, RUTH, YOU WANNA KNOW WHY I WAS OKAY WITH US FRAMING HECTOR FOR--FOR HAYLEY HARPER?"

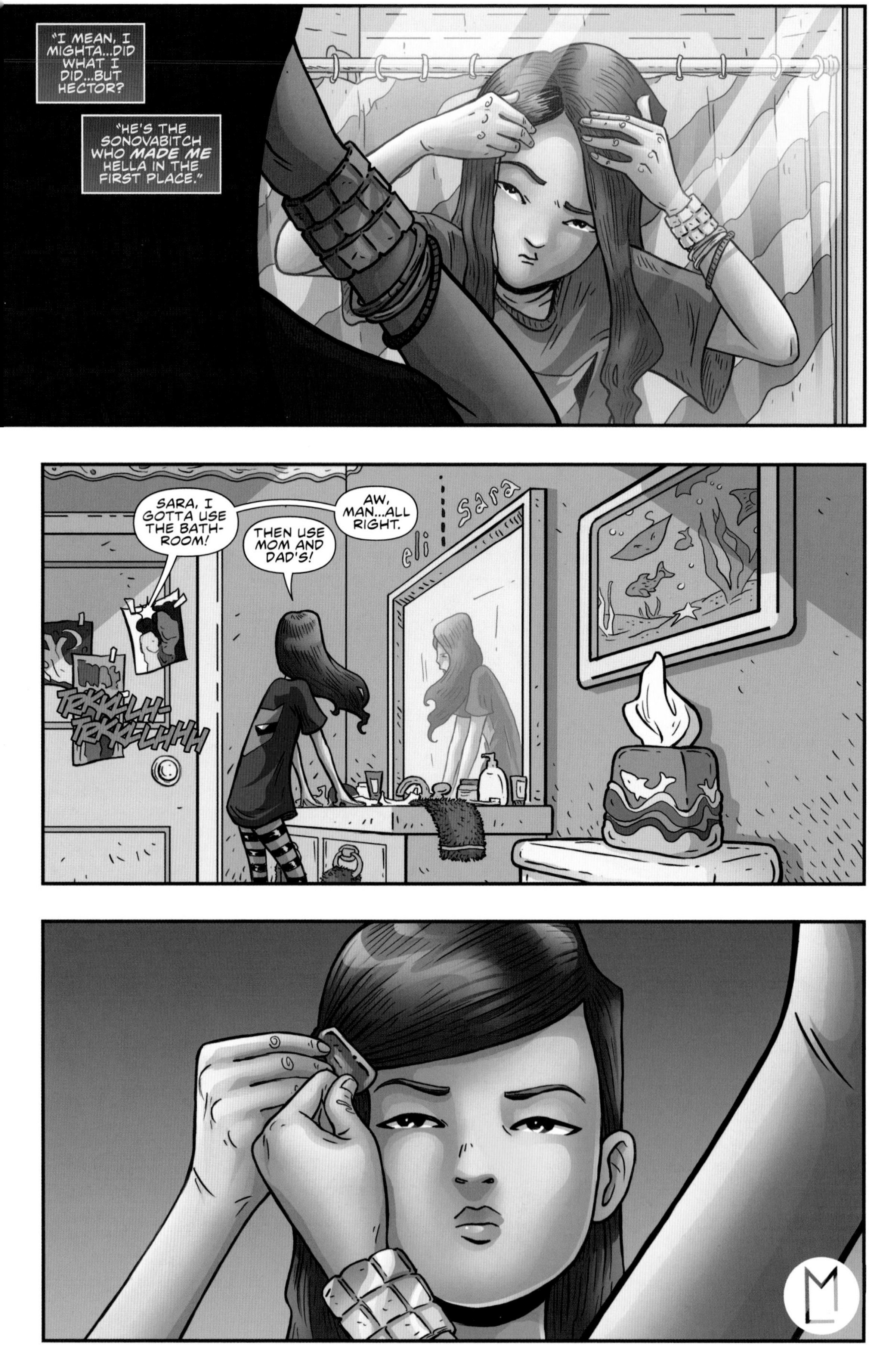
"I MEAN, I MIGHTA...DID WHAT I DID...BUT HECTOR?
"HE'S THE SONOVABITCH WHO *MADE ME* HELLA IN THE FIRST PLACE."
SARA, I GOTTA USE THE BATH-ROOM!
THEN USE MOM AND DAD'S!
AW, MAN...ALL RIGHT.
eli
sara
TRKKLH-TRKKLHHH

GRACE RANDOLPH'S

SUPURBIA™

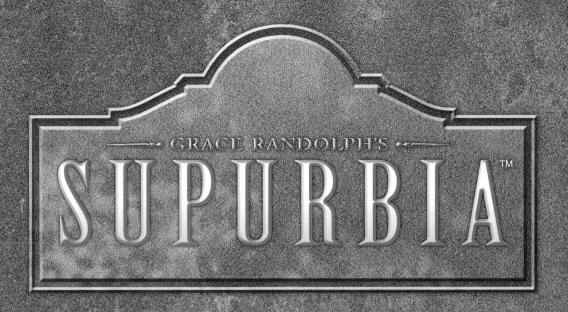

VOLUME THREE

TROUBLE IN PARADISE

COMING SOON

COVER GALLERY

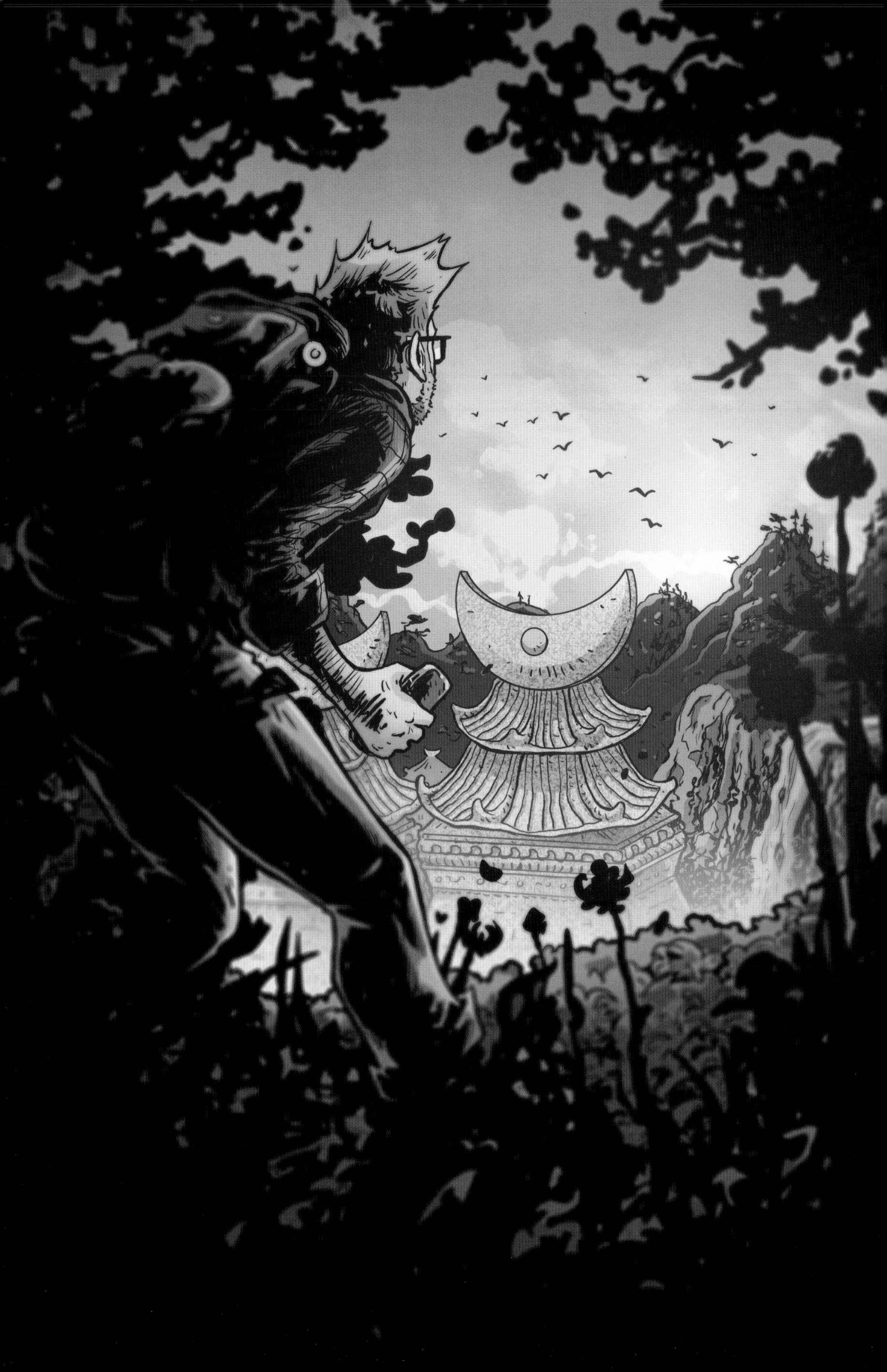

Issue One
Stephane Roux

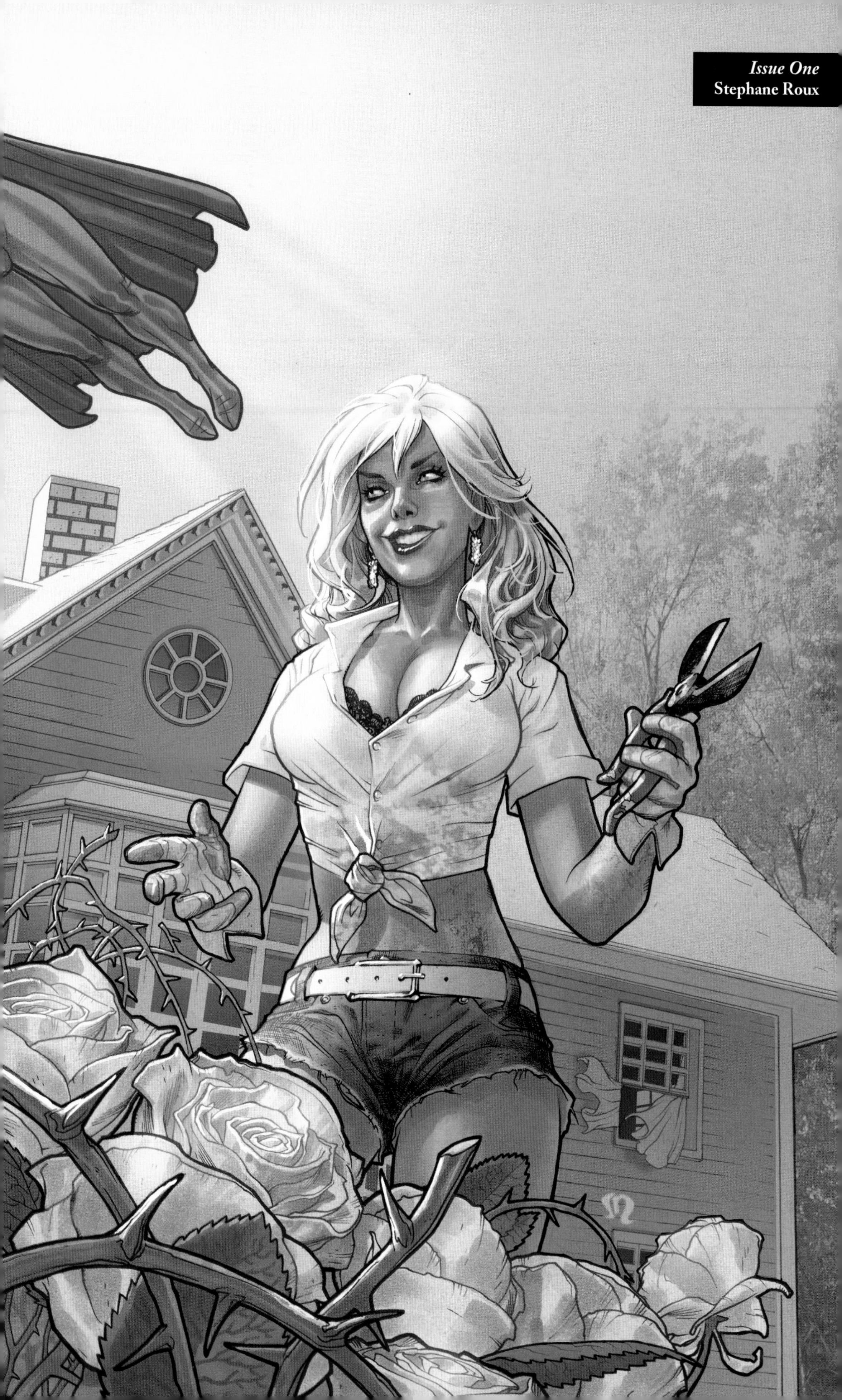

Issue One
Jonboy Meyers with colors by Gabriel Cassata

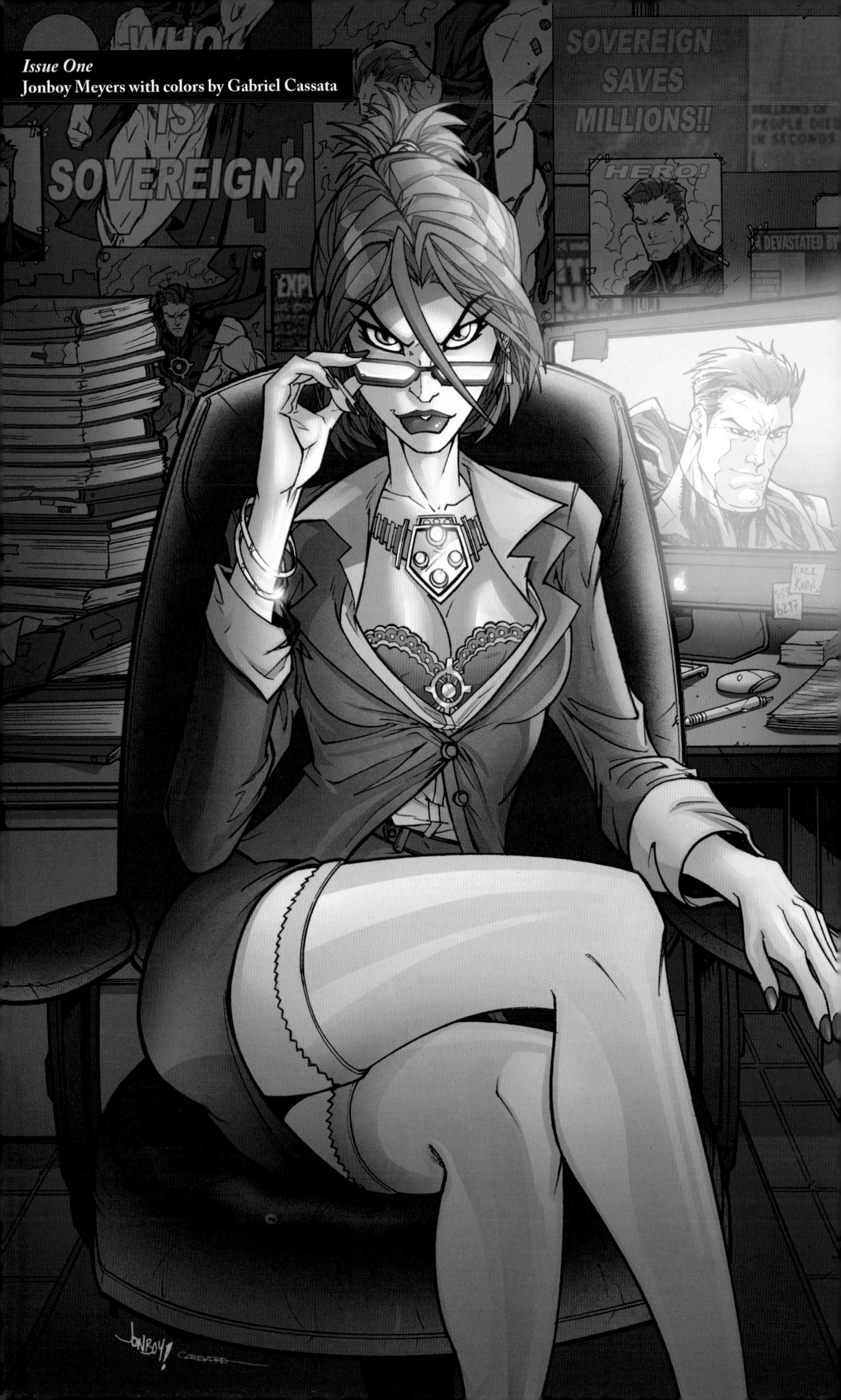
SOVEREIGN?
SOVEREIGN SAVES MILLIONS!!
HERO!
DEVASTATED BY
CALL KWAN
555 6217
JONBOY!

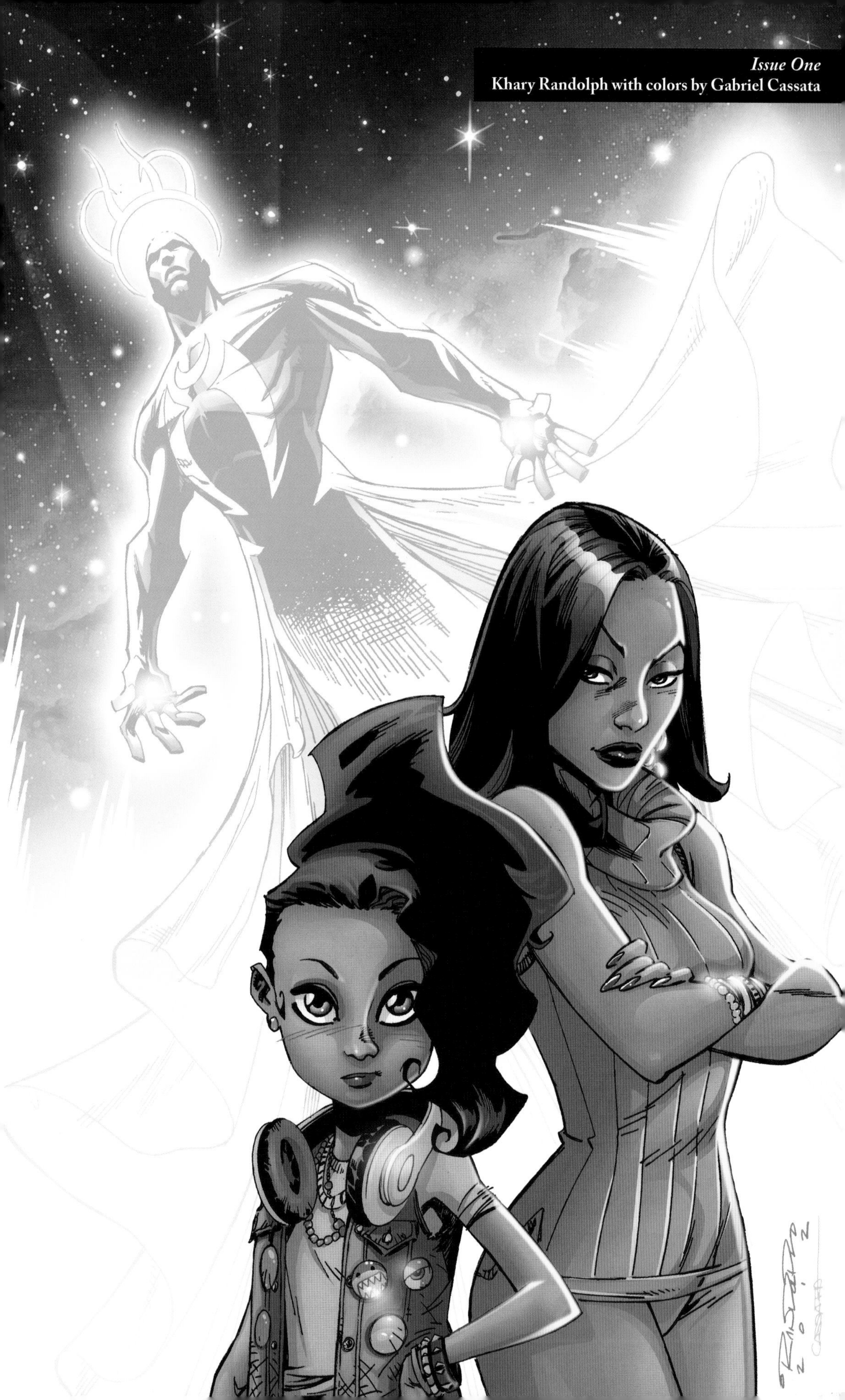

Issue One
Khary Randolph with colors by Gabriel Cassata

Issue One
Phil Noto

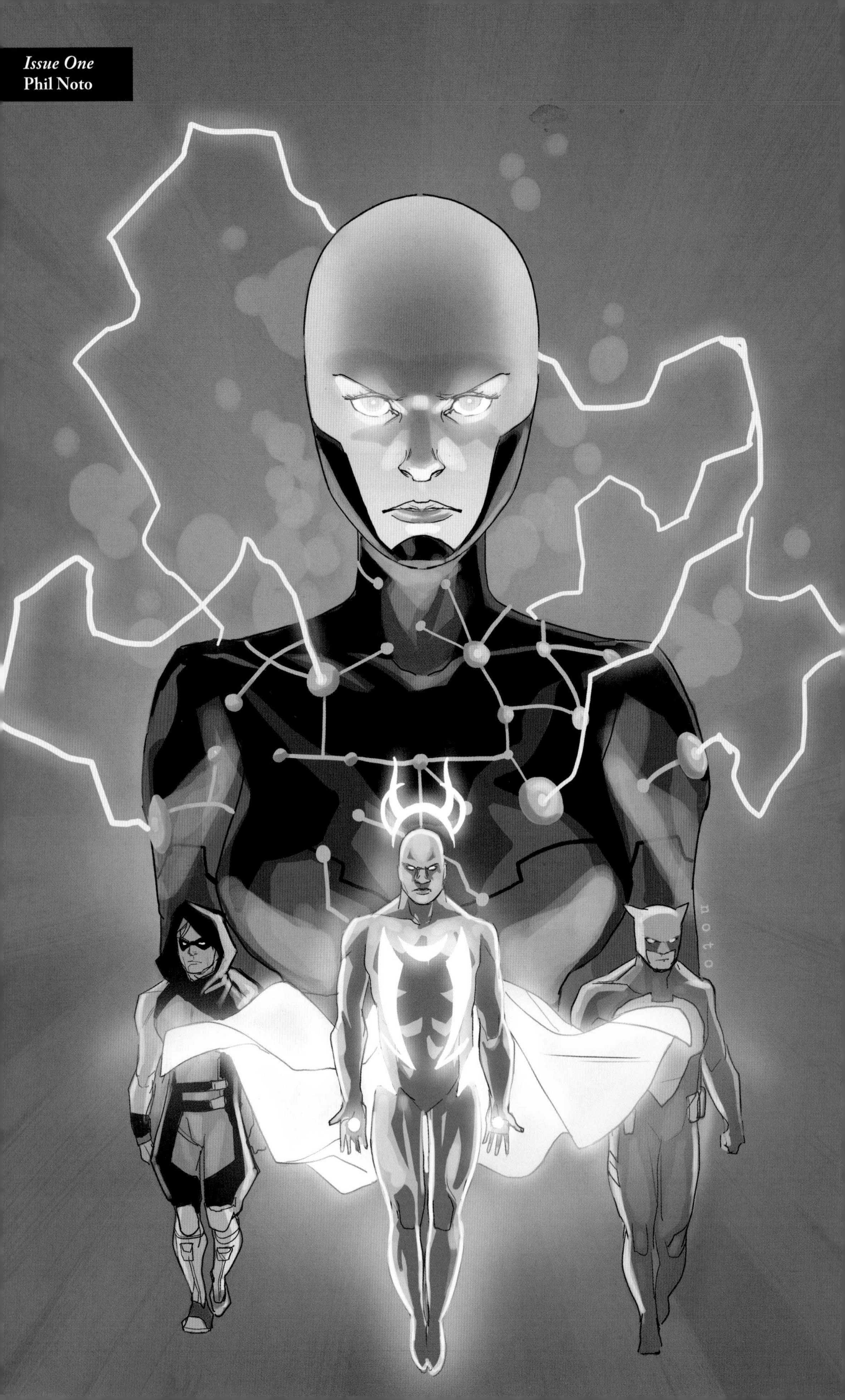
noto

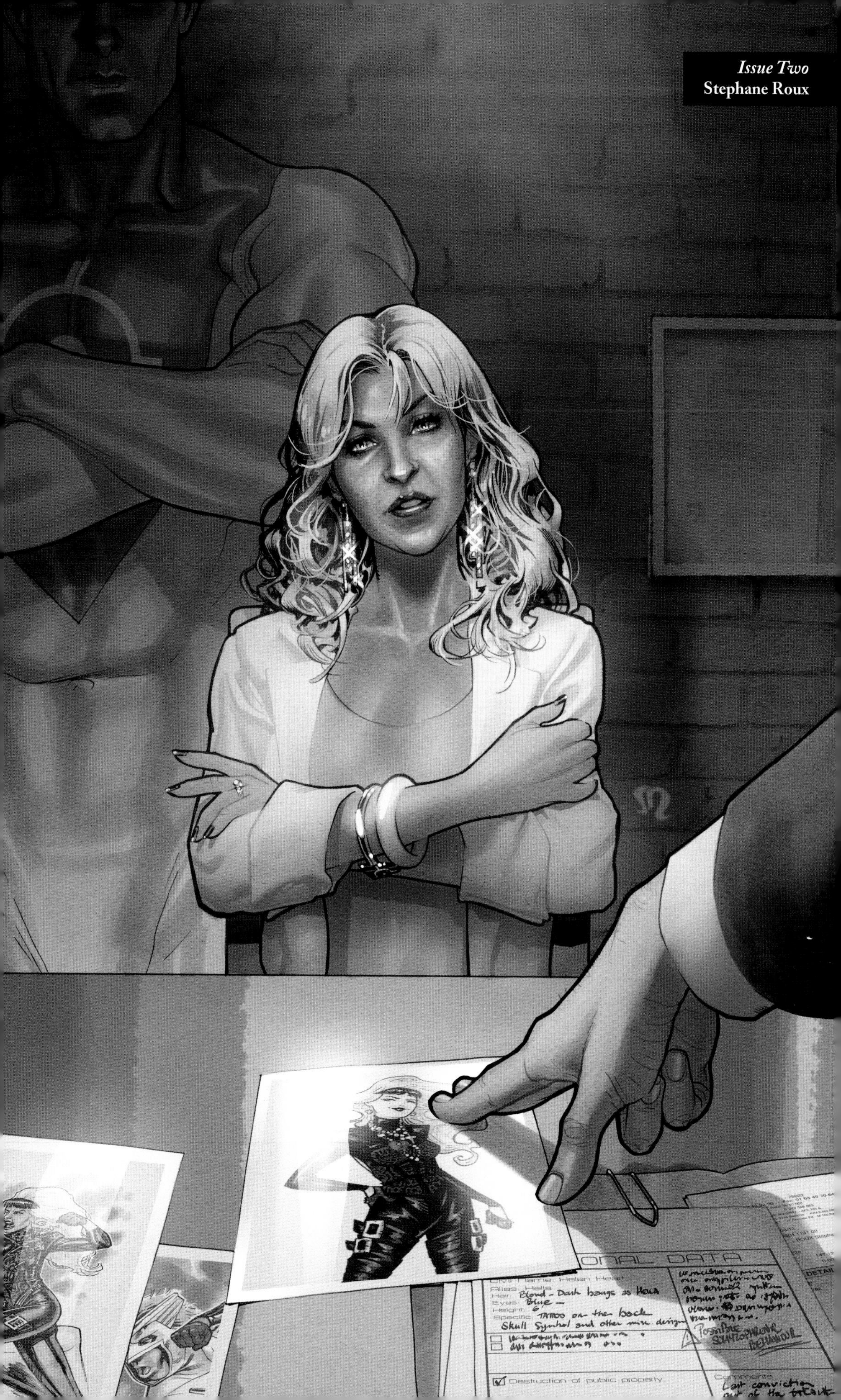
ONAL DATA
Civil Name: Helen Heart
Alias: Hella
Hair: Blond - Dark bangs as Hella
Eyes: Blue -
Height: 6'
Specific: TATTOO on the back
Skull Symbol and other misc. design
POSSIBLE SCHIZOPHRENIC BEHAVIOUR
Destruction of public property
Comments:
Last conviction

Issue Two
Stephane Roux

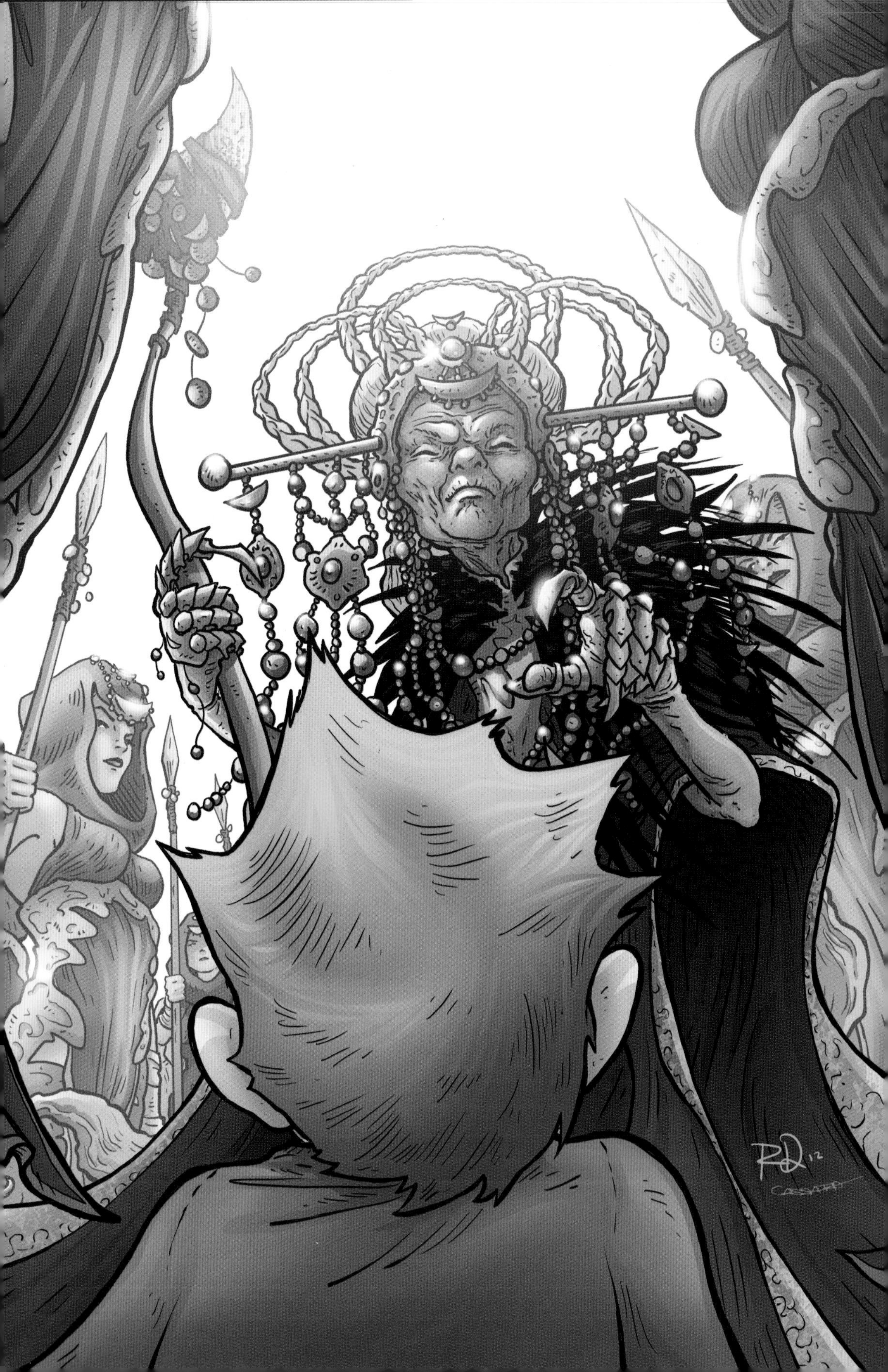

Issue Two
Russell Dauterman with colors by Gabriel Cassata

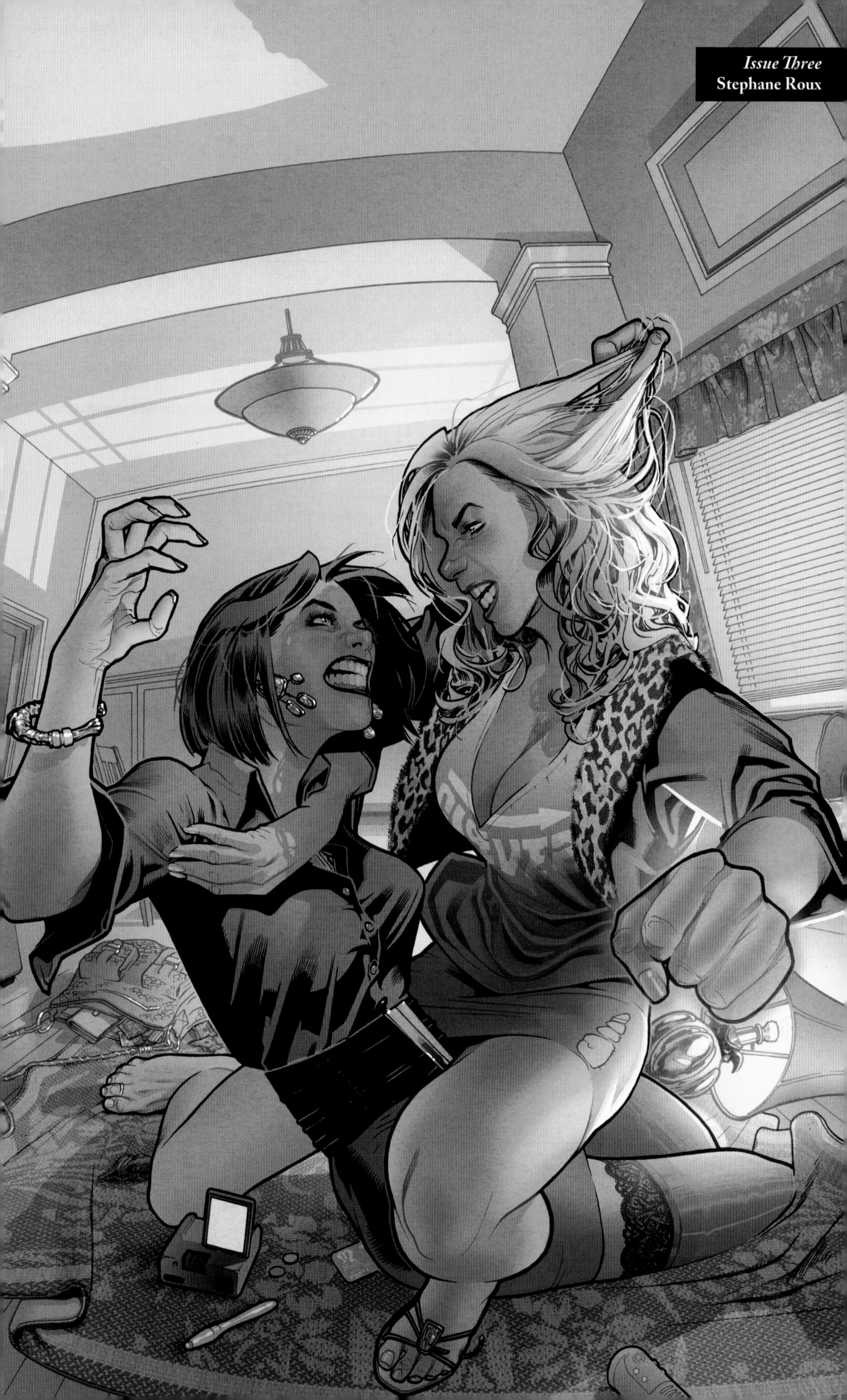

Issue Three
Stephane Roux

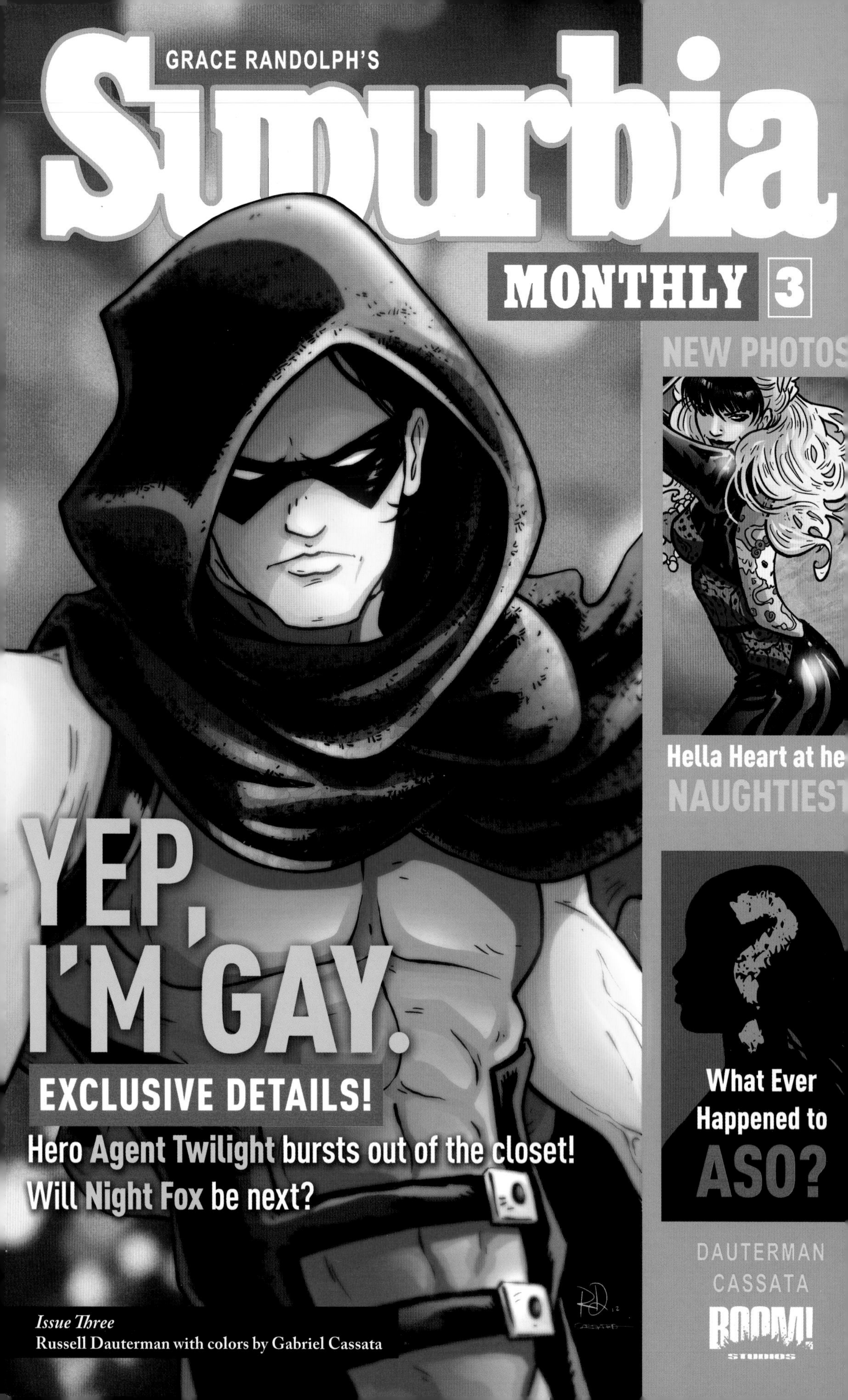
GRACE RANDOLPH'S
Supurbia
MONTHLY 3
NEW PHOTOS
Hella Heart at he
NAUGHTIEST
YEP, I'M GAY.
EXCLUSIVE DETAILS!
Hero Agent Twilight bursts out of the closet!
Will Night Fox be next?
What Ever Happened to
ASO?
DAUTERMAN
CASSATA
BOOM! STUDIOS

Issue Three
Russell Dauterman with colors by Gabriel Cassata

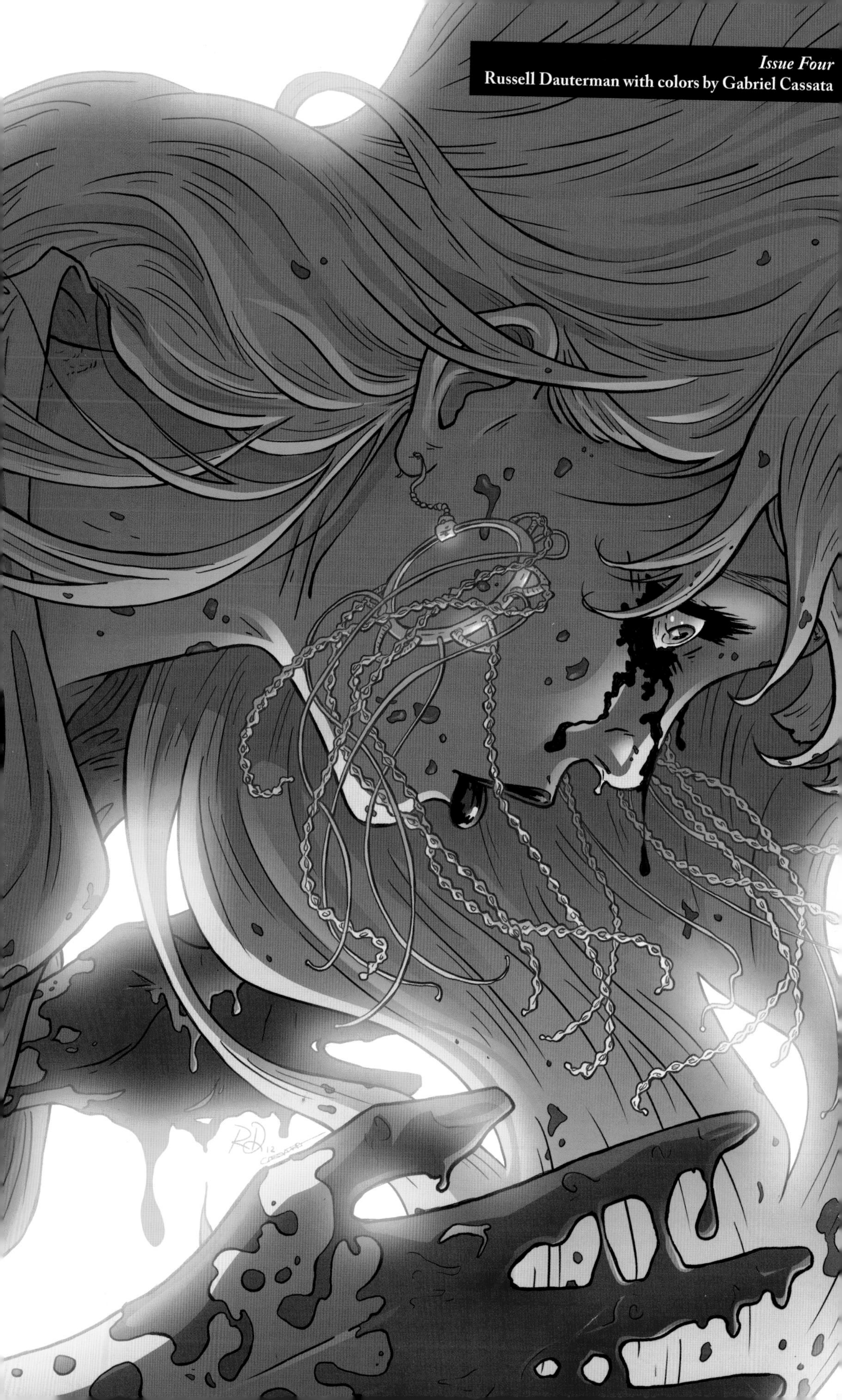

Issue Four
Russell Dauterman with colors by Gabriel Cassata

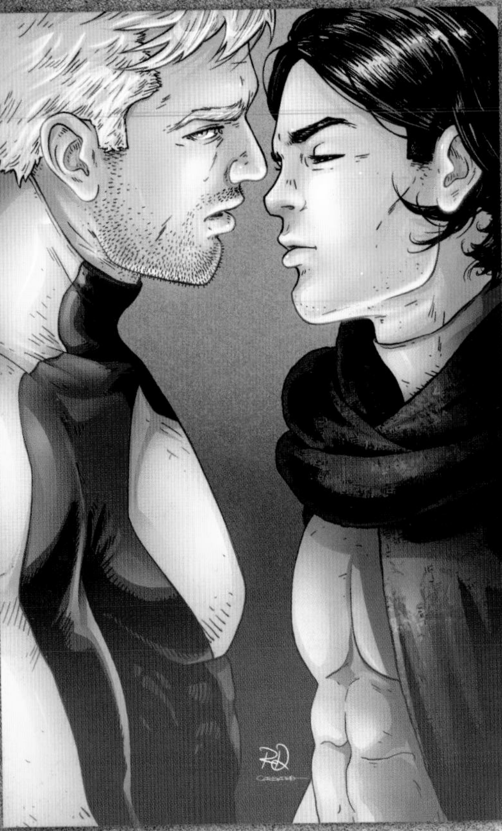

Issue One 2nd Print
Russell Dauterman with colors by Gabriel Cassata

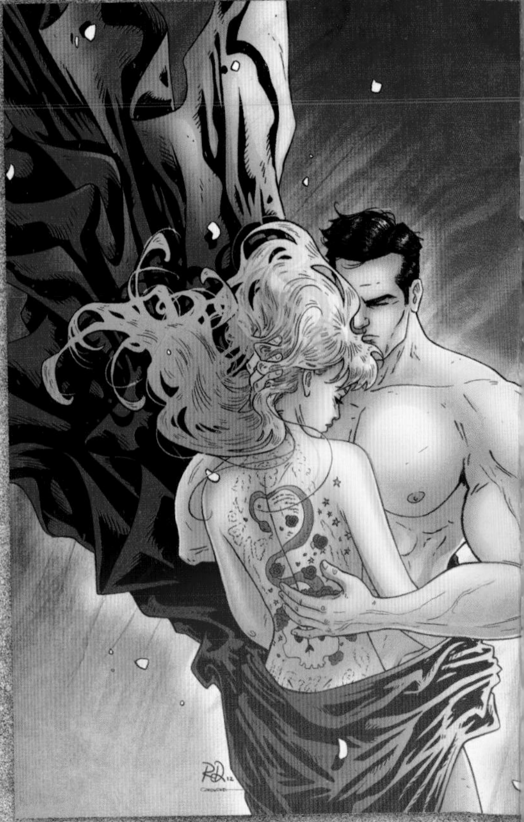

Issue One Long Beach Comic Con Exclusive
Russell Dauterman with colors by Gabriel Cassata

Issue One Third Eye Comics Exclusive
Jerry Gaylord with colors by Gabriel Cassata

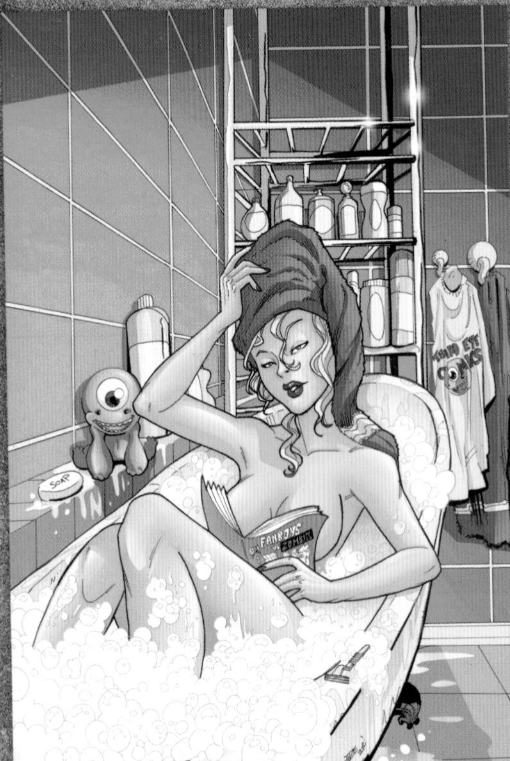

Issue Two 2nd Print
Joshua Covey with colors by Gabriel Cassata

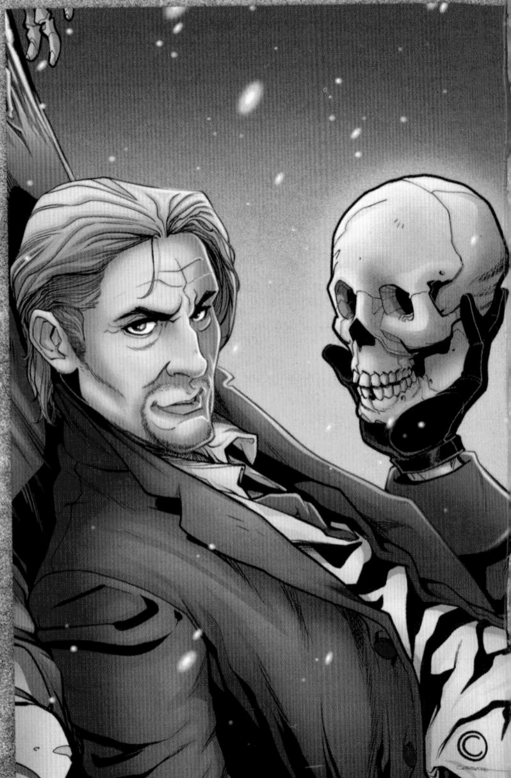